The Homeowner's Handbook to

ENERGY EFFICIENCY

Please work safely when following the procedures outlined in this book. If you cannot safely complete any of the procedures suggested in this book, hire a professional to do the job, or skip the procedure altogether. Your failure to heed this warning could result in injury, death, or damage to your home. Please perform only those tasks for which you are willing to assume responsibility.

Published by Saturn Resource Management, Inc.
324 Fuller Avenue, Helena MT 59601

For more information about improving the efficiency of your home, visit:
www.homeownershandbook.biz

Distributed by Greenleaf Book Group LP

For ordering information or special discounts for bulk purchases, please contact Greenleaf Book Group LP at 4425 Mopac South, Suite 600, Longhorn Building, 3rd Floor, Austin, TX 78735, (512) 891-6100

Design and Cover design by Greenleaf Book Group LP
Other artwork and photos by Steve Ballew, Anthony Cox, Terry Davenport, Chris Dorsi, Eric Doub, Troy Ford, Mike Kindsfater, John Krigger, Craig Miller, Maureen Shaughnessy, Marko Spiegel, Bob Starkey, and Paul Tschida.
This edition was compiled by Darrel Tenter using Adobe FrameMaker®. The text is set in Sabon Light and News Gothic Standard.

The following names appearing in this book are trademarks: AirCrete®, ENERGY STAR®, IECC®, International Energy Conservation Code®, Teflon® tape, Tyvek®, V-seal®.

Publisher's Cataloging-in-Publication (Provided by Quality Books, Inc.)

Krigger, John.
    The homeowner's handbook to energy efficiency : a
guide to big and small improvements / John Krigger,
Chris Dorsi.
    p. cm.
    Includes index.
    ISBN-13: 9781880120187
    ISBN-10: 1880120186

    1. Dwellings--Energy conservation--Amateurs' manuals.
    2. Dwellings--Maintenance and repair--Amateurs' manuals.
    I. Dorsi, Chris. II. Title.

TJ163.5.D86K749 2008   644
                    QBI08-600141

ISBN 10: **1-880120-18-6**
ISBN 13: **978-1-880120-18-7**
$24.95 USD Softcover.

Printed in the United States of America with vegetable-based inks on acid-free paper containing 50% or more recycled waste.

08 09 10 11 12 13   10 9 8 7 6 5 4 3 2 1

First Edition

The Homeowner's Handbook to

ENERGY EFFICIENCY

A Guide to
BIG AND SMALL IMPROVEMENTS

John Krigger
Chris Dorsi

RESOURCE MANAGEMENT

Contents

Introduction

We consume huge amounts of energy in North America. More than twenty percent of that energy flows through our homes, and if you include commercial and industrial structures, our buildings account for over forty percent of our total energy consumption. The energy we use also has an environmental impact—much of the pollution we create is emitted by the construction, maintenance, and operation of those structures.

More than ever before, the economic and environmental burdens of supporting our buildings presents a major challenge to each of us as individuals and to society at large. It is hard to imagine how any of us could have an impact on such large issues. Yet the management of our own homes does present such an opportunity, because we can each reduce our energy consumption at home through careful planning and investment. Helping you do so is the goal of this book.

Energy, Dollars, and Carbon Dioxide

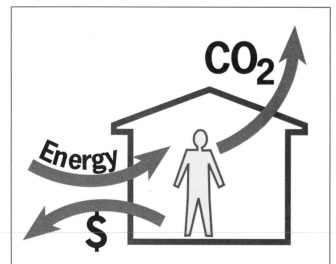

The energy you consume costs money. It also results in the release of carbon dioxide (CO_2) and other "greenhouse gases" that contribute to climate change. When you improve the efficiency of your home, you save money and reduce your carbon footprint at the same time.

THE BENEFITS OF ENERGY EFFICIENCY

We have long had the technical ability to minimize the energy consumption of our buildings. But this knowledge has not always made its way into mainstream construction practice. We believe that it's now time to bring this expertise to bear on our homes.

Many of us are ready to invest in the energy-wise renovation of our homes in order to provide future energy security for our families. Efficient homes offer many benefits to their owners.

- Efficient homes are cheaper to operate. You'll save money, and you'll be less vulnerable to price fluctuations.
- Efficient homes have a smaller carbon footprint. You'll be doing your part to control climate change.
- Efficient homes are more comfortable. Your home will be less drafty and the temperature will be more even.
- Efficient homes are more valuable. You'll get top dollar at the time of sale for a well-designed home with small utility bills.

This book will help you evaluate your home and embark upon improvements that allow you to reap all these benefits.

ALL HOMES CAN BE IMPROVED

The projects in this book are targeted toward typical single-family wood-frame homes in North America. These homes are most likely heated by forced-air furnaces or by boilers. If they are located in a hot region, they may be cooled by a central air conditioner. Hot water is probably provided by a standard storage water heater.

Most of these homes are supplied with a fossil fuel such as natural gas, propane, or oil. This fossil fuel is likely used for heating, water heating, cooking, and/or clothes drying. Almost all North American homes rely upon the electrical grid to power air conditioning systems, lights, appliances, and sometimes heating systems.

There are perhaps ninety million of these single family homes in the U.S. today, and another nine million in Canada. Most of them offer an abundant crop of energy waste that can be turned into savings. Why are these homes so inefficient? Weren't they constructed according to building codes? The answers are buried in history and economics.

Energy in North America has been relatively inexpensive for several generations now, owing to the discovery of large fossil fuel reserves both at home and abroad. Government subsidies have helped keep fuel prices artificially low. During and after the oil embargoes of the mid-1970s, the U.S. and Canadian governments and private sectors launched initiatives to improve energy efficiency. From about 1976 through 1986, the energy-efficiency of homes increased. New buildings were constructed to improved efficiency standards, and owners of existing homes invested in insulation, storm windows, and improved heating systems. But with the discovery of new oil and gas reserves in the 1980s and the stabilization of foreign energy supplies, energy costs dropped and the trend toward energy efficiency stalled. For the last few decades, energy concerns have faded from public consciousness.

Meanwhile, we've built millions of inefficient homes and installed millions of inefficient heating and cooling systems. Most have been built according to the latest building codes, and a few even exceed those standards. But building codes establish the minimum legal standards for health, safety, and energy efficiency—they define what a builder must do to avoid breaking the law. Despite recent revisions, today's building codes fail to provide wise guidance on building or remodeling for energy efficiency. The end result is that most of our homes are quite inefficient, and offer ample opportunities for improvement.

HOW THIS BOOK CAN HELP

Our primary goal is to present proven methods for reducing your home's energy consumption. Many of the projects we describe will also improve your home's comfort, safety, and durability. In each case, we offer clear explanations of the possible options, we describe the necessary commitments of time and money, and we present basic methods for estimating energy savings.

Throughout this book, we also describe how your home operates. We hope that by explaining some building science principles, we can help you analyze home improvement tasks beyond the ones we're discussing. This knowledge will also help you cut through the sometimes conflicting claims made by vendors of home improvement products and services.

It's possible to make reductions of up to eighty percent in your home's energy consumption. The projects described here are a good start toward that goal. But we also recognize that the most important step for each of us is to simply get started on whatever level we can. We've included both big and small improvements here, so you can find projects that fit both your budget and your personal commitment. An investment of any size in your home's efficiency will reduce both your monthly energy expenses and your environmental footprint.

The projects you choose from this book will also depend on the characteristics and current condition of your home. Some improvements are relevant to every home, while others may apply to only a few. But we'll show you how to craft a plan that suits your home. Whatever progress you make toward improving the energy efficiency of your home will benefit us all in the long run. We thank you for your commitment.

John Krigger
Chris Dorsi

1 Developing a Plan for Your Home

We presume you're reading this book with the intention of improving the energy efficiency of your home. We hope to help you do that and more.

Improvements to your home's efficiency are among the best financial investments available. The projects described here yield returns in utility cost savings that range from five to fifty percent annually, exceeding the interest yielded by many traditional investments. These economic returns will only improve as energy prices increase.

Most of the projects described here also offer benefits beyond energy efficiency. Many will increase your home's comfort, safety, and durability. And the resale value of efficient homes continues to climb in comparison to homes with high utility costs.

The best time to start improving your home's energy efficiency is now. Your savings won't begin until you take time to analyze your energy consumption, formulate your own solutions, and upgrade your home.

ENERGY CONSUMPTION VERSUS CARBON EMISSIONS

Your consumption of energy has an effect on the planet, which varies widely depending upon the amount and type of energy you use. The primary environmental factor we evaluate in this book is the emission of carbon dioxide (CO_2), a normal byproduct of the combustion process that is released when you burn hydrocarbon fuels such as coal, oil, or natural gas. Combustion takes place within your home heating equipment, and at the central power plants that produce most of our electricity. When carbon dioxide is released, it traps heat in the atmosphere through the process called the greenhouse effect. When you improve the efficiency of your home, you produce less carbon dioxide and other pollutants, saving money *and* reducing your environmental impact.

Comparing Emissions of Various Energy Sources

It's not difficult to estimate the amount of CO_2 released by the natural gas, propane, or oil you consume in your home. Your utility bill shows you how much fuel you consume. Burning that fuel releases predictable amounts of CO_2 up the chimney of your heating system.

It's more difficult to evaluate the carbon emissions that result from your electricity consumption because electricity is produced by a variety of methods. The fuel most commonly used to generate electricity in North America is coal, though natural gas and fuel oil are also used. These are burned to produce steam that spins electric generators. The combustion of these fuels, for both heat and electricity, accounts for the majority of greenhouse gas emissions that we produce.

Hydroelectric plants use falling water to generate electricity. Hydropower emits no carbon directly, though the associated construction and maintenance of dams, generators and transmission lines do incur a large environmental cost.

Even nuclear power can be described as "carbon neutral," since nuclear reactors don't burn fossil fuels and so don't release CO_2. Yet the operation of nuclear power plants and the disposal of their waste incurs large environmental and economic costs. Carbon emissions are not the only way to measure the desirability of potential energy sources.

One of the most promising ways to generate electricity today is with photovoltaic (PV) systems. You may have seen banks of PV solar panels on the roofs of buildings, or even in large arrays operated by utility companies. PV systems convert sunlight to electricity. But even this is not a perfect technology: PV systems are still relatively expensive and their manufacturing process consumes energy and incurs other environmental costs. Wind power and other renewable energy sources are also becoming a part of the mix as we develop sustainable energy systems.

When it comes to generating electricity, there is no perfect solution. The improvement of existing buildings, to make them more efficient, still produces a better economic return than the construction of almost any type of power plant. That's why using less energy is the best way to save money and trim your carbon footprint.

EMBODIED ENERGY AND DURABILITY

Your home leaves an environmental footprint beyond its carbon emissions from daily energy consumption. Two other factors carry great weight: the embodied energy in its materials, and the durability of the structure.

Embodied energy is the sum of energy inputs a material requires over its lifetime. Several organizations have proposed indexes of embodied energy that allow comparison among building materials. Not everyone agrees on what inputs should be included in these indexes, making comparisons difficult. But most such indexes account for the energy consumed in some or all of these activities.

- Mining or harvesting the raw materials
- Shipping the raw materials to the manufacturing facility
- Processing the raw materials into building products
- Shipping the materials to the job site
- Installing the building materials
- Performing needed maintenance over the material's lifetime
- Disposing of or recycling the material when it is replaced or the building is demolished

Other considerations may affect embodied energy, making a reliable estimate difficult to calculate. For example, should embodied energy include the energy required to build the manufacturing facility? Should it include the energy required to build the vehicle used to transport the material? What about the energy used by housebuilders to commute to the job where the material is installed?

The longevity of a material must also be considered when assessing its environmental impact. For example, PVC plastic roof gutters that last for ten years or less cannot be compared pound-for-pound to PVC plastic plumbing that remains functional for fifty years or more. And if a material is recycled when the building is demolished—common for aluminum in today's market but not for concrete—then some or its embodied energy is reclaimed by recycling.

You can minimize the embodied energy in your home by following these general guidelines:

- Build small. It's best to use less of any building material. Smaller homes have less impact on the environment both during their construction and throughout their lifetimes.
- Remodel your home rather than building a new one. You'll avoid the cost and environmental impact of buying an entire houseful of new materials. Focus your efforts on improving the efficiency of an existing building instead.
- Choose long-lived high-quality building materials. Materials with a long lifespan have less environmental impact than those that wear out quickly, plus they require less maintenance.

But remember that embodied energy is only part of the picture. Your home's operational energy—the electricity, gas, and other fuels used year after year to operate and maintain your home—are still your biggest concern. This is a simple matter of scale. Most research that compares the embodied energy and operational energy of homes shows that embodied energy accounts for only ten to twenty percent of the total energy consumed by the building over the years. Operational energy consumes the other eighty to ninety percent. The goal of this book is to help you control that ongoing energy consumption.

DEVELOPING A PLAN

The first step in crafting a home improvement plan is to decide how to improve your home. The characteristics of efficient homes vary from one region to another, depending on climate, the type of construction, the kinds of fuel that are available, and many other factors. But the best homes share these common traits:

- They have building shells that are airtight and extremely well insulated.
- They have small heating and cooling systems.
- Their windows are oriented to collect solar heat in winter and reject it in summer.
- They have appliances and lighting that are the most energy efficient available.
- They may use solar power to generate electricity (photovoltaic systems), or to produce hot water (solar thermal systems).

Your existing home may already include some of these traits. As you work your way through this book, you'll gain an idea of how your home compares to the ideal home. But don't be discouraged by your home's shortcomings. The best time to start any investment program—whether opening a savings account or starting home efficiency projects—is right now. There are plenty of small projects in this book that you can accomplish right away.

BIG VERSUS SMALL IMPROVEMENTS

As you review the projects in this book, you'll see that they cover a large range of cost and complexity. You could probably save a hundred dollars a year, for example, by installing compact fluorescent light bulbs in your home this weekend. But you could benefit from even more impressive savings by stripping the siding off your home, applying two inches of foam insulation, and installing new siding, windows, and doors. Though this big project would require advance planning and an investment of tens of thousands of dollars, it could be an equally wise investment in your future, especially considering both the improvement to your comfort and the economic benefits. We take this view of these large projects: the current energy crunch

will likely become permanent, and home improvements of this magnitude will be needed to bring our existing housing stock up to modern standards.

We suggest that you get started on some small energy improvement projects right away. At the end of this chapter we've outlined ten of the simplest ways to save energy without spending too much money. But do not neglect the big projects. We've found that these major undertakings produce the best package of overall benefits when you consider reduced utility expenses, lowered carbon emissions, improvement in comfort, and increase in home resale value. These biggest and most important projects usually include improvements to your home's shell—the walls, ceiling, floors, doors and windows. These major projects are worth the effort because most heating and cooling energy waste occurs through these areas.

Moreover, neglecting shell issues because they are too difficult will likely make other efforts less productive. It often doesn't make sense to replace your heating or cooling system, for example, without making major improvements in the building shell. That's because improvements in the shell will result in the need for far less heating and cooling capacity. Once you've made shell improvements, your new heating and cooling system can be smaller, and so will be less expensive to purchase, install, and operate. Over the lifespan of your home, reduced utility costs could easily pay for the upgrades you performed to the building shell.

HOW TO USE THIS BOOK

We recommend that you develop a written energy upgrade plan for your home. This can be as simple or complex as you'd like, but it will be worth the effort to gather your ideas on paper.

- Take time to review this book. You could read it all at once or just a chapter at a time, but you'll want to return to it occasionally when you start a specific project.
- When you read about a project that could be relevant to your home, make an entry in your written plan.

- Do some additional research. You may want to search the Internet for additional information, or ask questions of the service staff at your favorite hardware store. Get prices for materials, and enter them in your written plan.

- Consider how much money you want to invest in your home. For many of us, home maintenance is already a major expense, though we may be spending our money on cosmetic improvements. Consider how to piggyback energy upgrades onto cosmetic projects. Could you seal your ductwork, for example, before installing new drywall on your basement ceiling?

- Once you have assembled a wish list of projects, consider which ones would be most efficiently performed as a group. If you need to upgrade both your attic and floor insulation, for example, it makes good sense to get bids for both and to have them done at the same time.

- Identify projects that conflict with one another, so you don't spend money now on improvements that won't be needed once you complete future projects. You wouldn't want to spend money sealing ductwork, for example, that might be replaced when you upgrade to a high-efficiency furnace.

- Prioritize your assembled projects. Decide which ones you can perform with confidence yourself. Get written proposals from experts for those you don't plan to do personally. Budget money for the big improvements, and develop a savings plan, if necessary, that will allow you to do the big projects sometime in the future. Ask your lender about Energy Efficiency Mortgages that can be applied to a refinance.

- Identify the small improvements that you can make right away, and get started on them.

- If you have big improvements on the list, decide which one you'd like to start with. If you'll work with contractors on the project, inquire about schedule and budget. Make a commitment by marking your projects on your calendar.

The process of improving your home's efficiency will never be complete. Just like maintaining your home with tasks such as repainting or replacing a roof, you cannot afford to ignore your home's energy efficiency. At this point in history, our relationship to energy is changing, too, driven by the cost of fuel, climate change, and shifting housing markets. The sooner each of us gets started on the projects outlined in this book, the sooner we can each reclaim control of our energy costs and our housing. We wish you luck in this endeavor.

ANALYZING YOUR ENERGY CONSUMPTION

The first challenge you face in setting goals for reducing your energy consumption is to understand your current energy usage. With this knowledge in hand, you'll be prepared to analyze the potential savings you can reap from your home improvement efforts. You'll also be able to estimate your emissions of carbon dioxide and other pollutants.

The best way to analyze your consumption is by reviewing your utility bills. The utility bill analysis we describe in *Analyzing Your Utility Bill* on page 8 will take an hour or two, but will be well worth your time. You could complete all of the tasks described in this book without performing that analysis, but your work will be more successful if you know where to apply your efforts. If you choose to skip this procedure for now, be sure to review *Ten Sure-Fire Ways to Improve Your Home's Efficiency* on page 16, near the end of this chapter.

You may receive one utility bill that includes both gas and electric accounts, or you may receive separate bills for each of these types of energy. If you live within reach of the nationwide grid of underground gas lines, you probably use natural gas in your home. If you live in a rural area, you may use propane instead (propane is a type of liquefied petroleum gas, or LPG). In some regions, fuel oil is still widely used for heating. And some all-electric homes use electricity for both heat and appliances.

Measuring Electrical Consumption

Electrical energy is measured in kilowatt-hours (kWh). One kilowatt-hour is the amount of electricity consumed by a 100-watt bulb in 10 hours of operation.

- If you inspect your electric bill, you may see this unit of measurement written variously as kilowatt hour, kilowatt-hour, kWh, or kwh. These terms all refer to the same measurement.
- The cost to the consumer of a kilowatt-hour of electricity typically ranges from 10 to 20 cents (2008).
- The average family in the U.S. uses about 11,000 kWh of electricity per year. Those with electric heat use more, those with gas or oil heat use less.

We refer to electric consumption in kilowatt hours throughout this book. Though your rate will vary depending upon your region, time of year, and in some cases time of day, we have chosen to use an average current electrical rate of 15 cents per kilowatt-hour (2008).

Measuring Natural Gas Consumption

All measurements of heating fuels — natural gas, propane, and fuel oil — are ultimately based upon the British thermal unit (BTU). A BTU is a measure of heat, and is approximately equal to the heat released when burning a common stick match.

There are several different quantities of BTUs used by utility companies. Inspect your gas bill to see which is used by yours.

- The most common units for measuring natural gas are *therms* (100,000 BTUs) and *decatherms* (1,000,000 BTUs, abbreviated dkt). Some utility companies also use the designation MMBTU (a thousand thousand, or 1,000,000 BTUs, the same as a decatherm).

- Many utilities sell natural gas by the cubic foot. This the unit of volume actually measured by your gas meter. These bills don't show BTUs or therms, but rather 100s of cubic feet (100 cubic feet is abbreviated CCF). Since 100 cubic feet of natural gas produces approximately 100,000 BTUs when burned, 100 CCF equals 1 therm.
- The cost of a therm of energy to a North American consumer usually ranges, with a few exceptions, from $1.00 to $1.80 (2008).
- The average household in the U.S. uses about 920 therms of gas per year. Those who live in cold regions use the most.

Units of Measurement for Natural Gas

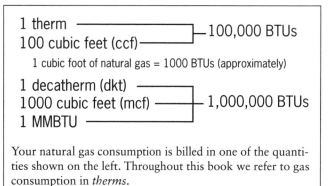

Your natural gas consumption is billed in one of the quantities shown on the left. Throughout this book we refer to gas consumption in *therms*.

Though the rate you pay for natural gas will vary depending upon your region and the time of year, we have chosen to use a average natural gas rate of $1.50 per therm when we do calculations or make comparisons in this book (2008).

If your gas bill is stated in therms or CCF (shown in the top of the chart above), our measurements are parallel and can be compared directly. If your bill is in decatherms or MMBTU (shown in the bottom of the chart), you'll need to multiply our measurements by 10 to draw comparisons to your utility bill. When we refer to the average price of natural gas at $1.50 per therm, for example, the equivalent price would be $15.00 per decatherm or MMBTU.

Measuring Propane and Oil Consumption

The costs of propane and fuel oil are more volatile than natural gas because they are refined from crude oil and so are more vulnerable to supply disruptions.

- Propane and fuel oil are sold by the gallon. A gallon of fuel oil or propane produces 130,000 to 140,000 BTUs when burned.
- The current cost of propane and fuel oil ranges from $1.50 to $3.00 per gallon (2008).

Comparing Heating Energy Sources

A furnace or boiler burns fossil fuels, such as natural gas, propane, and oil fuel, to heat your home. A combustion water heater burns fossil fuel to heat domestic hot water. Burning these fuels inevitably wastes some of the heat of combustion. Some heat escapes up the chimney and some through the cabinet of the appliance. Older furnaces or boilers may operate at only 65 percent efficiency, while modern high-efficiency appliances operate at 90 percent efficiency or higher.

Electricity can also be used as a home heating energy source. But it's always more expensive as a heat source than combustion heating fuels because its production has such a poor efficiency. The primary losses occur at electrical generating plants where coal or oil is burned to make steam that spins turbines which drive electrical generators. Just like a home furnace, a large amount of waste heat is released up the smoke stack of these facilities. Large electrical losses are also incurred at transformers and in electrical transmission lines. By the time electrical energy is delivered to your home, the entire process has an efficiency of only about 30 percent, with 70 percent of the original energy being lost.

That's why electricity is not usually an economical heating fuel. There are a few exceptions, though. One is in homes with minimal need for heat. If you live in San Diego, for example, you probably need heat so infrequently that the inefficiency of electric heat doesn't translate into much additional cost. The other situation in which electric heat can be an economical choice is when it is provided to one room at a time, and it is operated instead of central heat. In some climates, there may be times of the year, for example, when you could get by using only a small electric heater (either built-in or portable) in your kitchen each morning. If you can do so without operating your central gas-fired furnace, you may actually incur less expense since you aren't heating your entire home.

The table *Cost Comparison Among Heating Sources* shows how the cost of energy purchased is not the same as energy delivered to your home.

ANALYZING YOUR UTILITY BILL

It's worth spending a few minutes to learn how to read the utility bills for your home. Gather a set of bills, a calculator, and a pencil. A single month's bill is a good place to start, but a year's worth of bills allows you to perform a more useful analysis. Some utility companies include a recap of the previous twelve months' consumption in each bill—this simplifies your task. If you don't have a complete set of utility bills, call your utility company and ask them to send you a year's worth of records.

When analyzing your home's energy consumption, it's helpful to divide your energy use into two broad categories: seasonal consumption and baseload consumption. This is true of both electric and gas consumption.

Your seasonal consumption includes the energy used for heating and cooling. Consumption may vary dramatically from season to season, and is largely dependent on the outdoor temperature. Your baseload consumption includes the energy used by appliances operated throughout the year: your water heater, refrigerator, stove, washer and dryer, computer, television, lighting, and various small appliances.

The dollar figures you derive here will help you evaluate the cost effectiveness of proposed home improvement measures. If, for example, your heating bills are three times greater than your cooling bills, you will likely see a greater benefit from adding wall insulation than you would from installing awnings on your south-facing windows. But if you live in a mild climate and your baseload consumption accounts for three-quarters of your total utility cost, you may get the most benefit from retrofits to your lighting and water-heating systems.

Cost Comparison Among Heating Sources

Energy type and how purchased	Cost per unit of purchased energy	Cost per therm of delivered heat
Natural gas	$1.50/therm	$2.14
Propane	$2.10/gallon	$3.00
Fuel oil	$2.70/gallon	$3.86
Electricity	$0.15/kWh	$4.35

The third column shows the cost of delivered heat for typical home heating systems with efficiencies of 70% for gas, oil, and propane. Electricity has a delivery efficiency of 100% within your home. Costs are averages for U.S. and Canada. (2008).

Baseload Versus Seasonal Energy Consumption

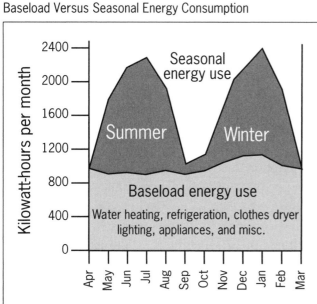

The home profiled here uses about 1000 kilowatt-hours monthly for baseload uses. It shows a winter peak for heating, and a summer peak for cooling. During the months of March, April, and September, the home uses little energy for heating or cooling. This home uses electricity only, but you can perform a similar analysis for a home that uses both gas and electric by totaling both bills for each month.

BASELOAD VERSUS SEASONAL CONSUMPTION

Refer to the chart *Analyzing Your Utility Bill* on page 11 to follow the case study we describe here. We first profile a cold-climate home, with its large heating load and no cooling load. But the process will be the same wherever you live.

- **Monthly baseload gas cost.** Note that the gas consumption for the sample home is lowest in June ($48), July ($48), August ($42). These months are composed of mostly baseload uses, when no heat was used. In this home, the baseload uses include a gas water heater and a gas clothes dryer. If a furnace had been the only gas equipment in this home, the baseload might have been near-zero for these months. In this case, we've identified three baseload-only months, so we calculate an average cost for those months.

  $48 + $48 + $42 = $138 for three months
  $138 ÷ 3 = $46 average monthly gas baseload

- **Annual baseload gas cost.** To calculate your annual baseload gas cost, multiply your estimated monthly baseload consumption by 12.

  $46 x 12 = $552 annual gas baseload

- **Total annual gas cost.** To calculate your *total* annual gas cost, add the gas bills from all 12 months.

  276 + 266 + 170 + 75 + 68 + 48 + 48 + 42 + 56 + 172 + 276 + 305 = $1802 annual gas cost

- **Seasonal gas cost (heating).** Finally, to calculate your annual gas consumption for heating, subtract your annual baseload gas cost from your total annual gas cost.

  $1802 - 552 = $1250 seasonal gas cost (heating)

Next we run a similar calculation for electric consumption to determine how much electrical energy is consumed by the heating system. If you have electric heat and no gas heating, this will be your primary heating expense. If you have a gas-fired furnace or boiler, you'll still have some small electrical expense for operating the system's fans or pumps. Once you perform a similar calculation for electric consumption, you can add the two up to determine the total cost of heating your home. Here we summarize the electrical consumption for the same cold-climate home. This procedure is identical to the one for gas consumption.

- **Monthly electric baseload cost.** The electric consumption is lowest in May ($86), June ($86), and July ($100). The electric baseload that is reflected here is lighting, a refrigerator and freezer, a kitchen range, a clothes washer (for the pump and motor—the hot water is gas heated), a dryer (for the motor—the heat is provided by gas), and miscellaneous appliances. In this case, we've identified three baseload-only months, so we calculate an average cost for those months.

  $86 + $86 + $100 = $272 for three months

  $272 ÷ 3 = $91 average monthly gas baseload

- **Annual electric baseload cost.** To calculate your annual baseload electrical cost, multiply your estimated monthly baseload consumption by 12.

  $91 x 12 = $1092 annual electric baseload

- **Total annual electric cost.** To calculate your total annual electric cost, add the electric bills from all 12 months.

  115 + 96 + 110 + 105 + 86 + 86 + 100 + 119 + 126 + 122 + 118 + 128 = $1311 annual electric cost

- **Seasonal electric cost (heating and other winter uses).** To calculate your annual electric consumption for heating, subtract your annual baseload electric cost from your total annual electric cost.

$1311 - 1092 = $219 seasonal electric cost

Summary For This Case Study

The annual baseload gas cost for this home is $552 (from the first procedure above). The annual baseload electric cost is $1092 (from the second procedure above). The *total baseload energy cost* of $1644 (total of both) is the cost of operating baseload equipment such as lighting, refrigeration, kitchen range, hot water heater, appliances, and miscellaneous loads. Improvements to these systems, such as installing compact fluorescent lamps, replacing a refrigerator, or insulating a water heater, would reduce this amount.

The annual seasonal gas cost, primarily heating for this home, is $1250 (from the first procedure above). The annual seasonal electric cost is $219 (from the second procedure above). The *total seasonal energy cost* of $1469 (total of both) is the cost of heating the home. This includes both gas and electricity to operate the heating system, and also the slight increase in consumption for lighting and appliances that is typical for most families in winter. You can reduce your seasonal consumption by adding insulation, air sealing your home, or by improving the efficiency of your heating system.

The process for analyzing the utility consumption of any home is the same. In the case of the hot-climate home profiled in the figure, the seasonal consumption shows a winter peak in gas consumption for heating, and a summer peak in electric consumption for cooling.

Analyzing Your Utility Bill

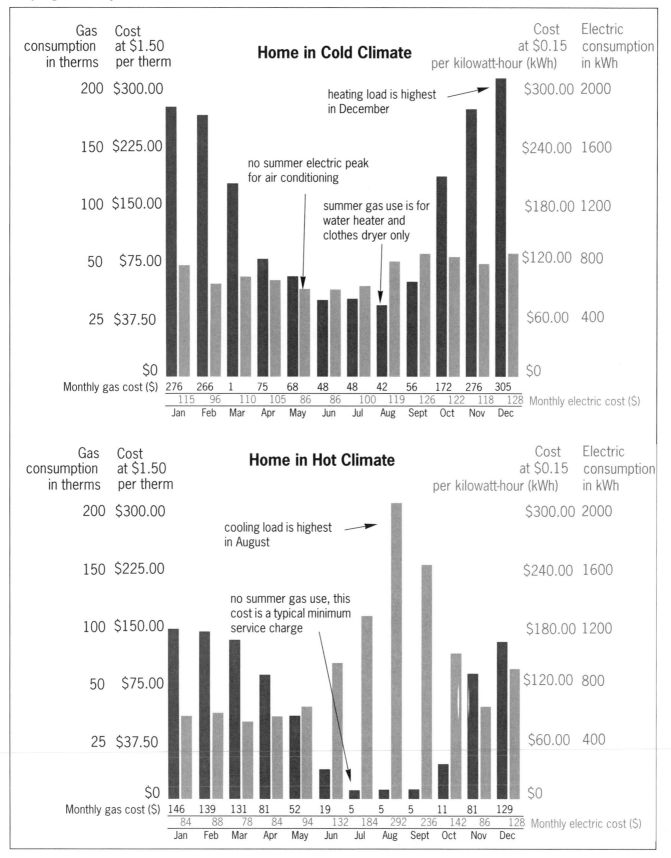

Home in Cold Climate

Gas consumption in therms | Cost at $1.50 per therm

heating load is highest in December

no summer electric peak for air conditioning

summer gas use is for water heater and clothes dryer only

Cost at $0.15 per kilowatt-hour (kWh) | Electric consumption in kWh

Monthly gas cost ($)	276	266	1	75	68	48	48	42	56	172	276	305
Monthly electric cost ($)	115	96	110	105	86	86	100	119	126	122	118	128
	Jan	Feb	Mar	Apr	May	Jun	Jul	Aug	Sept	Oct	Nov	Dec

Home in Hot Climate

Gas consumption in therms | Cost at $1.50 per therm

cooling load is highest in August

no summer gas use, this cost is a typical minimum service charge

Cost at $0.15 per kilowatt-hour (kWh) | Electric consumption in kWh

Monthly gas cost ($)	146	139	131	81	52	19	5	5	5	11	81	129
Monthly electric cost ($)	84	88	78	84	94	132	184	292	236	142	86	128
	Jan	Feb	Mar	Apr	May	Jun	Jul	Aug	Sept	Oct	Nov	Dec

Annual Natural Gas Consumption for U.S. Homes

Use	High	Average	Low
Space Heating	1000	450	100
Water Heating	700	250	100
Clothes Drying	100	60	0
Cooking	50	25	10
Totals	1850	785	210

All measurements in therms (100,000 BTU). To convert to decatherms (dkt), divide by 10. Summary from US EPA and other sources. For U.S. homes.

Calculating Your Consumption in Kilowatt-Hours and Therms

You may also want to estimate your electrical consumption in kilowatt-hours, or your gas consumption in therms. This can be useful for a few reasons. First, you can compare your consumption over a period of years. Since the cost of utilities typically increases over time, a comparison of cost will be skewed by rate inflation. Once you learn how to analyze your utility bill, you will find it more useful to compare your consumption in kilowatt-hours and therms rather than in dollars. Cost is important to all of us, but its variability makes cost a poor point of comparison at a time when the cost is rising.

The other reason to calculate actual consumption rather than cost is so you can make a comparison among homes that are profiled here or elsewhere in the press. That's why we've provided tables that show typical consumption for U.S. households.

To calculate your actual gas or electric consumption (rather than cost), follow this procedure:

- Compile your utility bills as for the cost analysis procedure above. Separate out the electric and gas accounts.
- Identify the lowest month for each type of energy.
- Multiply the monthly baseload times twelve for each type of energy. This is your annual baseload for each.
- Total up all twelve months for each type of energy. Subtract the baseload calculated above to determine your seasonal consumption for each.

These baseload figures (in kilowatt-hours and therms) will provide insight into your home's equipment. For your gas bill, if you have a gas furnace and gas water heater, your summer gas bills reflect only the cost of water heating. If instead you have gas heating and electric water heating, then you may see a summer baseline gas consumption of zero. For your electric bill, if you have air-conditioning, your highest bills will be in summer; if you have no air conditioning, then your bills show only baseload consumption for several summer months.

Comparing Your Home to Others

You'll find it helpful to know how your home compares to others. The table *Annual Natural Gas Consumption for U.S. Homes* shown here gives a rough idea how much natural gas is consumed in the average North American home. The table *Range of Annual Consumption for All-Electric Homes* on page 13 profiles an all-electric home. For homes that also use gas, fuel oil, or propane, the comparison is more complicated, but the general proportions still hold true.

The tables show a range of consumption that illustrates how little energy is consumed by the most efficient homes. The High Use figures are for large or poorly built homes. The Low Use figures reflect small homes that are built according to reasonably stringent standards. The Passive House standard has been developed in the European markets, and has recently been adopted by a few progressive builders in North America. Homes built to Passive House standards exemplify how well modern homes can perform.

These tables may help you understand how the energy you consume can be separated into specific uses within your home. To estimate how much energy you use in each category, you must analyze your home, your appliances, and your behaviors. We'll discuss this in more depth later.

Range of Annual Consumption for All-Electric Homes

Type of use	High usage	Low usage	Passive House[a]
Heating and ventilation[b]	20,000	4000	3000
Air-conditioning[b]	7000	600	0
Water heating	8000	2400	1000[c]
Refrigeration	2000	600	400
Clothes drying	2000	700	0[d]
Lighting	2000	700	400
Other	3000	2000	1400
Annual totals (kWh)	44,000	11,000	6200
Annual consumption (kWh per square foot)	26	6.4	3.6

a. The Passive House standard establishes guidelines for extremely efficient homes.
b. Highly variable depending on climate, occupants' temperature sensitivity, and personal preferences.
b. Presumed solar hot water system, includes energy for pumping and backup heat.
d. Clothes dried on clothesline.
A kilowatt-hour of electricity in the U.S. and Canada cost between 10 cents and 20 cents (2008). Figures are for an average single-family home of about 1700 square feet.

Estimating Your Carbon Emissions

Most of us use energy that comes from just a few sources. The table *Carbon Emissions Per Unit of Energy and Per Therm* on page 14 shows two ways to measure how much carbon dioxide is emitted by various energy sources:

- How much CO_2 is emitted per unit of fuel consumed.
- How much CO_2 is emitted as a result of generating one therm of energy.

Note that, of all fossil fuels, natural gas creates the smallest CO_2 emissions per therm of heat created. Electricity in general produces the highest CO_2 emissions per therm of heat, though this varies based upon how the electricity is generated. For this reason, electricity is not usually the cheapest energy source for heating, especially if natural gas or other combustion fuels are available. Electricity is best applied to uses for which it is the only choice, such as lighting and appliances.

Carbon Emissions for Typical U.S. Households

Type of energy	Typical use	Typical CO_2 emission
Natural gas	920 therms	11,000 lbs.
Fuel oil	660 gallons	14,500 lbs.
Electricity	10,800 kWh	16,300 lbs

Your household probably uses natural gas or fuel oil, but not both. Virtually all households use electricity. From Energy Information Administration *A Look at Residential Consumption.*

This table allows you to estimate the carbon dioxide emissions you produce with your current energy use:

- Compile your utility bills, and calculate your total annual consumption of heating fuel (in therms or gallons) and electricity (in kilowatt-hours).
- Find your heating fuel in the chart, and multiply your annual consumption in therms by the CO_2 emission per therm of the fuel you use. This product is your annual CO_2 output in pounds for that fuel.
- Multiply your annual consumption of electricity in kilowatt-hours times the appropriate emission per kilowatt-hour. This product is your annual CO_2 output in pounds for electricity.

For example, the average U.S. household uses about 920 therms of natural gas annually. This represents an output of about 11,000 pounds of carbon dioxide. The average U.S. household uses about 11,000 kilowatt-hours of electricity annually, an output of about 16,500 pounds of carbon dioxide.

You may note that the weight of CO_2 produced by the combustion of fuel is greater than the original weight of the fuel itself. That's because atmospheric oxygen combines with fuel in the process of combustion, and so its weight is added to the weight of the carbon dioxide byproduct.

Carbon Emissions Per Unit of Energy and Per Therm

Type of energy	CO_2 per unit	CO_2 per therm
Natural gas	12 lbs./therm	12 lbs.
Propane	13 lbs./gal.	14 lbs.
Fuel oil	26 lbs./gal.	19 lbs.
Wood	5000 lbs./cord	21 lbs.
Electricity from gas	1.3 lbs./kWh	39 lbs.
Electricity from oil	2.2 lbs./kWh	63 lbs.
Electricity from coal	2.4 lbs./kWh	69 lbs.
Electricity: average from all U.S. sources	1.5 lbs./kWh	45 lbs.

From American Council for an Energy-Efficient Economy and Energy Information Administration.

HOME ENERGY AUDITS

Once you've evaluated your energy consumption and costs, you'll have a general idea where to direct your home improvement efforts. But if you'd like to fine-tune your analysis, you should consider hiring a professional to do a home energy audit. Energy audits can take several forms.

Utility Company Audit

Many utility companies offer free energy audits to their customers. This offer may apply to all customers, though it is sometimes reserved for low-income customers. The utility audit usually offers a brief snapshot of the home, with the intention of helping homeowners decide where to apply their conservation efforts. The utility auditor will sometimes install a few measures such as water heater wraps or compact fluorescent lamps. Contact your utility company to schedule this type of simple audit.

Comprehensive Energy Audit

Comprehensive energy audits are usually offered by private consulting firms. The auditor will perform a room-by-room assessment of your home, evaluating insulation, air leakage, heating and cooling equipment, appliances, doors and windows, and other systems. He

or she should perform a blower door test to evaluate air leakage, and make recommendations for air sealing. If you have combustion heating or water heating equipment (burning gas, propane, or oil), the auditor should perform a combustion safety evaluation. If you have a forced air heating or cooling system, the auditor should test the duct work for air leakage.

The auditor should evaluate your utility bills, and provide a written report that describes the home's components, and makes recommendations for energy upgrades. This report can serve as a blueprint for your future home improvement projects.

See the *Resources* on page 173 for more information about locating an energy auditor in your area, or contact your State Energy Office.

Home Energy Rating System

The Home Energy Rating System (HERS) provides a standardized method of measuring the energy efficiency of residential structures. HERS ratings can be used in several ways: to help lenders qualify both new and existing homes for Energy Efficiency Mortgages (EEMs), to identify new homes that meet Energy Star standards, to qualify homes for federal tax credits, and to help consumers compare homes that they are considering purchasing. A HERS rating can also be used to evaluate the likely savings from home efficiency upgrades such as those described in this book.

To assign a HERS rating to your home, an energy auditor will visit your home to gather data. He or she will analyze this information with an approved software program, and produce a numerical rating for your home. A lower number is better on this scale. A rating of zero is given to a zero-energy home, one which requires no net use of external energy. A rating of 85 or lower earns the home the ENERGY STAR label for new homes in much of the U.S. A rating of 80 or lower is required for ENERGY STAR homes in the north-central region. A rating of 100 is the basis for the HERS index, and represents a hypothetical home that is built in compliance with the International Energy Conservation Code (IECC). The average home today in the U.S. has a HERS rating of 130.

If you plan to perform major energy retrofits to your home, we recommend that you have a HERS rating performed as part of the design process. Be sure to ask for a prioritized list of improvements that would reduce your home's HERS rating. You may be able to add the projected cost of these improvements to an Energy Efficiency Mortgage (EEM). Ask your lender.

See the *Resources* on page 173 for more information about HERS raters, the Residential Energy Services Network (RESNET), and Energy Efficiency Mortgages.

SETTING GOALS FOR YOUR HOME

Throughout this book, we illustrate a variety of ways to improve your home. The projects all focus on energy savings, but each will have the added benefit of reducing your carbon emissions. Some will also improve the durability of your home by controlling the flow of moisture both from within your home and from outdoors. This careful management of moisture can benefit your health by reducing the occurrence of mold and mildew in your home. Finally, many of these projects will improve the safety of your home, especially those that include testing or upgrades of your heating system.

The Passive House Model

Homebuilders in Germany and Austria have recently established new standards of energy efficiency for homes. The Passive House provides outstanding comfort, requires very little heating, and uses no energy for cooling. We've compared these ultimate homes to our existing housing stock in the graph *Evolution of Home Energy Savings*. It illustrates how efficient the best modern homes can be. It's a vision we should all keep in mind as we adapt our existing housing stock to meet the challenges of the future.

The success of the Passive House design results from setting clear numerical goals for these extremely energy-efficient homes.

Heating capacity. Install no more than one watt of heating capacity per square foot of floor space. Under this standard, a 1500-square-foot home would be insulated so well that a single electric space heater could heat it during the coldest weather.

Evolution of Home Energy Savings

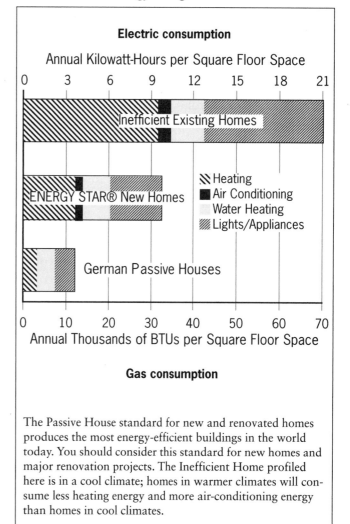

The Passive House standard for new and renovated homes produces the most energy-efficient buildings in the world today. You should consider this standard for new homes and major renovation projects. The Inefficient Home profiled here is in a cool climate; homes in warmer climates will consume less heating energy and more air-conditioning energy than homes in cool climates.

Annual heating consumption. Use no more than 1.5 kilowatt-hours per square foot annually to heat the home.

Annual overall consumption. Use no more than four kilowatt-hours per square foot annually in total energy use.

Thousands of such buildings have recently been built or renovated to meet this standard in Germany and Austria. A few hundred North American homes probably also meet the Passive House standard. It serves as an example of a successful energy conservation initiative and provides a useful goal for the U.S. design and construction industries.

TEN SURE-FIRE WAYS TO IMPROVE YOUR HOME'S EFFICIENCY

There are some principles that never change when improving the efficiency of a home. The ten items listed here are guaranteed to reduce your energy consumption and reduce your carbon emissions. We offer detailed advice about each item elsewhere in this book.

Adjust Your Habits

Many families could shave at least 25 percent off their energy costs by adopting energy-conserving habits. Furnaces and air conditioners typically log many hours of operation during times when heating and air-conditioning aren't really necessary. Appliances are often left running when not needed. Hot water consumption for many families can be reduced one-half through simple changes in habits.

What you can do Control your thermostat faithfully, or install a programmable thermostat and learn to program it. Turn lights and appliances off when not needed. Use less hot water. Wash your clothes in cold water. Use a clothesline instead of a dryer.

Improve Lighting Efficiency

Old-fashioned incandescent lamps are still the norm in many homes, yet compact fluorescent lamps (CFLs) are inexpensive and easy to install.

What you can do Convert all your incandescent light bulbs to CFLs or tubular fluorescents. Install occupancy sensors and timers if necessary to turn lights off when not needed.

Improve Appliance Efficiency

Your refrigerator and washing machine typically are the most inefficient appliances in the home. Computers and entertainment centers usually draw "phantom loads" even when in the "off" position.

What you can do Replace your refrigerator if it was manufactured before 1993. Buy a model with an ENERGY STAR rating. When you next replace your washing machine, buy a front-loading machine with an ENERGY STAR rating. When you next replace your dryer, buy one with a moisture sensor and an ENERGY STAR rating. Install switched plug strips at computer stations and entertainment centers and turn them off at the switch when not in use.

Improve Water-Heating Efficiency

Most of our homes have water heaters that include a storage tank. Those that consume gas or oil operate at less than 60 percent efficiency, meaning that 40 percent of the fuel you consume goes up the chimney or is lost at the storage tank. This year-round expense will become more important with rising energy costs.

What you can do Lower the thermostat on your water heater. Install a water-heater blanket. Insulate your hot water pipes. Install a water-saving shower head. Invest in a solar water-heating system.

Provide Summer Shade

Blocking solar heat is the best way to control air-conditioning costs. The best shading comes from trees. Sun screens, awnings, and window films are also very effective.

What you can do Shade your roof and your hottest windows with trees, awnings, trellises, or other shading devices. When you next change your siding or roofing, choose reflective surfaces for the roof and walls.

Seal Air Leakage

Air leakage wastes energy by allowing expensive heated or cooled air to leak out of your home. It also causes uncomfortable drafts, and can carry pollutants into your home. The most significant leaks are in hidden areas like attics and crawl spaces. Windows and doors aren't usually the main problem.

What you can do Hire an energy auditor who can do a blower door test to locate air leaks. Seal the biggest leaks in your attic and crawl space.

Add Insulation

Almost all modern homes have too little insulation in the attics, walls, and floors. There is no better energy-saving measure than installing more insulation.

What you can do   Insulate your attic to at least R-40 (14 to 16 inches). Insulate your walls until they are full. Fill floor cavities with insulation or insulate foundation walls with one to two inches of foam insulation.

Upgrade Windows and Doors

The doors and windows in most homes are a major gap in the building's thermal boundary, allowing heat to escape in winter and enter in summer.

What you can do   Replace your windows and doors, but only as part of a major energy renovation which includes adding insulation to the exterior of the building. Don't just install new windows and doors without adding wall insulation at the same time.

Improve Heating and Cooling Equipment

Your heating and cooling equipment may account for the majority of your utility expense. Old low-efficiency equipment may be part of the problem, but duct leakage, inadequate airflow, and malfunctioning controls are also to blame.

What you can do   Shop for a good contractor and ask for a complete heating and cooling tune-up. Have your technician seal your home's duct system if appropriate. If you plan to install a new furnace or air conditioner, ask for a smaller unit that has a higher efficiency rating.

Seal Your Duct System

Most duct systems are not sealed during installation. If the ducts run through unconditioned areas like crawl spaces, attached garages, or attics, duct leakage can be a major energy problem. Besides the leakage of heated and cooled air, duct leakage may draw moisture and pollutants into the home.

What you can do   Have your duct system professionally tested for air leakage. Seal the leaks by starting at the furnace and working your way outwards.

Lighting and Appliances

Lighting, appliances, and water heating—the types of consumption we call baseload—account for up to two-thirds of the energy consumed in North American households. If you've analyzed your utility bills as described in *Analyzing Your Utility Bill* on page 8, you've estimated how much of your utility bill goes to baseload uses and how much goes to heating and cooling. This will show you how much you can potentially save by improving the efficiency of your baseload uses.

The size of your baseload varies depending on your climate, your home, and your habits. If you live in a very hot or very cold climate, for example, your total utility costs will be relatively high, with your baseload accounting for a smaller portion of those bills. If you live where both winters and summers are mild, or if your home has an efficient building shell with good insulation and air-sealing details, your total utility costs may be low, but your baseload will account for a larger portion of your bill.

In this chapter, we'll show you some easy ways to improve the efficiency of your existing lighting and appliances. In many cases, you can make improvements that save energy right away. We'll also consider upgrades to your lighting system and replacement strategies for your appliances. We dedicate all of Chapter 3 to water heating since it is the most complicated of the baseload uses.

Let ENERGY STAR® Be Your Guide

The ENERGY STAR® label has emerged as one of the best ways to identify the most energy-efficient appliances available in both the U.S. and Canada.

EVALUATE YOUR LIGHTING AND APPLIANCES

How many of your light fixtures are fitted with old-fashioned incandescent light bulbs? Replacing incandescents with compact fluorescent lamps usually has a payback of less than two years. This is one of the best investments described in this book.

What is the wattage of the lamps installed in your fixtures? If you have fixtures that provide more light than you need, you can easily install smaller lamps and save energy. This is especially true of lights that are left on all night, such as nightlights and outdoor fixtures.

Do you have light fixtures installed over work areas that can be used instead of overhead fixtures? Task lighting that is installed close to your work provides illumination more efficiently than ceiling fixtures. Try using task lighting without turning on overhead fixtures to get the maximum benefit.

Do you have light fixtures that tend to be left on when they are not needed? The easiest solution is to turn the lights off when you don't need them. But lighting controls such as motion detectors and timers can also reduce this consumption.

How old is your refrigerator? Does it have an ENERGY STAR rating? Recent technological advances have made new refrigerators and freezers two to three times more efficient than older models.

Does your clothes washer have an ENERGY STAR rating? Newer front-loading washing machines use less hot water, cold water, electricity, and soap.

Do you use a clothesline or drying rack? You can reduce your drying cost to zero with this simple and effective approach.

If you have a dishwasher, does it have an ENERGY STAR rating? Dishwashers use cold water, hot water, and electricity. The best new machines allow you to trim consumption by giving you control over cycle length, water consumption, and drying cycle.

If you have groups of appliances at a desk or entertainment center, can you put them all on a control strip? Most of these appliances consume electricity even when they aren't in use. Control strips let you shut them off.

LIGHTING BASICS

The first step toward improving your lighting efficiency is to learn how to compare various types of lamps. In lighting terminology, a lamp is the tube or bulb that emits light. A fixture holds the lamps or bulbs. The output of those lamps is measured in lumens, which we perceive as brightness.

Lighting efficiency is described by the term "efficacy" (pronounced EFF-u-ke-see). Efficacy is the measure of lumens emitted per watt of electricity consumed. A higher efficacy is better.

- A 100-watt incandescent lamp that emits 1200 lumens of light has an efficacy of 12.

$$1200 \div 100 = 12$$

- A comparable 28-watt compact fluorescent lamp that emits 1200 lumens has an efficacy of 43.

$$1200 \div 28 = 43$$

The compact fluorescent lamp has an efficacy more than three times higher than the incandescent, and so uses less than one-third the electricity while emitting the same amount of light. When shopping for lamps, choose those with the highest efficacy possible to save energy.

Incandescent Light Bulb

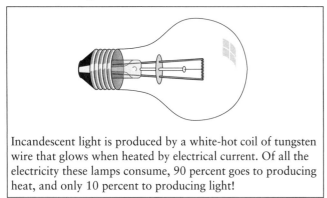

Incandescent light is produced by a white-hot coil of tungsten wire that glows when heated by electrical current. Of all the electricity these lamps consume, 90 percent goes to producing heat, and only 10 percent to producing light!

TYPES OF LIGHTING

To craft a plan for improving your lighting efficiency, first inspect your light fixtures to see what sort of lamps you currently have installed. Your lighting upgrades will likely focus on lamp replacement, though replacing fixtures is also a good upgrade.

Standard Incandescent Lamps

Incandescent light bulbs are the oldest style of lamp. They are also the least efficient, and so are increasingly prohibited by both building codes and government bodies. Standard incandescent lamps have efficacies of 10 to 17 lumens per watt. Incandescent lamps have the shortest service life of the common lighting types, lasting only 750 to 2000 hours. They are the cheapest of the lamps at less than $1 for most types. But they are a poor value because of their short life and poor performance.

Halogen Lamps

Halogen lamps are a specialized type of incandescent bulb. They are filled with halogen gas that allows them to burn hotter and somewhat more efficiently. But they still run at an efficacy that is scarcely higher than standard incandescent lamps.

Halogens lamps produce a whiter light than is emitted by standard incandescents. They are always installed in dedicated fixtures, and are mounted under cabinets, as wall scones, and as ceiling fixtures.

Halogens have an efficacy of 12 to 22 lumens per watt, and their lifespan varies from 2000 to 4000 hours.

Comparison Among Types of Lamps

Type of Lamp	Efficiency (lumens/watt)	Typical lifespan (hours)
Incandescent	10–17	750–2500
Halogen	12–22	2000–4000
Fluorescent tube lamp	30–100	7000–24,000
Compact fluorescent lamp (CFL)	50–70	8000-10,000

Fluorescent Tube Lamps

Fluorescent tube lamps are among the most efficient lamps available, with efficacies that run as high as 100 lumens per watt. They are often installed in kitchens, laundry rooms, and other utility areas. Fluorescent lamps have a service life of 7000 to 24,000 hours.

The quality of fluorescent tube lights has dramatically improved in recent years. Early fluorescent lamps cast a blue pall over a room, and were prone to flicker and hum. Modern fluorescents are quiet, and are available in models that produce natural colors of light.

Older tube fluorescents were known by the designation T-12 ($^{12}/_8$ or 1-$^1/_2$" in diameter). The most efficient new fluorescent lamps are slim T-8 tubes (1 inch). They fit in standard fixtures, and are 10 to 15 percent more efficient than the old T-12s.

Many new T-8 fixtures are equipped with high-efficiency electronic ballasts, which increase the fixture's efficiency by 30 to 40 percent compared with the older fixtures. These efficient T-8 fixtures provide a great replacement option for the inefficient multi-bulb fixtures found above many bathroom mirrors. Fluorescent fixtures also work well for indirect lighting when installed in a wall-mounted valance, which bounces light off the ceiling. Four-tube ceiling-mounted fixtures are a common choice in kitchens, where they produce handsome savings in this most frequently used location.

Fluorescent tube fixtures vary in price from $100 to $200. In most cases, installation will take about an hour if wiring is already in place.

Compact Fluorescent Lamps

Compact fluorescent lamps (CFLs) range in efficacy from 50 to 70 lumens per watt. They consume only one-quarter to one-third the energy of incandescent lamps. They are somewhat less efficient than fluorescent tube lamps, but can be fitted into standard light fixtures.

CFLs have a service life of up to 10,000 hours. However, some cheaper CFLs have a poor service record and may fail after only a few thousand hours. We suggest purchasing CFLs only from the major manufacturers. Good quality CFL lamps cost $2 to $5 each.

The most common CFLs have threaded bases that allow you to retrofit them to existing fixtures. Most homes have many incandescent lamps that can be easily upgraded to CFLs.

Install CFLs in light fixtures that you use the most. Start by replacing incandescent lights that are on four hours a day or more, such as those in your kitchen, bathrooms, and living room.

If you plan to replace an entire light fixture, or are choosing fixtures for a new home, select fixtures that are designed for CFLs. CFL fixtures have plug-in replaceable CFL bulbs rather than screw-in bases. They include improved reflectors that distribute light more efficiently, and they come in a wide range of designs. Many energy codes require dedicated fluorescent fixtures in high-use areas such as kitchens.

Dedicated CFL fixtures cost $50 to $125. Installation will take about an hour if wiring is already in place.

Fluorescent Lamp Operation

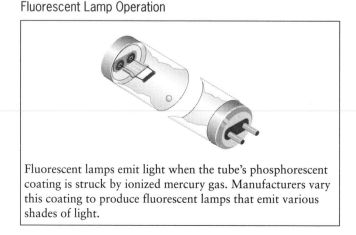

Fluorescent lamps emit light when the tube's phosphorescent coating is struck by ionized mercury gas. Manufacturers vary this coating to produce fluorescent lamps that emit various shades of light.

Compact Fluorescent Lamps

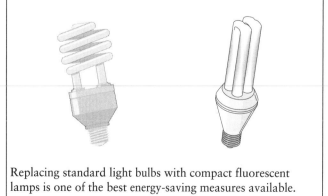

Replacing standard light bulbs with compact fluorescent lamps is one of the best energy-saving measures available.

OUTDOOR LIGHTS

Many of us use outdoor lights for safety and security. But leaving outdoor lights on all night uses a lot energy, and there are several ways to reduce your outdoor lighting expenses.

The first step is to change any incandescent bulbs to fluorescent lamps. If you live in a cold climate, check the minimum service temperature of the CFL, since some CFLs operate poorly in temperatures below 15°F. Choose fluorescent "wall packs" that are designed for outdoor use. They cost $25 to $75 each, and are installed in a half hour or less if they replace an existing fixture.

Photocells and occupancy sensors, discussed next, can reduce the operating hours of outdoor lights.

Solar-powered lights are another good option for reducing outdoor energy consumption. These stand-alone units are simply pushed into the ground or fastened to a fence where you need light. They utilize a small solar panel to charge a built-in battery during the day. Though not as bright as line-powered lights, solar-powered yard lights provide enough light for outdoor entertaining, or for safe night-time navigation around your yard.

The cost of solar yard lights ranges from less than $50 for single units to $200 or more for groups of fixtures that are powered by a single solar panel.

Solar-Powered Yard Lights

Solar yard lights are a cost-effective substitute for standard line-voltage outdoor fixtures. They can also be installed where electrical wiring is not available.

INSTALLING LIGHTING CONTROLS

Adding additional controls beyond the traditional on-off switch to your lighting can save both energy and effort. Making the change is also fairly simple. The most common residential lighting controls are occupancy sensors and photocells that turn lights on and off, and dimmers that allow you to operate lamps at a lower wattage.

Occupancy Sensors

Occupancy sensors sense heat or motion and activate lights when a person enters the area and shut off the lights after detecting no human presence for a period of time. Outdoor occupancy sensors offer security advantages over continuous lighting—the abruptly switched lights startle intruders and alert residents and neighbors to activity in the area. The savings can total $20 to $40 per year if these are installed where lights would otherwise operate all night. Most hardware stores sell exterior fixtures with built-in occupancy sensors. Outdoor fixtures with built-in motion detectors cost $50 to $100. Installation is simple if you are familiar with electrical wiring. An electrician should be able to install one in less than an hour.

Photocells

Photocells can switch on outdoor lights at dusk and switch them off at dawn. This often results in increased consumption if the lights were not previously on through the night, and so these controls should be used only where outdoor lights absolutely must be operated all night. Most outdoor fixtures that utilize motion detectors also have integrated photocells so the lights operate only at night *and* when someone is present.

Timers

Timers are used to automatically control lights that might otherwise be left on. Timers might be appropriate in children's rooms or rarely used rooms such as basements. Timers come in two general types: the simple wind-up timer that you twist to a selected period of time, and digital timers that allow you to select a fixed period of time such as 10 or 20 minutes. Most timers cost less than $50, and they can be installed in a half-hour or less.

Dimmers

Dimmers save energy by reducing the consumption of fixtures when a low output of light is acceptable. They allow you to use the same fixture to illuminate activities that require high light levels, such as cleaning and cooking, and those that require only minimal illumination such as night-time navigation.

The best choice of lamps for fixtures with dimmers is CFLs. Buy CFLs that are designed to be dimmed—read the fine print on the box or in the manufacturer's literature.

Dimmable CFLs cost $8 to $15 each. Their additional cost over standard CFLS will be returned in savings if you regularly dim them.

Dimming incandescent lamps, on the other hand, reduces their light output more than their wattage, making them less efficient when dimmed. For this reason, dimmers are not an effective energy-saving measure for incandescent lamps.

APPLIANCE BASICS

You can save a surprising amount of money by simply changing the way you operate your appliances. Some simple adjustments and maintenance can be very effective, too.

Setting Refrigerator and Freezer Controls

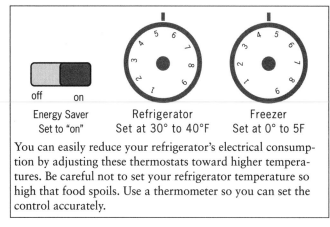

Energy Saver
Set to "on"

Refrigerator
Set at 30° to 40°F

Freezer
Set at 0° to 5F

You can easily reduce your refrigerator's electrical consumption by adjusting these thermostats toward higher temperatures. Be careful not to set your refrigerator temperature so high that food spoils. Use a thermometer so you can set the control accurately.

Refrigerator and Freezer

In most homes, the refrigerator consumes more electricity than any other appliance, accounting for 8 to 15 percent of the total electrical consumption.

Follow these tips to reduce the cost of running your refrigerator and freezer:

- Use a thermometer to measure your refrigerator and freezer temperatures. Adjust the thermostats inside the refrigerator until the thermometer reads 38° to 40°F for the refrigerator and 0° to 5°F for the freezer.
- Activate the Energy Saver switch if your refrigerator has one. This controls the anti-sweat heaters that are sometimes needed in moist climates to control condensation and frost that would otherwise form near the gaskets around the door. Deactivate the Energy Saver switch only if you actually perceive a moisture problem.
- Don't open the doors more than necessary. Decide exactly what you want to get out, open the door and get it, then close the door.
- Use a soft brush or vacuum to clean the coils on your refrigerator or freezer periodically. They are located either on the back or on the bottom of the unit.

Clothes Dryer

One of the best ways to reduce the cost of doing laundry is to avoid using your dryer. By setting up an outdoor clothesline or indoor drying rack, you can reduce your clothes drying expense to zero. This will save $100 to $200 per year for most households.

Follow these guidelines when you do use your dryer:

- Run your dryer with full loads only. This may increase the time needed to dry each load, but the energy consumed will be less than for running multiple smaller loads.
- Clean your dryer's lint filter after each cycle to maximize the airflow through your clothes.
- If your dryer has an Automatic Dry or Moisture Sensor cycle, use that setting instead of the timer. This will save 10 to 15 percent on energy usage

because the dryer will turn off when the load is dry rather than running for a fixed period of time. For the first few loads, set the control near the bottom of the range offered (less dry), and see if your clothes are dry enough. Inch it upward to find the minimum setting that still does the job. Mark this optimum setting once you find it.

- When possible, position your clothes dryer on an outside wall of your home to minimize the length of dryer duct leading outdoors. Every foot of dryer vent, and every bend in the vent, reduces the amount of air that passes through the dryer, and increases your drying time and expense. Use smooth aluminum vent pipe instead of flexible plastic tubing for your dryer vent since it has far less airflow resistance. If you must use a flexible vent, keep it short, support it to prevent drooping, and make sure it has no kinks.

About 90 percent of the energy used by washing machines is contained in the hot water they consume. Water-saving tips are included in *Adjusting Your Water-Heating Habits* on page 28.

Entertainment Centers

Many modern appliances consume electricity even when they are off. This energy is used by transformers, remote controls, clocks, and timers. These always-on "phantom" loads use electricity costing $50 to $100 annually in many homes.

For all appliances that draw phantom loads—such as computers, TVs, VCRs, stereos, cable boxes, and other entertainment devices—you can install a power strip with a switch that you can turn off when you are not using them.

If you need to keep some appliances on all the time, perhaps to retain the programming in a VCR, you can still run all the other appliances on the plug strip while plugging the needed appliance into an always-on outlet. Some plug strips now feature a single always-on receptacle for this purpose.

Clotheslines and Clothes Racks Save Energy

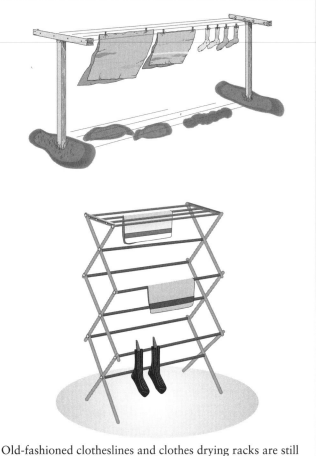

Old-fashioned clotheslines and clothes drying racks are still some of the best energy saving devices available.

Plug Strips Control Phantom Loads

Many electrical appliances draw power 24 hours a day. By connecting groups of appliances to a plug strip, you can turn them all on or off at the same time.

REPLACING APPLIANCES

When purchasing new appliances, the best way to identify the most energy-efficient models available is to look for the ENERGY STAR. This designation is used by both the U.S. and Canadian governments to show consumers which appliances are the best in their class.

You should also examine the Energy Guide labels posted on the models you're considering. They are posted on all major appliances and help you compare the annual energy use of the model you're considering to the most efficient appliance available. But the presence of a yellow Energy Guide label does not mean that you are looking at an efficient appliance. Only the Energy Star label offers that assurance.

To help you make wise decisions about new appliances, we recommend you read the *Consumer Guide to Home Energy Savings,* published by the American Council for an Energy Efficient Economy. See the *Resources* on page 173 for more information.

Replacing Refrigerators and Freezers

Recent technological advances have allowed the manufacture of vastly improved refrigerators. New units consume as little as one-third the energy of models sold ten years ago, yet they cost little more than the older models.

Replacing an older refrigerator with an ENERGY STAR model is a sure way to reduce your electricity costs significantly. But remember that the ENERGY STAR designation, and the comparison among refrigerators on the yellow Energy Guide label, is for models with similar features (size, configuration of doors, presence of automatic defrost, presence of through-the-door dispensers). To buy the most conservative refrigerator, shop for models with the features noted below, then choose a specific model that has both an ENERGY STAR designation and a good ranking on the Energy Guide label.

- Buy the smallest model that will sufficiently serve your family. Big refrigerators always consume more due to the increased surface area and longer door gaskets.

- Buy a unit with an upper freezer compartment. Side-by-side refrigerator/freezers tend to use more energy because of the longer door gaskets.

- Avoid units with ice and water dispensers in the door. These features create a weakness in the thermal insulation that will cost you money every month.

Resist the temptation to move an old refrigerator out to the garage or to sell it. Older refrigerators are very inefficient and should be recycled. Ask your appliance dealer about disposal. They are required to recycle refrigerators in a way that prevents the refrigerant from escaping into the atmosphere, where it could damage the ozone layer.

Read the Energy Guide Label

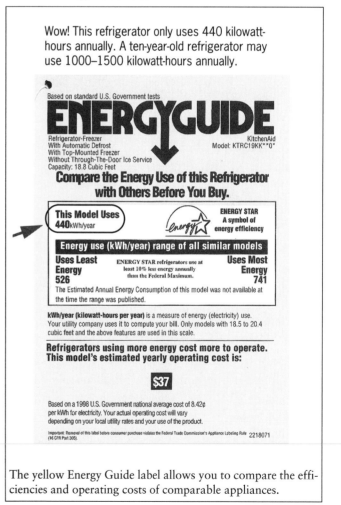

The yellow Energy Guide label allows you to compare the efficiencies and operating costs of comparable appliances.

Electrical Consumption of Typical Appliances

Appliance	Annual usage (kWh)	Annual cost
Ten-year-old refrigerator or freezer	1250	$188
New ENERGY STAR refrigerator or freezer	500	$75
Television	100–1000	$15–$150
Clothes dryer	1200	$180
Well pump	500	$75
Furnace fan	500	$75
Computer	50–400	$8–$60
Hot tub, spa	2300	$345
Water bed	1000	$150

Data from Lawrence Berkeley Laboratory and others. Based on 15¢ per kilowatt-hour for electricity.

Replacing Washers and Dryers

Front-loading, or horizontal-axis, washing machines use far less energy and water than top-loading machines. According to recent field tests, a front-loading machine can save you 60 percent of the energy, 40 percent of the water, and 20 percent of detergent that you would use with a top-loading machine. Front-loading washers also spin faster, wringing more water out of the clothes than a top-loading washer. This saves approximately 20 percent of the energy needed for clothes drying.

Front-loading washers cost approximately 50 percent more than conventional top-loading models, with the average front-loader costing about $1200. You can usually re-coup this initial investment in two to five years, especially if you have a large family or an electric water heater.

For dryers, be sure to look for the automatic temperature or humidity-sensing option. This will save you 10 to 15 percent on the cost of running your dryer.

THE BOTTOM LINE

The decisions you make in the management of your lighting and appliances will have an effect on your utility bills that will be apparent in the first month. You can start by making some simple changes in your habits. You can make additional improvements with small projects such as installing new fixtures. Finally, do some research before you buy any new appliance to make sure you are taking full advantage of the best current technologies.

- Whenever you shop for appliances, always choose models that display the ENERGY STAR label. If you buy a refrigerator, be sure to also buy the smallest model that will fit your needs.
- Turn the lights off when you don't need them. Install motion detectors or timers in areas where you tend to leave lights on for long periods of time.
- Install CFLs in any fixtures you use more than a few hours per day. Choose wattages of about one-third that of the incandescent bulbs they replace.
- Install dedicated fluorescent fixtures where you use the most lighting.
- Use a clothes line to reduce your drying costs to zero. Clean the lint out of your dryer's ducting. Be sure the ducting leads to the outdoors. Use the Automatic Dry feature on your dryer.
- Clean the coils on the outside of your refrigerator and freezer. Adjust your refrigerator thermostat to 38 to 40°F. Adjust your freezer thermostat to 0 to 5°F.
- Set up a plug strip wherever you have groups of appliances so you can shut them all off at once.

Water Heating

Heating water is the largest baseload use in most households. In mild climates, such as California, many families spend as much or more on water heating as they do on heating or air-conditioning.

In this chapter, we describe how to reduce hot water consumption through both simple adjustments to behavior and improvements to your water-heating system. We also outline the current options for upgrading your equipment.

EVALUATE YOUR WATER-HEATING EFFICIENCY

What type of water heater do you have: a storage tank, a tankless or on-demand system, or a solar system? Traditional storage water heaters are the least efficient type of system, and so offer the best opportunities for improvement. Tankless on-demand systems are more efficient, and offer few opportunities for improvement. Solar water heating is the paradigm of efficiency.

If you have either a storage or tankless system, does it use electricity, gas, or oil? If you have electric water heat, your current high cost of water heating will improve the payback of your efficiency improvements. If you heat with gas or oil, your improvements will have a less favorable return.

What is the temperature of hot water at the taps in your home? If your water is delivered at more than 120°F, you can easily save money by adjusting your water heater thermostat downward.

What is the flow rate of the showers in your home? If your showers deliver more that 3 gallons per minute, you can save both water and the energy used to heat water by installing low-flow high-efficiency showerheads.

Are the lines between the water heater and your fixtures insulated? If your hot water lines are not insulated, you're wasting many gallons of water each day.

If you have a storage water heater, how many inches of built-in insulation does it have? If you have an older water heater with only an inch or two of insulation, you can save energy adding an external blanket.

Have you considered installing a solar water heater? Solar water heaters are not inexpensive, but in many climates they produce a good economic return.

WATER-HEATING BASICS

Water heating systems present opportunities for effective conservation in three categories: demand, standby, and distribution. Trimming each category requires a different set of efficiency measures:

- **Demand** is the actual hot water used in your shower, washing machine, dishwasher, and other fixtures. You can reduce your demand by installing low-flow showerheads, upgrading appliances to models that use less hot water, or by simply adjusting your habits to use less hot water. When you conserve hot water, you save both water and the energy that would be used to heat the water.

- **Standby** loss includes the heat lost through the walls of your water heater tank. You can reduce standby loss by installing a water heater blanket, by installing a new water heater with better built-in insulation, or by insulating the water lines near your water heater tank.

- **Distribution** loss includes the heat lost through the sides of your hot water pipes when you are using hot water. You can reduce distribution loss by insulating your hot water pipes.

A vast majority of North American homes have storage water heaters that include an insulated tank and a gas burner or electric element. Recent improvements in storage water heaters include better tank insulation and improved combustion systems.

Tankless or on-demand systems include a large gas burner or electric heating element but no tank. These heat water only as you use it. They are more expensive to purchase than storage water heaters, but they use less energy since they don't incur the standby losses of storage systems.

Water can also be heated with solar systems that use no fuel for heating, though some systems consume a small amount of electricity for pumps and controls. These are the most expensive systems to install. The economic feasibility of solar water heating systems is greatest in warm climates.

ADJUSTING YOUR WATER-HEATING HABITS

The quickest way to reduce your water-heating expenses is by adjusting your habits. Some of these tips can make a surprising difference in consumption without causing much hardship.

- Use cold water whenever possible.
- Take shorter showers. Avoid running the shower for longer than necessary before you get in.

Typical Hot Water Consumption

Number of residents	Electric annual kWh	Gas annual therms	Gallons per day
1	2700	180	25
2	3500	230	40
3	4900	320	50
4	5400	350	65
5	6300	410	75
6	7000	750	85

For single-family homes in the United States. Compiled from the Energy Information Administration, Lawrence Berkeley Laboratory, and others.

- Run your washing machine with full loads. If you must do a small load of wash, adjust the machine's water level to match the load size.

Don't use the hot water setting on your washing machine. Modern detergents work perfectly well in warm or cold water, and your clothes will last longer.

- Run your dishwasher with full loads. Set it to Air Dry to save additional electricity. Avoid pre-washing dishes when loading your dishwasher.

SIMPLE IMPROVEMENTS

You can also make some inexpensive improvements to your water heating system that will produce a handsome payback. Taken together with the above changes in habits, these improvements can help most households save a third or more of their water-heating costs.

Lowering Your Hot-Water Temperature

One of the most effective conservation measures for water-heating is to reduce the temperature of water in your storage tank. That's because many storage water heaters are set to keep water at 140°F or more, causing more heat to conduct through the walls of the tank than would occur at lower temperatures. High water temperatures also encourage scale and corrosion to form inside the tank, shortening its lifespan. And extremely hot water increases the risk of someone getting scalded.

We recommend that you reduce your hot water temperature to about 120°F. Avoid adjusting your thermostat lower than this, since harmful water-borne microbes can thrive at cooler temperatures.

Follow this procedure to adjust the temperature of gas water heaters:

- Measure the hot water temperature at the tap that is farthest from the water heater. The goal is to get this water to approximately 120°F.
- Find the thermostat on the water heater—it is usually a round knob near the bottom of the tank.
- Turn the thermostat a small amount toward the correct temperature.
- Wait a few hours for the water in the tank to stabilize. Use your thermometer to again measure the water temperature at the faucet.

- Readjust the thermostat as needed.
- When you find the setting that corresponds to 120°F, mark that setting on the thermostat with a permanent marker.

Follow this procedure to adjust the temperature of electric water heaters:

- Measure the hot water temperature at the tap that is farthest from the water heater. The goal is to adjust this water temperature to approximately 120°F.
- Turn the power to the water heater off at your home's electrical panel.
- Use a screwdriver to open the two access panels on the front of the water heater tank. You'll find a separate thermostat under each panel.
- Use a small screwdriver to adjust both thermostats a small amount towards the correct temperatures.
- Wait a few hours for the water in the tank to stabilize. Use your thermometer to again measure the water temperature at the faucet.
- Readjust the thermostats as needed.
- When you find the setting that corresponds to 120°F, mark those settings on the thermostats with a permanent marker.

Adjusting Your Water Heater Temperature

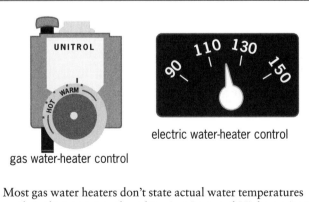

gas water-heater control

electric water-heater control

Most gas water heaters don't state actual water temperatures on their thermostats—they show just Low and High, or similar descriptions instead. Electric water heaters sometimes show actual temperatures, but they aren't very accurate. It's best to measure water temperature with a thermometer at the faucet.

You can also collect some additional savings by turning your water heater down to a lower temperature if you'll be away from home for more than a few days. Adjust it to the "Vacation" setting if your water heater has one. Or simply turn the thermostat to a lower temperature, and when you return adjust it back to the mark you've made on the dial.

Evaluating Your Showerheads

Showering is typically the biggest hot-water use in the home, and so should be one of the first places you turn to reduce your consumption.

Modern low-flow showerheads must by law deliver less than 2.5 gallons per minute (GPM). Most can do this while still producing a satisfying shower—a design advance that includes controlling the size of the droplets and mixing air into the water. With these new showerheads, you'll never know you're saving energy and water.

The savings can be substantial. With an old shower head that uses 5 GPM, a family of four that each takes a daily six-minute shower will use about 43,000 gallons of hot water per year! Low-flow showerheads will cut that use in half, saving up to a few hundred dollars per year.

It is worth installing a new showerhead if your existing one uses more than 3 GPM. Follow this procedure to determine the flow rate of your existing showerhead:

- Find a one-gallon plastic milk jug, and cut a hole in the top so it will fit over the showerhead. Or use any vessel that can hold a gallon.
- Hold the jug over the showerhead, note the second hand on your watch, and start the shower.
- If the jug fills in less than 20 seconds, your flow rate is more than 3 GPM, and you could significantly reduce consumption by installing a new showerhead.

You'll have a lot of choices when shopping for showerheads, though most of the features don't decrease consumption. One energy-saving feature, though, is the addition of a small valve on the side of the showerhead that allows you to adjust the flow of water without touching the main mixing valves. You can use this to slow or shut off the water while you lather up, then turn it on full-force to rinse off. You could probably reduce your water consumption per shower by one-third with this simple device alone.

New low-flow showerheads range in price from $20 to $100, plus installation.

Installing a Showerhead

Installing a showerhead is easy if you are comfortable with using hand tools. You need a pair of slip-joint pliers or vise-grips, an adjustable crescent wrench, and a roll of plumber's teflon tape or pipe dope. All the tools and materials mentioned here are available at hardware stores.

- Inspect the existing showerhead and shower neck (the bent pipe protruding from the wall). Some showerheads have a setscrew on the back to keep them from turning—loosen the setscrew if you find one.

- Turn the showerhead counterclockwise by hand to see if it comes off easily. Warning: do not twist the shower neck, which could cause it to leak or break inside the wall.

- If you can't remove the showerhead by hand, look on the back of it to find the flat places that accommodate a wrench. Fit the adjustable wrench to these flats.

- Fit your adjustable slip-joint pliers to the shower neck. Cover the pliers with tape or a cloth to avoid scarring the shower neck.

- Stabilize the shower neck, and carefully turn the showerhead counterclockwise to remove it.

- Clean the threads on the shower neck and apply a few wrappings of teflon tape or a dab of pipe dope on the male threads of the neck.

- Thread the new showerhead into place until it is hand tight. Stabilize the shower neck with the slip-joint pliers.

- Run the shower and look for leaks around the base of the showerhead. Tighten the showerhead additionally as needed to seal any leaks. Do not overtighten the showerhead.

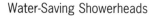
Water-Saving Showerheads

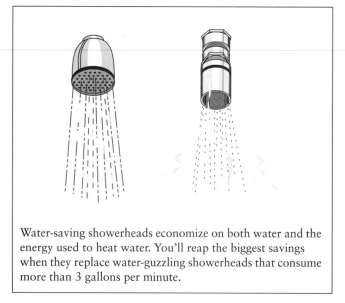

Water-saving showerheads economize on both water and the energy used to heat water. You'll reap the biggest savings when they replace water-guzzling showerheads that consume more than 3 gallons per minute.

Installing a Water-Heater Blanket

Water-heater blankets reduce standby losses. Water heaters that are more than ten years old usually have only one inch of built-in fiberglass insulation (about R-3), which is not really sufficient to control heat loss. Adding a blanket to these older tanks will cut consumption by 5 to 10 percent. Newer water heaters usually have two to three inches of foam insulation (R-10 to 15), which reduces standby losses significantly. Adding a blanket to newer tanks is still a good idea, but it will have less of an impact than on older tanks. On older tanks, you'll recoup the cost of a blanket in a year or less; on newer tanks it may take a few years.

Inspect your water heater to see if the R-value of its built-in insulation is listed on a yellow Energy Guide label or on the manufacturer's data plate. If the R-value is not listed, the tank is probably old enough to have no more than R-3 insulation.

Water-heater insulation blankets are available in most hardware stores for $10 to $20. Choose one that is at least 3 inches thick, or listed as R-8. These blankets are fairly easy to install if you are comfortable working with hand tools. You'll need a tape measure, a sharp knife, and a pair of scissors for this project.

- Open the blanket and read the manufacturer's instructions. Remember that safety is an important consideration for this project.

Pipe Sleeves Slow Standby Loss

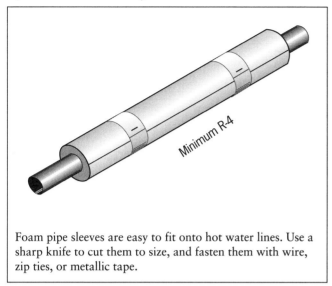

Foam pipe sleeves are easy to fit onto hot water lines. Use a sharp knife to cut them to size, and fasten them with wire, zip ties, or metallic tape.

- Turn off an electric water heater at the house electrical panel. Turn a gas water heater to the pilot setting so it can't fire up while you're working on it.

- Measure the distance from the top of the tank to the drain valve located near the bottom of the tank. Cut the blanket if necessary so it doesn't extend below the drain.

- Fasten the blanket into place with the tape that is included in the kit. Cut around the brass pressure relief valve on the top of the tank and the drain at the bottom.

- Electric water heaters: run the blanket over the top of the tank.

- Gas water heaters: do NOT insulate the top of the tank. Do NOT cover the thermostat or burner cover at the bottom of the tank. Keep the blanket and tape at least six inches away from the chimney.

- Secure all edges with additional tape. Install at least three straps or wires around the tank to hold the blanket firmly into place. Do not rely on tape alone since it often fails.

When you're done, make a final inspection to confirm that you've left the proper clearances around the pressure relief valve, the drain, the thermostat and chimney if you have a gas heater. Turn the electric or gas service back on.

Installing Water Heater Blankets

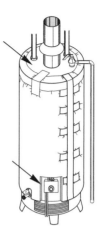

Gas Water Heaters
Do NOT insulate the top of gas water heaters. Maintain 6" clearance to the chimney.

Electric Water Heaters
DO insulate the top of electric water heaters.

Keep insulation away from the gas valve and burner door of gas water heaters.

Cut out small flaps over the elements and controls of electric water heaters.

Gas and electric water heaters have different safety requirements for external blankets. Read the instructions that come with the blanket.

Insulating Hot-Water Lines

You can also reduce energy consumption by insulating your hot water lines. You should be able to buy enough pipe insulation to do all your accessible piping for $10 to $30, and the installation is simple. Savings from pipe insulation should repay this investment within five years.

- Choose pipe sleeves that are at least R-4, or about 3/4 inch thick. Measure the diameter of your existing pipes to determine if you have 1/2 inch or 3/4 inch piping. Note that plumbing lines are specified by inside diameter, so both sizes of piping will be slightly larger at their outside diameter than the specified size suggests.

- Install pipe insulation on all the accessible hot water lines between your water heater and plumbing fixtures. This will reduce the temperature drop that takes place when you're drawing hot water at your fixtures. It will also help hold hot water in the lines at a warm enough temperature that you may not have to purge the lines if you need hot water again within a few minutes. Don't worry about lines you can't get to.

- Insulate the first five feet of your cold water line as well, starting at the water heater. You should insulate this line because you lose some heat here in standby mode—when no one is home—since hot water circulates by convection up into the lines near the water heater on both the hot and cold sides.

- If you have a gas water heater, be sure to keep the sleeves at least six inches away from the chimney.

REPLACING WATER HEATERS

Water heaters have a lifespan of ten to twenty-five years. The variation depends upon the type and quality of heater, the chemistry of the local water (some waters are more corrosive or full of minerals than others), and the thermostat setpoint (lower is better). When you do need to replace your water heater, you'll have an opportunity to install a more efficient system.

Most of us replace our water heaters when they spring a leak, or perhaps because they just stop working. This is unfortunate, because it's difficult to make an informed purchase decision under such duress. If your water heater is more than ten years old, consider working with a local plumber now to evaluate your system and possibly perform an upgrade before your existing equipment fails.

Comparing Storage Water Heaters

Storage water heaters that consume electricity, gas, or oil are the most common types of water heating systems in North America. They are also the least expensive to install, though they incur more operating expense over time than other systems due to their low efficiency. Storage water heaters cost $150 to $300, plus installation costs of $100 to $150.

Energy Factors: Required and Best Available

Water Heater Fuel*	Legally Required	Best Available
Electric	0.90	0.93 to 0.95
Natural Gas	0.59	0.63 to 0.67
Oil	0.59	0.62 to 0.68

Energy Factor

The efficiency of storage water heaters is described by a measurement known as their Energy Factor. This accounts for the energy consumed to actually heat the water and the standby losses through the walls of the storage tank. For gas systems, it also includes heat lost up the chimney and the fuel used to operate a pilot light. Energy Factor is always a decimal of less than 1.0, and the higher the better. An Energy Factor of 1.0, which is not achievable, would imply no losses. The current minimum energy factors are 0.59 for gas and oil water heaters and 0.90 for electric water heaters.

Electric water heaters will always have a higher Energy Factor than combustion water heaters that burn gas or oil. That's because combustion appliances must allow air to circulate up through the burner and flue, carrying heat away from the water and up the chimney.

Standard gas and oil water heaters have a pilot light that burns around the clock. Electric water heaters require neither a chimney nor a pilot light, so their only losses are in standby mode as heat passes through the walls of the tank whether or not you are even using hot water. But even with the favorable Energy Factors of electric heaters, they will be more expensive to operate than gas or oil due to the higher cost of electricity.

As when purchasing any appliance, always study the detailed information on the yellow Energy Guide labels. Choose a water heater with a low annual consumption, and the highest Energy Factor available. Note that there is at present no ENERGY STAR designation for water heaters, since it is difficult to draw a comparison among the vastly differing types of technology (gas versus electric versus solar, and storage versus demand).

Water-Heater Tank Insulation

Most older storage water heaters have only an inch of fiberglass insulation (about R-3) installed between the inner tank and outer shell. Many new gas water heaters have two inches of foam insulation (R-10 or more), and better electric models have three inches of foam (R-15 or more). More insulation helps reduce the heat loss through the walls of the tank. Be sure to look for higher levels of insulation when researching a new unit. This R-value information is found on the specification label attached to the water heater and on the Energy Guide label. The level of insulation is factored in when calculating the Energy Factor.

Chimney Safety Issues

Some storage water heaters that burn gas or oil can have draft problems that result in combustion gases leaking into your home. This often happens when their weak chimney draft is overcome by negative air pressure in the home. This depressurization can be caused by nearby exhaust fans or by leaky ducts that draw air out of the home. When you next have your water heater or furnace serviced, ask your installer to perform safety checks of chimney draft for any fuel-burning appliances to confirm that combustion gases are carried safely out of your home.

Some newer models of storage water heaters counteract these potential problems. These safer models are considerably more expensive, but they are less likely to spill combustion products into the home. Upgrading to these models is increasingly appropriate as you improve the insulation and air sealing elsewhere in your home.

Induced-Draft Water Heaters   These heaters use a fan to pull combustion gases through the flue that runs through the center of the tank. Though this design can solve some problems, such as weak chimney draft, it draws indoor air for combustion which can interfere with other combustion appliances such as a nearby furnace. This makes it less desirable than the sealed-combustion design.

Safer Storage Water Heaters

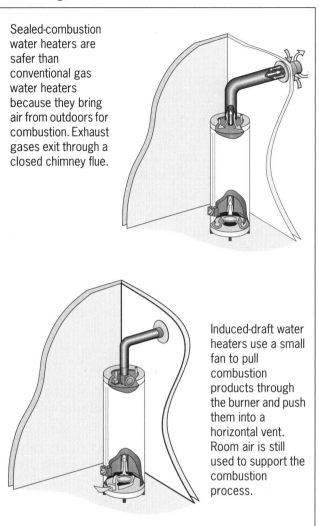

Sealed-combustion water heaters are safer than conventional gas water heaters because they bring air from outdoors for combustion. Exhaust gases exit through a closed chimney flue.

Induced-draft water heaters use a small fan to pull combustion products through the burner and push them into a horizontal vent. Room air is still used to support the combustion process.

Water heater technology is currently in evolution. Conventional gas storage water heaters often have venting problems that are solved by the two heaters shown at the top. Unfortunately, these units still have low energy factors of 0.65 or less.

Sealed-Combustion Water Heater   These heaters use a combustion and venting system that is sealed off from the house. It brings air in from outside for combustion and exhausts flue gases into the outside. This type of unit offers additional safety and greater savings because less airflow is necessary.

Both induced-draft and sealed-combustion water heaters achieve an Energy Factor only slightly better than conventional water heaters.

Tankless Gas Water Heaters

Tankless gas water heaters—also called demand or instantaneous water heaters—are a good solution for improving energy efficiency. They heat water as it flows through the heater, eliminating the storage tank. The absence of a storage tank eliminates standby losses through the walls of the tank.

Tankless water heaters can provide a continuous flow of hot water, but might not serve the simultaneous needs of two or more fixtures. Taking a hot shower and running the dishwasher at the same time, for example, could stretch a tankless water heater to its limit. Nonetheless, they can provide good service if you are willing to make the small adaptation of staggering hot water uses among family members.

Most older gas-fired tankless water heaters were designed with open combustion chambers. These draw air out of the home to support the combustion process. Open-combustion units are prone to backdrafting and spilling combustion gases into the home. The newer models draw combustion air from outdoors, a much safer design. We recommend these sealed-combustion water heaters in all cases.

Tankless heaters are much more expensive to purchase than conventional water heaters, costing $1000 to $2000 plus installation.

Tankless Electric Water Heaters

Tankless electric water heaters generally serve just a single fixture, such as a shower or sink. The largest electric tankless water heater will produce only about two gallons of hot water per minute.

Since standard storage electric water heaters have energy factors as high as 0.95, that doesn't leave much room for improvement by tankless models. Tankless electric units are best reserved for use at remote fixtures far from the main water heater, or in vacation homes with minimal use.

Advanced Storage Water Heaters

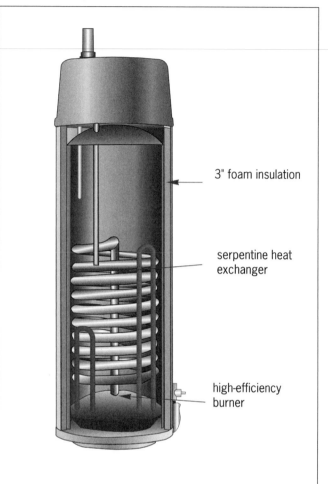

3" foam insulation

serpentine heat exchanger

high-efficiency burner

This high-efficiency water heater is representative of storage water heaters of the future. It has an improved combustion system, high levels of insulation, and an energy factor of around 0.90. Unfortunately, it has a price tag many times greater than conventional storage water heaters.

Choosing Tankless Water Heaters

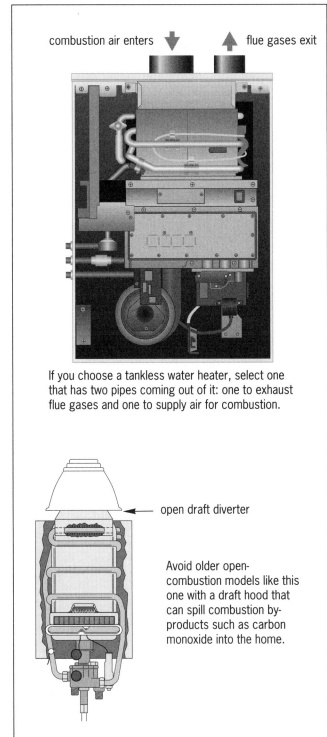

combustion air enters → | ↑ flue gases exit

If you choose a tankless water heater, select one that has two pipes coming out of it: one to exhaust flue gases and one to supply air for combustion.

open draft diverter ←

Avoid older open-combustion models like this one with a draft hood that can spill combustion by-products such as carbon monoxide into the home.

Tankless water heaters cost more to purchase and install, but will return your investment over time. Sealed-combustion models provide an extra margin of safety by drawing combustion air from outdoors.

SOLAR WATER HEATING

Solar water heating is a practical technology that has undergone several generations of development. These systems often have a lifespan of thirty years or more, depending on the quality of their components.

If you live in a climate where freezing temperatures are rare, a simple solar water-heating system, backed up by your old storage water heater, may be your best water-heating choice. If you live in a cloudy or northern climate, solar water heating can still work for you, but it will cost more initially for a larger collector area, a design that includes freeze protection, and higher-quality components.

To employ solar water heating successfully you need a good unshaded southern exposure on your house to mount the solar collectors. You can learn more about siting all types of solar systems in *Solar Site Assessment* on page 147.

To get the best benefits of a solar system (or any water heating system), your home should be designed with a concentrated plumbing system, with the bathrooms and kitchen close to one another, and a central indoor location to install a solar storage tank. Solar water-heating systems that are spread out (with too much distance among collectors, storage tank, and fixtures) tend to be less effective.

Solar water heating systems are not inexpensive, and so are most economically viable if you live beyond the reach of natural gas lines. That's because households with gas water heat typically spend $200 to $300 per year on water heating, while households with electric water heat spend $400 to $600 per year. If electric heating is your only other option, your potential savings from solar water heating will be much higher.

Remember that solar heating is the icing on the cake for the most efficient homes. Dedicate your first dollars to the other projects in this book that save more money per dollar invested. This is especially true of water conservation measures: make sure you have low-flow shower heads, water-efficient appliances, and insulated water pipes before you consider installing a solar water heating system.

Batch Solar Water Heating System

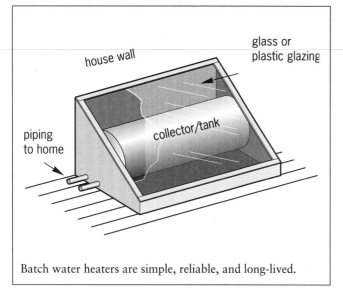

Batch water heaters are simple, reliable, and long-lived.

Thermosiphoning Solar Water System

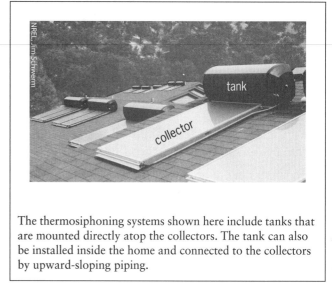

The thermosiphoning systems shown here include tanks that are mounted directly atop the collectors. The tank can also be installed inside the home and connected to the collectors by upward-sloping piping.

Batch Solar Water Heaters

Batch heaters, also known as breadbox heaters, are a simple and relatively trouble-free system for climates where freezing weather is rare. Water is heated passively, with no circulating pumps.

Batch heaters are built around a black steel tank that acts both as the collector and storage vessel. The tank is encased in an insulated box covered with glazing.

Batch heaters may survive occasional freezing temperatures, but they are most practical in frost-free climates. Batch water heaters are the least expensive solar water heating option because they don't require separate solar panels.

The batch water heater is usually charged with house water pressure. Domestic water is heated in the batch water tank and then usually feeds into a conventional water heater where heat is added when needed. In the summer, the conventional water heater is called upon infrequently because the batch heater provides water hot enough for direct use at the fixtures. In the winter, when water from the batch heater is cooler, the conventional water heater fires to provide additional heat. Batch solar water heaters typically cost between $2000 and $3000 for materials. Installation might run another $500 to $1000, depending on installation details. Many of these simple systems have also been constructed by do-it-yourselfers.

Thermosiphoning Water Heaters

These passive solar water heaters utilize collectors that are separate from the tank. Like batch water heaters, they work best in frost-free climates, although they can be drained for the winter months in cold climates.

Thermosiphoning systems are designed so the greater buoyancy of hot water will naturally move it from the collector to a storage tank mounted on top of the collector. The collector is similar in appearance to that in an active system. The hot water is sometimes piped directly to fixtures in the home, but thermosiphoning systems are often designed so hot water flows into a conventional tank to provide added heat as necessary. Thermosiphoning water heaters typically cost between $1500 and $3500 installed.

Active Solar Water Heaters

Active systems circulate water, glycol, or other fluids through the collectors by means of a pump. These are the most expensive solar water heating systems, and can come closest to providing year-round domestic hot water.

An electronic controller monitors temperatures throughout the system, and runs the pump when sufficient heat is available in the collectors. The pumps and controller can be powered by standard house current, or by integrated photovoltaic (solar electric) panels.

Active Solar Water Heating System

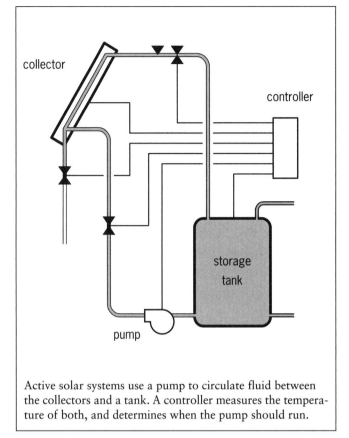

Active solar systems use a pump to circulate fluid between the collectors and a tank. A controller measures the temperature of both, and determines when the pump should run.

Where temperatures drop below freezing, solar water heating systems need freeze protection. Some systems circulate a water-antifreeze mix through the collectors for protection from freezing. If water is used for a circulating medium, the system is sometimes set up to drain automatically during freezing weather.

The storage tank usually utilizes a heat exchanger that allows the circulating medium—water or anti-freeze—to remain captive in the collection loop. Heat is transferred to the domestic hot water through the heat exchanger. Backup heat, for cloudy weather, is usually provided by a conventional gas or electric system that is installed in either the same tank or in an auxiliary tank. The materials for active solar water heating systems typically cost between $4000 and $10,000. Installation might run $1000 to $3000.

THE BOTTOM LINE

The measures described here—reducing your hot water usage, increasing the efficiency of your existing water heater, or installing a new water heating system—can substantially reduce your baseload energy consumption. Taking these important steps will reduce your current and future energy costs year-round:

- Repair any leaky faucets.
- Measure your hot water temperature. If necessary, adjust your water-heater thermostat down to about 120°F.
- Add an external blanket to your water heater.
- Insulate all your accessible hot water lines. Insulate the cold water lines near your water heater.
- Install a low-flow shower head if your existing one uses more than 3 gallons per minute.
- Install a solar water-heating system if you can afford the investment.

4 Heating and Cooling First Steps

The energy used by your heating and cooling systems probably makes up the majority of your utility expense for many months of the year. Several of the big improvement projects described elsewhere in this book—improving insulation, replacing heating and cooling equipment, or upgrading doors and windows—reduce these seasonal costs.

Here we describe the small steps you can take to improve the comfort of your home without embarking on those bigger projects. In some instances, particularly if your heating and cooling system is relatively new, these steps may be all you need to substantially reduce your seasonal energy consumption.

We describe guidelines for upgrading and replacing complete systems in *Cooling Systems* on page 117, and *Heating Systems* on page 129.

EVALUATE YOUR HOME'S COMFORT

Does the temperature of your home feel consistent in winter? If you notice large temperature swings in winter, it may indicate that your home has insufficient insulation or excessive air leakage.

Does the temperature of your home feel consistent in summer? If you notice large temperature swings in summer, it may indicate that your home is subject to excess solar gain through your attic or windows.

Are there individual rooms in your home that are too cold in winter or too hot in summer? You may be able to solve these room-by-room problems by improving the delivery of heated or cooled air. In summer, rooms that tend to overheat may benefit from window-shading devices.

Do members of your household have regular schedules? If so, you may benefit from the installation of a clock thermostat.

If you use central air-conditioning, do you ever use portable room fans as well? You can often trim your cooling consumption substantially by using fans to create a cooling breeze or to flush hot air out of the home at night.

If you use central air-conditioning, do you live in a dry climate? If so, you may be able to cut your cooling costs substantially by installing an evaporative cooler.

Do you have a dark-colored roof? If so, you may be able to trim your cooling costs by installing a light-colored cool roof that absorbs less heat.

Have you had your heating and/or cooling systems serviced recently? Poor maintenance can cause substantial deterioration in the efficiency of this equipment.

BASICS OF COMFORT

Your home should be comfortable. If it's not, you will likely adjust your thermostat to a more comfortable setting, forcing your heating or cooling system to operate, and making your gas or electric meter spin faster. It's a simple cause and effect relationship that all begins with human comfort. Sometimes a small adjustment that increases comfort can allow you to cut your energy consumption substantially.

Our perception of indoor comfort is primarily based upon four things: the air temperature around us, air movement within the room, the radiant temperature of our surroundings, and the humidity of the air. Your ability to control all of these factors in your home is a key to efficient heating and cooling. If one of these factors drifts beyond what is comfortable, most people compensate by adjusting the thermostat to a setting that increases consumption. Your comfort threshold is an important determinant of your utility costs.

What Determines Comfort?

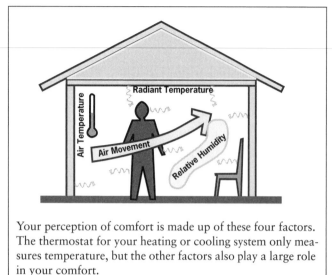

Your perception of comfort is made up of these four factors. The thermostat for your heating or cooling system only measures temperature, but the other factors also play a large role in your comfort.

Air Temperature

This most obvious factor is the one that is directly controlled by your thermostat. In winter, you spend more money to maintain the same indoor temperature because the greater temperature difference between indoors and outdoors will force more heat across the shell of your home—through your ceiling, walls, floors, doors, and windows—and force your furnace to run more. In summer, the indoor-outdoor difference increases the cost of cooling.

Radiant Temperature

Your home's radiant temperature is almost as important as its air temperature. Radiant temperature is the temperature of all the objects in the room: the ceilings, floors, and walls are of primary importance, though the temperature of the furniture and everything else in the room does have some effect. Your body gains or loses heat directly across space to these objects. It is uncomfortable to have hot objects in the room in the summer, and equally uncomfortable to sit near cold objects in winter. The radiant temperature of these objects determines how fast your body gains or loses heat from them.

The insulation level (R-value) of a house has a big effect on its radiant temperature. In summer, for example, the sun tends to heat up your attic, often to as high as 150°F in sunny regions. That heat eventually conducts down through your attic insulation and heats the ceilings in your home. The hot ceiling radiates heat down upon you. It is distinctly uncomfortable to sit in a room with a 100°F drywall ceiling over your head, no matter how cool the thermometer on the wall says it is in the room. Attic insulation helps slow this flow of heat down into your home, so your ceilings stay cooler.

In winter, you are uncomfortable in a home with poor insulation because the walls, ceilings, and floors are so cold. Again, the thermometer on the wall may say 75°F, but you can't shake the chill caused if your warm skin radiates heat to cold surfaces in the room. Insulation improves your comfort because it helps the interior surfaces of the walls, ceiling, and floor stay closer to the room temperature rather than sinking towards the outdoor temperature. But unlike summer, when attic insulation is most important, winter calls for good insulation in the entire building shell. That's because in winter your attic is close to the same temperature as outdoors. If you have a crawl space under your floors, it may be cold, too, though it will be somewhat tempered by the ground.

Shading affects radiant temperature in summer. Good shading keeps radiant temperatures low, promoting good comfort and low air-conditioning costs. Taken together, shading and insulation allow for a higher comfortable summer thermostat setting. In winter, insulation is most important.

How the Sun Heats Your Home

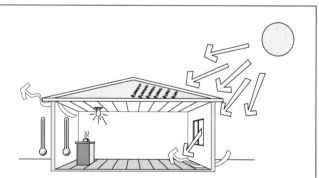

Solar energy heats your home by shining on the roof, entering through the windows, and heating outdoor air that travels into the home through air leaks. Internal gains, such as appliances and lighting, also release heat into your home.

Air Movement

In winter you perceive moving air in your home as a cold draft. If your home is drafty, you will likely raise your thermostat in response, requiring your heating system to run more often to keep you comfortable. In a drafty home, you may need to set your heating thermostat at 72°F. If you can control drafts inside your home, you may be just as comfortable at 68°F. This can make a huge difference in your heating bills.

In summer, moving air is your friend. If you seal up your home and run an air conditioner, you may not feel comfortable until the temperature is lowered to 78°F. Yet if you run a simple table fan at the same time, the cooling breeze may allow you to raise your cooling thermostat to 82°F with no notable reduction in your comfort. If you live where it is dry and not excessively hot, you could take it one step further: shut off the air conditioner, open your windows to take advantage of an outdoor breeze, and be comfortable at 86°F. It's all a matter of adjusting your environment to create acceptable comfort. Most importantly, moving air can help you save money by reducing your reliance on air conditioning.

Defining Dewpoint

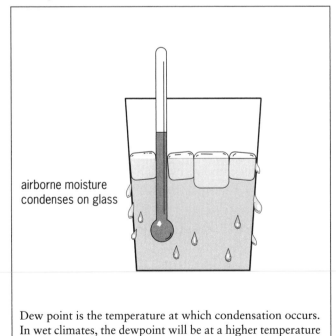

airborne moisture condenses on glass

Dew point is the temperature at which condensation occurs. In wet climates, the dewpoint will be at a higher temperature than in dry climates.

Relative Humidity

Relative humidity (RH) affects your comfort because it changes the rate at which moisture evaporates from your skin. Your sweat will evaporate more quickly in dry weather, and that's why 90°F is a more comfortable temperature in Tucson than it is in New Orleans. Whenever water evaporates, whether from your skin or from the surface of a lake, it absorbs heat and cools the area where the evaporation occurred. This cooling by evaporation is an important physical factor in human comfort.

Relative humidity describes the amount of moisture in the air. It is measured as a percentage: air at 100 percent relative humidity is saturated and can hold no more water vapor.

Dew point, sometimes included in summer weather reports, is the temperature at which the relative humidity is 100 percent and condensation begins to form. On a typical summer day in New Orleans, the temperature may be 90°F and the relative humidity 75 percent, but as the temperature of the air drops, it cannot hold as much moisture. Given these conditions (90°F and 75 percent RH), the air will reach dew point, or 100 percent relative humidity, at about 81°F. At this point, moisture will begin to form on outdoor surfaces. And sweating loses some of its cooling effectiveness because it evaporates slowly off your skin. But in Tucson, air at 90°F might be at 20 percent relative humidity. Given these conditions, the dew point would not occur until the air cooled to about 43°F. Sweating is a very effective cooling mechanism in dry climates.

Most people feel comfortable at relative humidity between 40 percent and 80 percent. At less than 40 percent, the air feels dry and full of static. Above 80 percent, the air feels clammy to most people, though we all have different perceptions of comfort.

Relative humidity does not play a large part in heating strategy except in cold climates, where we try to keep humidity low enough to avoid excessive condensation on windows and other cold surfaces. But this type of moisture management is important for occupant health and building preservation, and therefore covered in *Moisture Management and Ventilation* on page 153.

The Best Cooling System for Your Climate

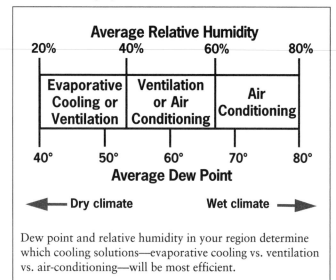

Dew point and relative humidity in your region determine which cooling solutions—evaporative cooling vs. ventilation vs. air-conditioning—will be most efficient.

Manual Thermostats

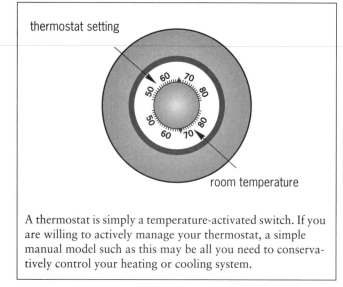

A thermostat is simply a temperature-activated switch. If you are willing to actively manage your thermostat, a simple manual model such as this may be all you need to conservatively control your heating or cooling system.

Relative humidity is extremely important in the choice of a cooling strategy during hot weather. In hot and dry climates, evaporative cooling and simple ventilation are effective cooling methods. In hot and humid climates, we are more often forced to rely on air-conditioning because it dries the air as well as cooling it.

ADJUSTING YOUR THERMOSTAT HABITS

Your thermostat is simply an automatic on-off switch for your furnace, heat pump, or air conditioner. Your choice of temperature settings determines how much you'll pay to heat or cool your home.

During the heating season, when your home's temperature dips a degree or two below your chosen temperature setting, the thermostat turns on the furnace. After the temperature rises to the desired level, the thermostat turns off the furnace. The lower the temperature setting on the thermostat, the less energy the furnace consumes to heat the house. During the cooling season, the thermostat switches on the cooling system when the temperature in your home rises above the setpoint and turns off when it reaches the setpoint.

There are many steps we can take to improve our energy consumption through better control of our air temperature and thermostats, beginning with temperature selection.

Selecting the Best Room Temperature

Your heating or cooling system will operate more efficiently if you avoid fiddling with the thermostat while you are home. Your family should agree upon a temperature that provides a reasonable level of comfort in the winter, another setting for the summer, and leave it at that. Family "thermostat wars" result in temperature swings that increase energy consumption.

During the winter, most people can be comfortable at a thermostat setting of 68°F or less. Wearing warmer clothing helps you remain comfortable at lower indoor temperatures, and it also saves energy. During the summer, most people are comfortable at a thermostat setting of 78°F or higher. Wearing light clothing in the summer helps you stay comfortable at higher indoor temperatures.

But when you are sleeping or away from home, you can reduce consumption by adjusting your thermostat away from your normal setting. In the winter, adjust your target temperature down 5° to 15°F when you go to bed or leave for work. In the summer, adjust it up 5° to 15°F when you leave home during the day. You may have heard that your heating or cooling system will "fall behind" as a result of these setbacks, and will use more energy as a result. It's just not true—setbacks save energy and money in both the heating and cooling seasons.

Programmable Thermostats

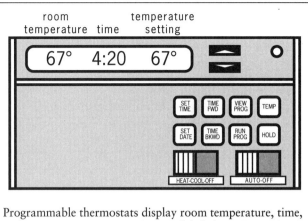

Programmable thermostats display room temperature, time, and temperature setpoints. Buttons labeled "set" or "view" display entry screens where you enter the temperatures you desire at times you specify. The hold button maintains the current temperature, overriding the program.

To avoid wasting energy when you return home or get up in the morning, remember that the thermostat isn't like the gas pedal of your car. Setting the thermostat's temperature higher or lower than you need doesn't speed up the system's heating or cooling ability. Most modern systems have no trouble bringing your home back to a comfortable temperature after setback periods.

Programmable Thermostats

Though you can gain substantial savings by regularly adjusting your manual thermostat to the most appropriate temperature, you may prefer to not have to constantly manage your thermostat. If so, we recommend you get a programmable thermostat that will make adjustments automatically when you are sleeping or away from home.

Programmable thermostats are most convenient and effective for families who have regular schedules. Most have the capacity to adjust the temperature twice daily and also to allow separate schedules for weekdays and weekends. Families who are gone during the day at work or at school will save the most because they can schedule two daily setback periods (when they are out of the house and when they are sleeping), saving energy for more hours per day.

In the winter, you can program the thermostat so your home will be cool while you sleep and warm when you wake up in the morning. You can also program your thermostat to change the temperature during the day, and then revert to a comfortable temperature before you return from work or school. For some families, a programmable thermostat will create savings of 10 to 15 percent on heating and cooling costs.

Programmable thermostats generally cost $50 to $100, plus the cost of installation. Depending on the type of system you have, their installation can vary from easy to moderately difficult. The manual process is simple, since you only need to drive a few screws, and strip and fasten some light wires. But you must read and follow the manufacturer's instructions, both for your safety and to assure that you don't damage your heating or cooling equipment.

Follow these steps to install a thermostat:

- Determine if the thermostat you'll replace is for a furnace, air conditioner, and/or heat pump. Buy a thermostat that is suitable for your particular equipment.

- Read the manufacturer's instructions.

- Turn off the electric power at the main switch for the furnace, air conditioner, or heat pump. This disconnect switch or circuit breaker should be visible from the unit. Do not just turn the power off at the thermostat.

- Remove the thermostat from the wall. There may be two separate pieces; the lowermost one will be screwed to the wall. *Important:* Before removing any wires, note the screw under which each is fastened and the color, number, or letter specified at that screw. Mark each wire with a piece of tape to record that information. Inspect the new thermostat at the same time to assure that you understand where to attach the wires. Stop here and get help if you are not certain.

- Attach the wires to the new thermostat, and fasten the assembly to the wall. Be sure the thermostat is level.

- Turn the power back on at each piece of equipment.

It can be tricky to program programmable thermostats properly, and each model is slightly different. It is important that you read the instructions carefully to ensure that you understand how to take advantage of all the available features. If you set up a programmable thermostat incorrectly, it's possible to use it to *increase* your energy consumption!

CIRCULATING AIR FOR SUMMER COMFORT

You can use moving air to great advantage during the cooling season. There are two principle strategies involved: using circulating fans to move air within the home, and bringing air in from outdoors. They cool by distinctly different methods, so it's worth learning when to use each.

Recent studies at the Florida Solar Energy Center showed that families who used circulating fans and also lowered their air-conditioning thermostat by just 2°F saved an average of 14 percent on their cooling bills. It's simple to see why: the average room fan consumes 25 to 100 watts, while the average air conditioner uses 2,000 to 5,000 watts. You could run three 50-watt room fans for sixteen hours a day, and over the course of a month they would consume only $11 worth of electricity (at 15 cents per kilowatt-hour). If you run a typical 3000-watt air conditioner for the same period, it will cost you $216.

Portable Room Fans

During hot weather, you feel cooler under a light breeze due to evaporative cooling as moisture evaporates from your skin. Circulating fans, whether portable room fans or ceiling fans, are a good way to create this breeze, and they can be very effective used by themselves during warm weather. If you are comfortable using circulating fans rather than air-conditioning for even part of the summer, you can save substantial electricity. These simple fans provide more comfort at less cost than any other electrically powered cooling strategy.

You can also use circulating fans in conjunction with air conditioners during truly hot weather. In this mode, you still want to leave the house closed up. Don't ever run an air conditioner with windows or doors open. Place your portable circulating fans wherever you spend time. Studies have shown that circulating fans will allow you to increase your air conditioner thermostat setting by at least 4°F with no decrease in comfort; this is the key to savings. If you run fans but don't adjust the thermostat for your air conditioner, you'll actually increase your consumption.

Fans Create Cooling Breezes

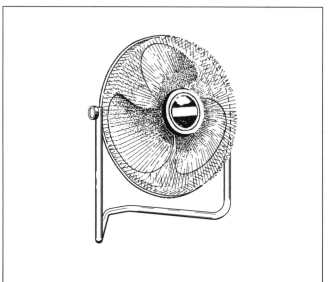

Portable fans can be moved to wherever you spend time in hot weather. They cool people, but don't change the air temperature, and should always be turned off when no one is in the room.

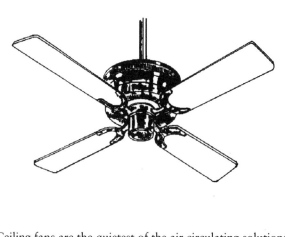

Ceiling fans are the quietest of the air-circulating solutions. Install them in the rooms where you spend the most time during hot weather.

Ceiling Fans

Ceiling fans are one of the most effective ventilation methods if you are willing to invest in a long-term cooling plan. They also move air with less noise than oscillating fans or box fans.

When choosing a ceiling fan, keep in mind that high-quality fans are often several times more effective than cheaper ones. Be sure to choose ENERGY STAR models and compare the information on the Energy Guide labels among the models you are considering.

Ceiling fans are sometimes said to reduce heating costs in winter by moving stratified hot air down toward the floor. This is generally not an effective energy-saving measure, since properly insulated homes don't tend to become stratified. The one exception would be homes with high ceilings of 12 feet or more.

Installing a ceiling fan is a moderately difficult task. You'll need to be familiar with electrical wiring to perform this project safely. You'll also need to confirm that the fan is securely fastened onto structural members in the ceiling since fans are heavy and move around when in operation. This is a good job for a licensed electrician.

A ceiling fan and associated hardware will cost $150 to $300. Installation should take two to four hours.

VENTILATING WITH OUTDOOR AIR

Ventilation brings fresh air into your home. During hot weather, it can save up to 50 percent of your cooling costs. Ventilation for cooling works when the temperature inside is higher than the temperature outside. Several factors determine its effectiveness:

- The temperature difference between inside and outside your home. Ventilation for cooling works best in regions with large temperature swings.
- The amount of shade around your home. Shade cools the outside air so it can be used more effectively to carry heat out of your home.
- The humidity of the outdoor air in your regions. Dry air is more effective for ventilating hot homes. In humid climates where air conditioning is often used, ventilating with outdoor air may not be as effective. That's because your air conditioner must remove moisture from the air in your home, and air that is introduced for ventilation carries humidity into the home. As a rule of thumb: if you use an air conditioner in a moist climate, wait until the outdoor air temperature drops below 70°F before ventilating with outdoor air. This is not an issue in dry climates.

You can move outdoor air through your home by several methods: natural ventilation, window fans, or whole house fans. We address these here. If you live in a hot and dry region, you can also use evaporative coolers, which are addressed under *Evaporative Coolers* on page 125.

Using Natural Ventilation

Natural ventilation can remove heat from your home for free. The most common routine for using natural ventilation is to ventilate during the coolest parts of the night, and close your windows and doors during the hottest periods of the day.

A little wind allows you to ventilate successfully without fans until daytime outdoor temperatures rise to 85°F or more. Wind creates areas of pressure and suction that will move air in and out of your house. Windows facing the wind will become pressurized so air will flow in when they are open, and windows facing away from the wind will be under suction, encouraging air to flow out. Wind blowing parallel to a window generally creates strong suction there. Fences, thick hedgerows, or other buildings near the home can direct the wind, creating pressure, or channel the wind along a wall, creating suction at its windows.

Inlets and outlets located directly opposite each other cool only those areas in the direct path of the airflow. More of your home is cooled if the air takes a longer path between the inlet and outlet. Remember that air from shaded outdoor areas is cooler, so try drawing this air in and exhausting air to hotter areas.

Ventilation in two-story homes can be increased by using the natural buoyancy of hot air. Using windows that are low on the pressurized (windy) side of the home for intakes and high windows on the leeward side for exhaust can enhance ventilation through two-story homes.

Experiment with different patterns of window venting to move fresh outside air through all the living areas of your home. This may involve leaving some windows closed if they interfere with moving air along a longer path through the house.

Ventilation Fans

When it's not windy, you can use fans to move air into and out of your home. Just as with room fans, you can save 50 percent or more on your cooling costs by ventilating with fans rather than an air conditioner.

Ventilation fans cool the home by circulating relatively cool outdoor air through the home. This cool outdoor air picks up heat that has accumulated in the home and expels it outdoors. Window fans, pedestal fans, and whole-house fans are the most cost-effective cooling devices you can buy when they work for your climate and heat tolerance.

Window fans are best used in windows facing the prevailing wind or away from it to provide cross ventilation. Window fans can augment breezes or create a breeze when the air is still. If the wind direction changes in your area, use reversible direction window fans so you can either pull air into the home or push air out, depending on which way the wind is blowing. Experiment with positioning the fans in different windows to see which arrangement works best. Two window fans, one pushing air and the other pulling it, at opposite corners of the home are often very effective at nighttime cooling. A two-story home might use two fans at opposite ends of the second story, both exhausting air that enters on the first story through open windows.

Use window fans to cool your home during the evening and night. The cool night air will flush out the heat your home collects during a hot summer day.

Window Ventilation Fans

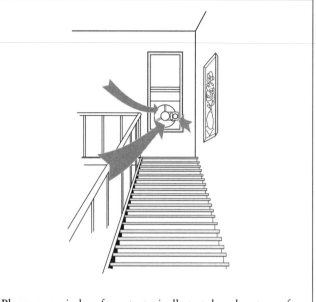

Place your window fans strategically to take advantage of outdoor air currents. Hot air will tend to rise toward the top of your home, so that is the best place to run an exhaust fan. To get the most cooling effect, open a window or door on the shady side of your home where cool air can be drawn into your home.

Whole-House Fans

Whole-house fans are large built-in ventilation fans that draw hot air out of the home and exhaust it into the attic. They are most effective in regions with hot, dry weather and cool evenings. You can achieve substantial reductions in cooling costs if you use a whole-house fan to avoid the use of air conditioning. They can also be used in conjunction with ceiling fans and portable fans.

Whole-house fans are installed in the ceiling in a central part of your house. They draw air in through open windows and exhaust house air out into the attic. They are usually designed so that roof vents allow hot air to leave the attic, though ducted models are also available that exhaust air directly out through a roof or wall opening.

You can determine which rooms will be cooled with a whole-house fan by simply opening windows where you want to draw cool outdoor air in, and closing windows in rooms you don't want to cool.

Whole-House Fans

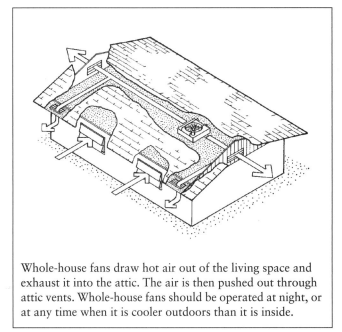

Whole-house fans draw hot air out of the living space and exhaust it into the attic. The air is then pushed out through attic vents. Whole-house fans should be operated at night, or at any time when it is cooler outdoors than it is inside.

Selecting Whole-House Fans Whole-house fans range in capacity from about 1000 to 10,000 cubic feet per minute (CFM). The smaller units have the advantage of lower initial cost, quieter operation, and lower electrical consumption. The larger sizes cool more quickly since they can move more air through your home.

The optimum size of whole-house fan depends on several factors: the hotness of your summer climate, the reflectivity of your roof, the amount of insulation in your attic, and the shading over your windows. In general, good home design in hot climates prevents heat from entering the home in the first place by utilizing these other solutions. But many homes do overheat on occasion, and during these times a whole-house fan can be an effective addition to your other low-cost cooling methods.

Traditional sizing guidelines for whole-house fans suggest that the fan should have enough capacity to change all the air in the home every minute or two. For a typical 1500-square-foot home, this would require a fan with 6,000 to 12,000 CFM capacity. This size would be excessive in all but the most poorly designed homes in the hottest climates. For homes that utilize other low-energy cooling solutions, smaller whole-house fans are usually sufficient. Fans with capacities of 1000 to 3000 CFM—exchanging all the air in a typ-

ical home several times per hour—are now considered sufficient in most areas.

Installing Whole-House Fans In regions with cool winters, whole-house fans should be fitted with a tight insulated cover so cold air can't enter the home through the fan during heating season. Some fans are made with built-in insulated doors that seal when the fan is not in operation. This saves you the task of covering the fan each autumn.

Traditional whole-house fans can be noisy. You can minimize this by installing them on rubber or felt gaskets to dampen vibration. When selecting a fan for your home, keep in mind that a large-capacity fan running at a low speed makes less noise than a small fan operating at high speed. A two- or three-speed fan control is a good option. You can then ventilate the entire house quickly at high speed, or just maintain gentle air circulation at a quieter low speed.

Whole-house fans generally should be installed by a professional. There are several reasons for this:

- Installing the fan will require structural modifications to your ceiling framing.
- You'll need to inspect the attic ventilation to see if it is sufficient to exhaust the large airflow produced by the fan. You may need to install additional attic vents.
- The fan must be wired into your home electrical system.

The cost of whole-house fans varies from $300 to $600 for traditional basic models, and $800 to $1500 for quieter, well-sealed units. Installation will run another $200 to $500.

Advanced Whole-House Fan

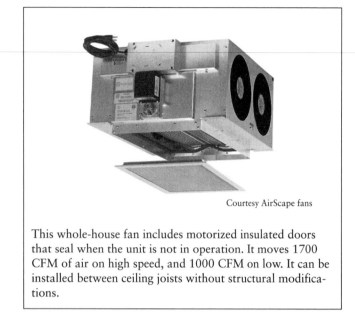

Courtesy AirScape fans

This whole-house fan includes motorized insulated doors that seal when the unit is not in operation. It moves 1700 CFM of air on high speed, and 1000 CFM on low. It can be installed between ceiling joists without structural modifications.

Powered Attic Ventilators

Powered attic ventilators move hot air out of your attic. They are sometimes confused with whole-house fans, but they are a much less effective cooling solution since they don't actually move air out of your living space. The most efficient homes don't utilize powered attic ventilators, but rely instead on light-colored reflective roofs to prevent attic overheating, passive (non-motorized) attic vents that encourage a moderate amount of ventilation, and ample attic insulation to keep attic heat that does accumulate from conducting down into your home.

Powered attic ventilators are controlled by thermostats that turn on at a set temperature, usually between 100 and 140°F. They are expensive to operate but are sometimes installed as a last resort in overheated attics under dark-colored roofs. If you do choose to use a powered ventilator, set the thermostat for 130°F or above so that it doesn't run unnecessarily and increase your electricity costs.

SHADING WINDOWS FOR SUMMER COMFORT

Shading windows is one of the most effective and practical low-cost cooling retrofits. The hotter your climate and the more you pay for air-conditioning, the more window shading you need. The challenge of designing window shading is to come up with a method that blocks most of the solar heat while preserving your view and allowing light into your home.

Shading devices are often rated by their shading coefficient (SC). The shading coefficient is the fraction of solar heat admitted by a window with the shading device compared to single-pane glass. For example, a 0.30 shading coefficient means the window with its window treatment admits about 30 percent of the solar heat of single-pane clear glass with no window treatment. Generally speaking, the lower the shading coefficient, the better the window treatment blocks solar heat.

The most common shading techniques are solar screens, reflective films, venetian blinds (exterior or interior), roller shades, and awnings.

Solar Screens

Solar screens are often the least expensive window-shading option. They absorb 65 to 70 percent of solar heat before it enters the home. They tend to obscure your view somewhat—you can always see that they're in place—but that is an acceptable trade-off for most people.

Solar screens are made by stretching nylon fabric, similar to insect screen, over an aluminum frame. They work particularly well for un-shaded windows facing west or east because they dampen glare in addition to blocking solar heat.

Solar screens must be installed on the exterior of the window to be effective. They are usually attached to the trim or window stop with clips or screws. If installed on outwardly opening windows, such as awnings or casements, they should be attached to the hinged sash.

Home improvement stores sell all of the materials you need to build solar screens yourself. It is not a particularly difficult project, but it does take good planning and patience. The light aluminum frames are cut to size, and are connected at the corners with metal or plastic corner pieces. Once the frame is complete, a piece of solar screen (purchased by the roll) is cut to fit the frame. The framing material has a groove on one side. A piece of spline (like rubber twine) is laid over the screen and then pressed into the groove with a spline roller, attaching the screen material to the frame. Once the screen has been attached on all sides, the excess material and ends of the spline are trimmed off. The cost of materials to build your own solar screens will range from $10 to $20 per window.

Purchasing ready-made solar screens isn't expensive, either. If you have a lot of windows to cover, or hard-to-access windows on a second or third story of your home, you may want to have them professionally installed. Most window or glass shops can make and install solar screens for your home for $50 to $75 per window. You could save probably $25 each by installing them yourself, if you are comfortable working on a ladder.

Reflective Films

Metallized plastic window films, similar to those applied to automotive windows, can block 50 to 75 percent of the solar heat that comes through single-pane glass. A microscopic layer of metal on the film reflects solar radiation.

The material comes in rolls, and is permanently applied to the glass. Installed on the interior side of single-pane or double-pane glass, reflective window films repel solar heat (reduce solar heat gain), reduce glare, and reduce wintertime heat loss. Films also reduce UV light, which protects fabrics and carpets from fading, and they make the glass shatter resistant. Tinted films that merely color the glass are not very effective at blocking solar heat. Clear, spectrally selective films can block up to 70 percent of the solar energy while stopping only 30 percent of the visible light.

Installing reflective window film is a difficult do-it-yourself project, so we recommend that you get professional help. These films require careful installation to an absolutely dirt-free glass surface. Selecting a contractor is probably the most important factor in the success of a window-film project, since installation quality is so important. Start by checking references of customers serviced in the past three years. Contractors usually charge $50 to $100 per window to install window films.

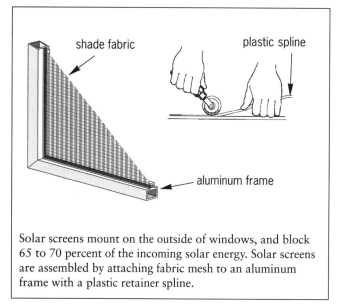

shade fabric

plastic spline

aluminum frame

Solar screens mount on the outside of windows, and block 65 to 70 percent of the incoming solar energy. Solar screens are assembled by attaching fabric mesh to an aluminum frame with a plastic retainer spline.

Venetian Blinds Block Solar Heat

Interior venetian blinds are popular for blocking solar heat and controlling light. Exterior venetian blinds provide superior solar shading, though they need to be hardy enough to withstand the elements.

Venetian Blinds

Venetian blinds can be installed on either the interior or exterior of your windows. They regulate both natural light and solar heat and also block glare with their movable slats. When designed for controlling light and solar heat, the slats should be bright white or polished aluminum.

When closed, interior venetian blinds can block up to 60 percent of the solar heat that would normally enter a single-pane window. When installed on the window's exterior, venetian blinds reduce air-conditioning costs even further because they block solar heat before it enters the building—fully closed exterior blinds block up to 90 percent of solar heat. Exterior blinds are practical only in areas that don't have extreme winds.

Venetian blinds cost $10 to $75 per window. Installation is easy, and should take no more than one hour each. This is a good do-it-yourself project that requires no more than a ladder, screwdriver, and tape measure.

Roller Shades

Interior roller shades have been used for years, though they fell out of favor for a while when new styles of window coverings came onto the market. Modern roller shades are made in a wide range of styles, including some that are very effective at reflecting and blocking solar heat.

Roller shades come in a wide variety of woven fabrics with different shading capacity. The exterior-facing side of the shade should be bright white or have a reflective metallized coating for blocking solar heat.

New specialized fabrics are designed to preserve the view, prevent glare, and block solar heat. These innovative fabrics have an open weave and are colored on the indoor side for glare-free outdoor viewing, and white or shiny metallic facing outdoors to reflect solar heat.

If you have a substantial overhang to protect outdoor shades from the weather, you can install a large roller shade on the exterior to shade large windows or sliding-glass doors.

South windows admit solar heat during the middle of the day, coming from high in the sky. If the building has overhangs, the bottom of the south-facing window glass needs shading more than the top. In this case, consider mounting the shades at the bottom of the window to provide shade at the window's bottom while allowing a view and natural light through the window's shaded top.

Roller blinds cost $25 to $100 per window. Installation should take no more than one-half hour each. This is a good do-it-yourself project that requires no more than a ladder, screwdriver, and tape measure.

Awnings

Awnings are usually the most expensive window-shading option. However, they are very effective at shading because they intercept the solar heat before it gets to the window. Awnings are popular in hot, sunny climates.

The amount of shade that an awning will cast over a window is determined mostly by the distance that it protrudes down from the top of the window. This distance is referred to as the "drop" of the awning. Awnings on the south side need a drop measuring 45 to 60 percent of the window height to block solar radiation coming from higher in the sky. Awnings on the east and west should have a drop of 60 to 75 percent to block solar radiation coming from lower in the sky.

Styles of Awnings

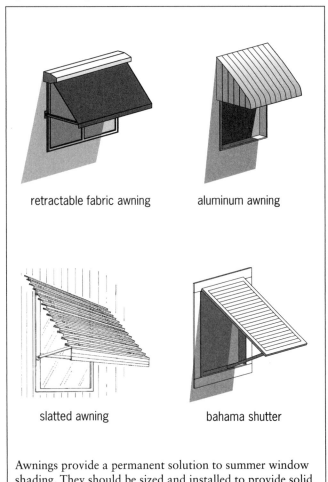

retractable fabric awning   aluminum awning

slatted awning   bahama shutter

Awnings provide a permanent solution to summer window shading. They should be sized and installed to provide solid summer shade while allowing low winter sun to enter. Retractable or folding awnings allow the best winter view.

Awnings with sides in addition to a top provide the most effective shade on south-facing windows. Do-it-yourself awnings usually do not have sides but you can partially compensate for this by making the awning wider than the window. The greater the drop of the awning the more the view is reduced, so you may have to compromise between shade and view.

Metal awnings have the longest lifespan, though many homeowners feel that canvas and other fabric awnings are more attractive. But fabric is also more expensive and slightly less effective because it absorbs more solar heat. Fabric awnings need more maintenance, too, and have a shorter life span than metal awnings.

It can be difficult to strike a perfect balance among the important factors of shade, view, appearance, and cost in selecting an awning. Awnings for tall narrow windows may need to be considerably wider than the window for a more balanced appearance. Awnings installed at a 45-degree angle seem most attractive. If a maximum amount of view is important, use sun screens and window films instead of awnings. Awnings with slats rather than a solid surface will allow some limited viewing through the top of the window.

Awnings vary widely in cost from $200 to $800 per window, depending on size. Installation is usually done by professionals at a cost of $50 to $100 each.

IMPROVING ROOF REFLECTIVITY

Your home overheats in summer, in part, because solar energy is absorbed through your roof. This heating of your roof can account for up to 50 percent of your home's cooling load.

Some types of roofing tend to absorb more heat than others. If you want your home to be cooler in summer, increasing the reflectivity of your roof is one of the best places to start.

Reflective roofs, or cool roofs, are made in many standard materials including metal, clay tile, concrete tile, or synthetic rubber membrane. These materials are installed during the process of re-roofing a pitched-roof building, and many of them are similar in appearance to traditional heat-absorbing roofs. If your existing roof is a type that will accept a coating, such as low-slope tar, bitumen, or synthetic rubber, you may

be able to install a simple white cool-roof coating directly over that surface without having to re-roof.

Measuring Effectiveness of Cool Roofs

Cool roofs must not only reflect solar heat, but should also effectively emit, or release, heat that accumulates. The concept of emittance is difficult to envision, but it is a fact that some materials reflect heat well but don't tend to release heat effectively. This prevents them from being efficient cool-roof materials.

Scientists at Lawrence Berkeley Laboratory have created an index for comparing the coolness of roofing materials that combines both reflectance and emittance into a rating more indicative of air-conditioning energy savings. The solar reflectance index (SRI) ranges from 0 to 100 (due to peculiarities in the rating system, some materials can be higher than 100 or less than 0). High SRI numbers are good.

Standard white asphalt shingles have an SRI of only 20 to 25 when new, and that will degrade significantly over time due to loss of white granules and dirt deposits. Darker asphalt shingle roofs have SRIs as low as 1.0 (they absorb almost all the solar heat that strikes them). White metal roofs, which are becoming more accepted in new construction, have good SRIs from 70 to 82 (they only absorb about one-quarter the solar energy that strikes them). Surprisingly, bare galvanized steel and aluminum aren't nearly as cool as white metal. Those shiny metals reflect solar heat well, but they don't emit heat effectively so they tend to heat up, resulting in SRIs in the 40s for bare galvanized steel and in the 70s for bare aluminum.

If you have high air-conditioning costs, we recommend that you install a cool roof with an ENERGY STAR rating when you next need to re-roof your home.

Effectiveness of Cool Roofing Materials

Roofing type	Reflectance	SRI index
White elastomeric coating (low slope)	.70 to .85	87 to 107
White EPDM rubber membrane (low slope)	.70 to .80	80 to 105
White clay tile	.70	90
White rubber membrane	.70	84
White metal	.60 to .70	82
New aluminum metal	.60	71
New galvanized steel	.60	46
Colored clay tile	.20 to .50	20 to 60
White asphalt shingles	.20 to .30	21 to 40
Colored asphalt shingles	≥0.20	−2 to 22
Black EPDM rubber membrane (low slope)	.06	−1

Higher numbers are better: a high reflectance or high SRI yields low cooling costs. An ENERGY STAR rating (in 2008) requires an SRI of 25 or higher for steep-sloped roofs, and an SRI of 65 or higher for low-slope roofs.

How to Apply a Cool-Roof Coating

You can apply a cool-roof coating directly over some types of roofing. If you have the right type of roof, this is the quickest and cheapest way to benefit from a reflective roof.

These coatings are usually water-based acrylic elastomers, and are applied with a roller. They can be applied over most low-sloped roofing materials such as metal, built-up asphalt, bitumen, or single-ply membranes. Some underlying materials require a primer to get proper adhesion—check the manufacturer's recommendations for asphalt-shingle roofs.

Cool-roof coatings qualify for an ENERGY STAR rating. Be sure to look for the seal when shopping for cool roof materials.

If you're considering installing a cool-roof coating on your home, the first step is to learn if the coatings available at your home improvement center are compatible with the roofing on your home. Read the manufacturer's instructions for guidance.

Surface preparation is critical when applying any coating. The underlying roofing materials must be clean so the coating will stick for many years. Roof coatings will not stick to dirty or greasy surfaces, and they cannot be used to repair roofs in poor conditions. Repairs should be performed if the existing roofing is cracked or blistered.

Follow this procedure to install a cool-roof coating:

- Clean the roof of debris such as dirt, leaves, and loose or detached roofing material.

- Wash the roof with water/trisodium phosphate (tsp) solution, or comparable mildewcide, and a scrub brush. Better yet, use a pressure washer.

- Reinforce any open joints around skylights, pipe flashing, roof drains, wall transitions, or HVAC equipment.

- Repair any cracks, blisters, or de-laminations in built-up asphalt or bitumen roofs. Use polyester fabric and roof coating for these reinforcements and repairs by dipping fabric patches in the roof coating and spreading them over the existing roofing. Or lay dry fabric into a layer of wet coating. Smooth patches down with a broad-knife or squeegee to remove bubbles or wrinkles. Allow any repairs to cure for one to two days before applying the topcoat.

- For metal roofs, sand any rusted areas down to sound metal. Install metal patches over any areas that are rusted through, followed by polyester patches as described above.

- Prime uncoated galvanized iron with the appropriate primer and ferrous metals with the appropriate primer.

- Assemble your tools. Use a shaggy 1- to 1½-inch roller on a 5- or 6-foot pole to apply coating to the broad areas. Use a large brush for the edges. Wear work clothes and shoes that you don't mind having permanently stained. Gather some disposable rags.

- Read the instructions to determine the proper coverage. You don't want the material to puddle in low places, yet you shouldn't try to stretch it so far that you leave thin places. Plan your work so you don't have to walk on the wet material.

- Use drop cloths or paper and tape to protect any nearby windows, siding, or automobiles from splatters.

- Install the coating when dry weather is predicted. Rain, heavy dew, or freezing weather within 24 hours of installation will weaken the bond between the coating and the underlying roofing.
- Use the brush to coat the edges, corners, and roof jacks around chimneys and pipes. Use the roller for open areas. Install at least two coats, allowing a day between coats for curing. Apply the second coat in the opposite direction to the first to get more complete coverage.

SIMPLE FURNACE MAINTENANCE

Gas furnaces should be professionally serviced periodically to ensure that they operate safely and efficiently. We cover those professional tasks in *Professional Heating System Service* on page 132. But you can perform some of the most important maintenance tasks yourself.

Cleaning Furnace Filters

Furnace filters should be changed or cleaned every few months so that the furnace airflow remains at its maximum. Check yours periodically to see how quickly it gets dirty. If you have both a furnace and a central air conditioner, the same filter may serve both systems. You should be able to replace your filter in ten minutes or less.   Furnace filters cost between $1 and $10.

Furnace filters are usually located in one of three places:

Replacing Furnace or Air Conditioner Filters

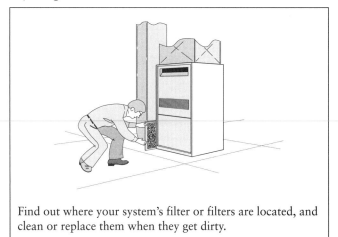

Find out where your system's filter or filters are located, and clean or replace them when they get dirty.

- In the cabinet of the furnace itself: you'll have to remove a sheet metal cover on the front of the furnace to access this filter location.
- Next to the furnace, behind an inch-wide slot in the main return-air duct: the filter slot may be covered with a small metal cover or strip of tape.
- Behind a central return air grille that draws air out of the living space: you will need to swing the grille open to access the filter at this location.

Once you've located your filter, inspect and clean or replace it as needed.

- Turn off both the furnace and air conditioner at the main disconnect switch(es). These should be located within view of the furnace or air conditioner. *Caution: Stop now if you aren't comfortable working around electrical equipment.*
- Remove the filter. It will be either a disposable fiberglass mat mounted in a cardboard frame, or a washable filter.
- Use a vacuum or wet rag to clean out the area surrounding the filter.
- If the filter is disposable, measure it and buy a new one, plus a few spares, at a home improvement or hardware store. Install the new filter, and replace any covers.
- If the filter is made of washable plastic fiber, wash it with soap and warm water, either in the bathtub or outdoors with a hose. Install the cleaned filter, and replace any covers.
- Turn the heating or cooling system back on.

Installing Carbon Monoxide Detectors

Furnaces, boilers, and water heaters that burn oil or gas release combustion gases such as carbon dioxide, water vapor, and sometimes carbon monoxide, which is poisonous and can be fatal. When the system operates properly, these gases are carried out of the home through a chimney. Under some conditions, however, the chimney can release combustion gases into your home. If you have any gas or oil-burning appliances in your home, we recommend that you install a carbon monoxide detector near this equipment to warn of any combustion venting problems. Follow the manufacturer's instructions regarding the number and location of these safety devices.

SIMPLE AIR CONDITIONER MAINTENANCE

No other home equipment is so prone to poor performance as air conditioners. Without regular maintenance, your air conditioner's efficiency can fall by as much as 50 percent. Proper maintenance saves energy and money, while extending the life of your equipment.

If you never clean your condenser coil, for example, your compressor will eventually fail. Many systems die this way and are simply replaced, when with proper service and maintenance they could have lasted much longer.

Air conditioners are complex. Repairing and adjusting them is strictly for professionals, and those complicated tasks are described in *Professional Air-Conditioning Service* on page 120. But you can perform some simple and essential maintenance tasks yourself.

Cleaning Filters and Coils

Perform these tasks to prolong the life and increase the efficiency of your central air conditioner. Always shut the unit off at its main disconnect switch, usually located outdoors near the compressor unit.

- Indoors: Clean or replace the filter that is located inside the metal air handler cabinet or behind a return air register. This is usually the same filter that also protects your furnace from dirt. The average air-conditioning system will lose about 1 percent efficiency per week because of decreasing air flow due to dirt on the filter.
- Outdoors: Clean the outdoor condenser coil. Heat that is collected by the air conditioner is carried outdoors to this coil—if the coil is dirty, it can't release heat as well and its efficiency will fall. Use a soft broom and water to gently remove dust and debris. This outdoor unit should be occasionally disassembled and cleaned

more thoroughly, but that is a task for a professional and covered in *Professional Air-Conditioning Service* on page 120.

- Outdoors: Remove plants and other debris from within three feet of the outdoor unit. Make sure the upward path of air leaving the unit is unrestricted for at least five feet.

Avoid activities that create airborne material that could be sucked into the condenser outdoors. Cutting grass near the condenser stirs up dust that can plug the coils—shut off the unit before mowing nearby grass. Dryer lint can also plug the coils, so be sure your dryer vent is located at least ten feet downwind from the condenser.

Maintenance for Central Air Conditioners

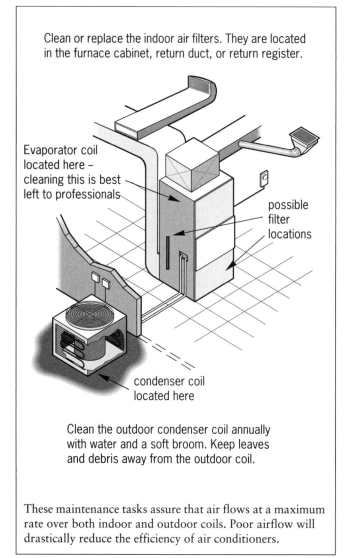

Clean or replace the indoor air filters. They are located in the furnace cabinet, return duct, or return register.

Evaporator coil located here – cleaning this is best left to professionals

possible filter locations

condenser coil located here

Clean the outdoor condenser coil annually with water and a soft broom. Keep leaves and debris away from the outdoor coil.

These maintenance tasks assure that air flows at a maximum rate over both indoor and outdoor coils. Poor airflow will drastically reduce the efficiency of air conditioners.

THE BOTTOM LINE

The tasks described in this chapter can help reduce your reliance on your heating and cooling equipment. They also assure that when you do use this equipment, it will be more reliable and efficient. Most of these measures cost far less in the long run than purchasing gas or electricity to run your equipment. By taking these first steps, you'll save energy, reduce expenses, and improve your home's comfort.

- If you use a standard manual thermostat, be sure to adjust the temperature to a more economical setting before you leave home or go to bed.
- If your family members have regular schedules, consider installing a programmable thermostat. Learn how to use it effectively.
- During hot weather, use room fans to circulate air and create a wind chill in occupied rooms. If you usually use air conditioning, try raising the thermostat a few degrees when you run room fans.

- During hot weather, move hot air out of your home at night using ventilating fans such as window fans or whole house fans.
- Provide shade for windows in rooms that tend to overheat. Draw the shades during the day during hot weather.
- If you live in a hot climate, install a cool roof or cool-roof coating that has an ENERGY STAR rating.
- Have your heating and/or cooling equipment professionally serviced. Ask questions about maintenance when the technician comes to your home.
- Inspect the filter in your furnace or air conditioner. Clean or change it if it's dirty.
- If you have central air-conditioning, clean the outdoor coils periodically.
- If you have heating or water-heating equipment that burns natural gas, propane, or oil, install a carbon monoxide detector to warn you of any combustion safety problems.

Landscaping

Landscaping should be included in your long-term plan for reducing heating and cooling costs. If your home is presently subject to glaring summer sun or blustery winter winds, you could see substantial savings from a well-crafted landscape.

Your plantings can also improve your privacy, reduce street noise, and control dust. Add these benefits to the beauty of mature landscaping, and it's no surprise that the presence of trees and shrubs can raise a home's resale value by 10 to 20 percent.

In this chapter, we illustrate the timeless principles of good landscape design. We show you how to choose trees and bushes that will thrive in your climate, and the best ways to plant them. We also include maintenance tips to assure that your plantings will increase in value over time.

EVALUATE YOUR LANDSCAPING

Do you have trees and shrubs already growing on your property? Are they evergreen or do they shed their leaves? What are their shapes? Your landscape plan will have to incorporate the existing plantings around your home.

Does your home overheat in summer? Are some rooms hotter than others? You may be able to reduce your heating costs by planting trees or shrubs so they shade the hottest parts of your home.

Is your home located in a region where it is hot and windy in summer? You may be able plant hedges that direct cooling breezes toward your home.

Is your home located in a region where it is cold and windy in winter? You may be able to plant a windbreak to shelter your home from cold winds.

Where is the sun's daily path over your home, and how does this path vary over the seasons? You may be able to design plantings that shelter your home from hot summer sun, while still allowing the welcome sun of winter to reach your home.

Does the ground slope away from your home or toward it? You should design your landscaping to protect your home's foundation from water.

LANDSCAPING BASICS

The benefits of landscaping are substantial and well-documented. Studies by the U.S. Department of Agriculture and Department of Energy illustrate how carefully positioned trees can reduce an average household's energy consumption by 20 to 25 percent, saving $300 to $400 each year.

Landscaping also has important positive environmental effects. Plants consume carbon dioxide and water through photosynthesis. This carbon is stored, or sequestered, in the plant itself and in the surrounding soils. Since carbon dioxide is a potent greenhouse gas that contributes to climate change, improving your landscaping also reduces your carbon footprint.

Summer Benefits

The shade cast by landscaping will typically reduce your home's summer air-conditioning costs by 15 to 50 percent. The savings may be up to 75 percent for small mobile homes. The savings are the greatest in hot climates and for homes with little existing shade.

You may have noticed that parks and forests are always cooler than nearby city streets. This is because trees block sunlight before it can reach the ground, and their canopies of leaves release cooling water vapor through a process called evapotranspiration.

Several studies show that summer daytime air temperatures in neighborhoods with mature tree are 3° to 6°F lower than in newly developed areas with no trees, and that large urban parks are up to 7°F cooler than surrounding neighborhoods.

Planting trees may be ten times more cost-effective than building new electrical generating plants to meet summer cooling demands. A 1992 study by the Lawrence Berkeley Laboratory estimated that building new power plants to meet electrical peak loads (such as those caused by air conditioners running on summer afternoons) cost an average of 10 cents per kilowatt-hour. The study showed that decreasing peak-load consumption by planting trees cost only 1 cent per kilowatt-hour. The numbers may have doubled since then, but the 10-to-1 ratio is still accurate.

The effectiveness of landscaping in reducing the cost of cooling your home will depend on several factors:

- The temperature of your summer weather.
- The color and reflectivity of your roof and walls.
- The number and size of windows on the sunny sides of your home.
- The amount of insulation in your attic.

If your home is located in a hot part of the world, and has large south-facing windows and a dark-colored roof, you'll have the greatest need for summer shading. If you live in the North and you rarely need air-conditioning, the shade cast by your plantings will be less significant.

Summer Landscaping Design

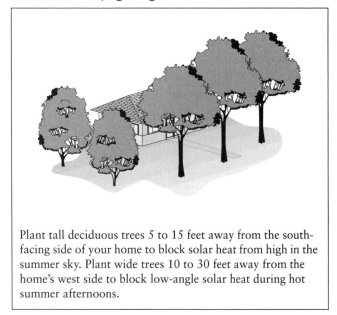

Plant tall deciduous trees 5 to 15 feet away from the south-facing side of your home to block solar heat from high in the summer sky. Plant wide trees 10 to 30 feet away from the home's west side to block low-angle solar heat during hot summer afternoons.

Winter Benefits

Landscaping can also reduce your energy costs in cold weather. Landscaping that creates a windbreak can reduce your winter heating bills by up to one-third.

Moving air carries heat much more quickly than still air. Wind blowing on your home will cool its exterior surfaces, causing heat inside the home to conduct through the walls and other surfaces more quickly. Wind will also work its way through cracks and other openings in the home's shell, causing drafts and driving up heating costs.

Owners of rural homes have long recognized this principle when designing shelter breaks around their buildings. One study conducted in South Dakota found windbreaks to the north, west, and east of houses cut fuel consumption by an average of 40 percent. With a smaller windbreak on only the windward side, the houses still consumed 25 percent less fuel than similar unprotected homes. An Oklahoma study found that a tall evergreen hedge on the north side of a house reduced that household's fuel consumption by 10 percent during lighter winds and more than 30 percent during high winds.

The effectiveness of landscaping in reducing the cost of heating your home will depend on these factors:

- The coldness of your winter weather
- The draftiness of your home
- The windiness of your site

Winter Landscaping Design

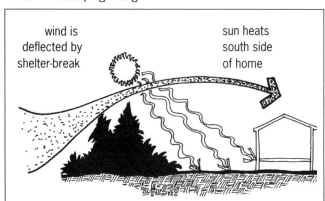

Design your landscaping to create an energy-saving microclimate around your home. To get the full benefit of solar heating, design your landscaping to allow full access to winter sun.

If you live in a drafty home out in the open in the far north, for example, you'll receive the most wintertime benefit from landscaping. You will benefit less if your home is well-sealed, sheltered by structures or trees, and located in a warm winter climate.

In all cases, whether you landscape to improve your home's efficiency in winter or summer, your landscaping will add value to your home and reduce your carbon footprint. It's always a good idea to spend time and money improving your landscaping.

Recognizing Your Microclimate

The climate in close proximity to your home is called its microclimate. If your home is located on a sunny southern slope, for example, it may have a warm microclimate, even though you live in a cool region. If you live in a hot and humid region, your home could still be situated in a comfortable microclimate due to dense shade and cool breezes.

Certain plants may do well in your microclimate, while others languish and never thrive. This could depend on the type of soil, amount of shade, and local ground moisture. To help assess these local factors, locate a trustworthy nursery tree specialist, county extension agent, landscape architect, or landscape contractor to help you choose appropriate plants and plant care. This knowledge is invaluable when it comes to planning and maintaining landscaping, and provides a good reason to choose full-service professionals rather than discount retailers.

CLIMACTIC REGIONS

North America encompasses five climatic regions that are generally described as temperate, hot-arid, hot-humid, cool, and cold. In interpreting the effect of your general climate on your home, you should also consider the effect of your microclimate. A high-elevation north-facing site, for example, may have the climatic characteristics of a region many hundreds of miles to the north. The energy-conserving landscape strategies you employ will be different for each of these regions.

Temperate

In most of the temperate region, you need to consider both the heating and cooling seasons. Seasonal winds can be expected in any season, and periods of high humidity are common.

- Create shade during summer by planting deciduous trees that will cast deep shadows on the home during midday. Choose tall trees with open trunks that allow the low winter sun to warm your home.
- Plant windbreaks that will deflect cold winter winds. Keep them far enough from your home to allow air circulation in summer.

Hot and Arid

This region has clear skies, dry air, and long periods of hot weather. Evenings are often cool, with large daily temperature fluctuations.

- Plant drought-resistant trees to shade walls and windows. They will also cool the air by evaporation from their foliage.
- Design plantings so natural breezes reach your home. Tall shade trees with open trunks, for example, will allow ground-level circulation.

Hot and Humid

This region has high temperatures and consistent high humidity. Wind speed and direction varies.

- Allow cooling summer winds to reach your home. Don't plant dense hedges near your home that will block breezes.
- Minimize humidity around your home. Don't plant trees or shrubs against your foundation that will require watering.
- Plant tall trees that will have spreading canopies and branchless lower trunks to maximize shade without interfering with air circulation around the home.
- If you live in a hurricane zone, select trees that can survive high winds.

Cool

This region has warm summers and cold winters. These locations receive less solar heating than southern areas.

- If you have a large lot, plant dense windbreaks of mixed conifer and deciduous bushes on the windward side of your home to protect it from cold winter winds.
- Shade your windows from direct summer sun. Focus on west-facing and south-facing windows in rooms that overheat in the afternoon.
- Design your landscaping so winter sun can reach south-facing windows.

Cold

This region has cool summers and very cold winters. Homes do not need cooling. Landscaping efforts should be directed at protecting your home from severe cold weather.

- If you have a large lot, plant dense windbreaks of mixed conifer and deciduous bushes on the windward side of your home to protect it from cold winter winds.
- Design your landscaping so winter sun can reach your south-facing windows.

Landscaping Climate Regions for U.S and Canada

Your climate determines the best landscaping strategy for energy efficiency. Your home's immediate surroundings—your local microclimate—may change which of these climate regions you fall within. If you live in the mountains of the temperate zone, for example, your local microclimate may be most similar to the cool region.

CREATING SHADE

Providing shade in the summertime over the sunniest parts of your home can reduce the cost of keeping your home cool. Solar energy that heats your roof and shines through your windows is the main reason that people resort to using air conditioners. Shading is the most cost-effective way to reduce solar heat gain.

In most regions, you can find landscape trees in sizes, densities, and shapes to fit almost any shading application. Nature accommodates our preference to block solar heat in summer and let it in during the winter with deciduous trees or shrubs. These shed their leaves in winter to allow passage of the sun's warm rays.

A tree can reduce incoming solar radiation by 25 to 60 percent, depending on the density of its foliage. Tall deciduous trees with a spreading canopy can be planted to the south, southeast, and southwest of your home to provide maximum shading from the summer sun. Shorter, broader trees are more appropriate to the east, and to the west where shade is especially needed from low-angle sun on hot afternoons.

A 10-foot deciduous tree planted near your home will begin shading nearby windows during its first year. Depending on the species and the home, the tree will shade the roof in 5 to 10 years. A single tree, located to provide shade during the afternoon, may reduce wall and roof temperatures as much as 20° to 40°F. An alternative to a single large shade tree with wide limbs is a row of narrow trees planted relatively close together.

A faster-acting option is to plant greenery closer to the building. Vines can provide shade to foundations and walls beginning with the first growing season. Either a trellis with climbing vines or a planter box with trailing vines will block the sun while allowing cooling breezes. Both annual vines (such as runner beans, sweet peas, and morning glories) and perennial vines (such as Virginia creepers or honeysuckles) serve this purpose well.

Shade and Microclimate

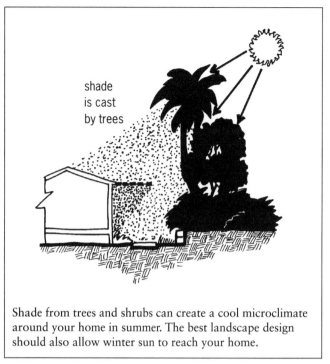

Shade from trees and shrubs can create a cool microclimate around your home in summer. The best landscape design should also allow winter sun to reach your home.

Shading with a Trellis

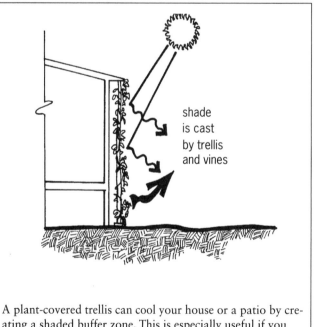

A plant-covered trellis can cool your house or a patio by creating a shaded buffer zone. This is especially useful if you have just one or two windows that cause overheating.

CREATING WIND PROTECTION

Besides providing shade in the summer, well-planned landscaping can also decrease your heating costs in the winter as windbreaks. A windbreak of trees and shrubs will reduce wind speed for a distance of up to thirty times the windbreak's height.

The best trees to block winter winds are evergreens planted on the windward side of your home. If your home's entryway faces cold winter winds, consider planting evergreen shrubs nearby to shelter it from winter's blasts.

Shrubs and vines planted next to your house (such as the trellises and low landscaping covered in the shading section) can also reduce heating costs by creating a dead air space that insulates your home in the winter.

Plant shrubs and vines so there will be at least a foot of space between the full-grown shrub and the house wall. In regions where the soil tends to be wet, foliage that's allowed to grow near your home can inhibit the drying action of the wind and sun. Irrigating against the side of a home can also lead to moisture problems. In damp locations, the best landscape design allows wind to flow around the home to keep the soil reasonably dry.

Be careful when planting evergreens on the south side of the house so they don't obscure winter sun. If winter winds from the south are a problem in your area, plant evergreens far enough away from your dwelling that they lift cold winds up and over the house without shading it.

PLANNING YOUR LANDSCAPE

The next step toward designing the right landscaping is to draw a simple sketch of your yard. Include all the buildings, walks, driveways, and utilities such as water, sewer, electric, gas, and telephone lines. Identify the potential uses for different areas of your yard: vegetable gardens, flower beds, patios, play areas, clothes line, and so on.

Draw arrows to show sun angles and prevailing winds for both summer and winter. Using different colored pencils or felt-tipped markers may help. As you sketch, circle the areas of your yard that need shade and/or protection from wind.

Altering Wind Patterns in Your Microclimate

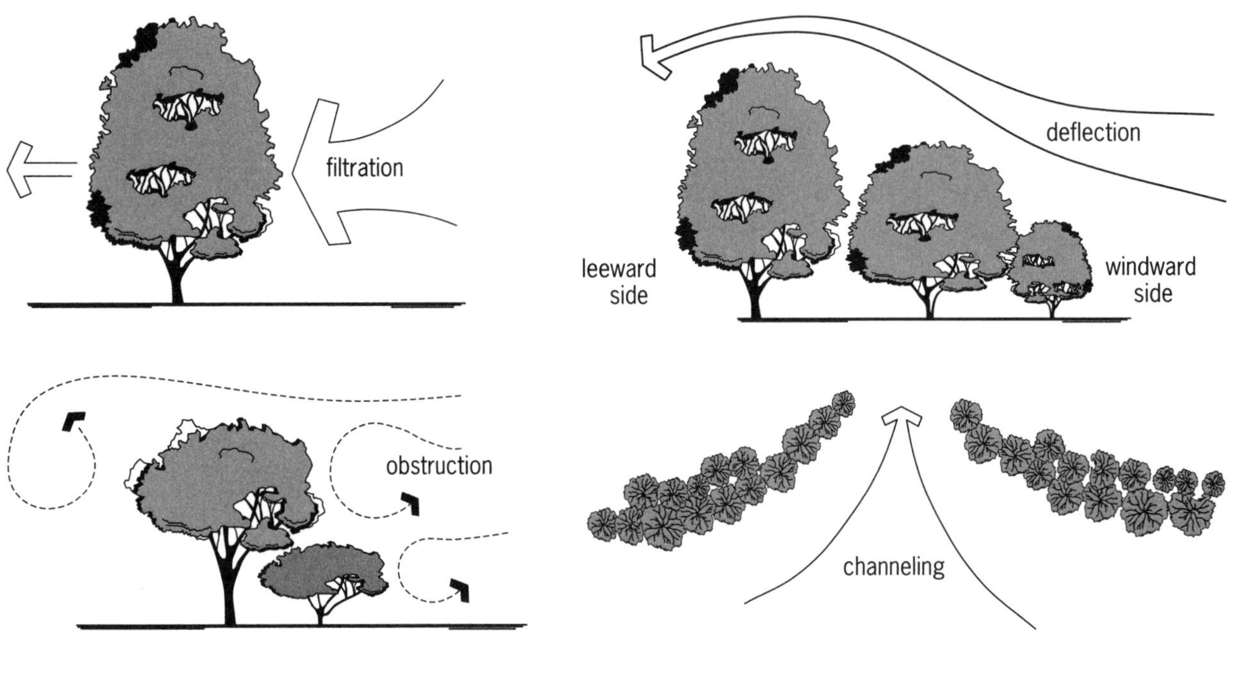

When planning your landscaping, position trees and shrubs so they alter the flow of air favorably through your site.

Paving near your home reflects or radiates solar heat onto the walls and windows. Note the location of all paved surfaces near your home, such as streets, driveways, patios, or sidewalks.

You may want to obscure a nearby house or street light, yet maintain distant views. Draw arrows to show how you want views to be maintained, screened, or framed. Mark routes of noise pollution you wish to block. Highlight areas where landscaping height or width may be restricted, such as under utility lines or along street corners.

The more you identify your goals and familiarize yourself with your yard's features—current and proposed—the more your landscaping projects will succeed. Your sketch will also help you communicate with landscape professionals.

Large expanses of lawn aren't necessary for a pleasing landscape. Lawns provide great areas for kids to play and families to relax. But areas not intensively used by people can be converted to a landscape of trees, shrubs, and perennials. You could cover some areas with an organic mulch, such as bark chips, or mineral covering such as gravel or scoria. Removing the lawn will reduce your water consumption. The new trees will provide a cooler microclimate.

If you need more shade, wind protection, or privacy, consider planting a living fence of dense trees and shrubs. Your living fence can provide an acoustic barrier, visual screening, windbreaks, food for your family, or wildlife habitat. And, once established, many living fences require less maintenance than conventional ones.

Nurseries and Landscape Specialists

The staff at your local nursery is often your best resource for planning and executing new landscape designs. They should know about area growing conditions from experience. They'll usually escort you through their lots for hands-on comparisons of different plant stock and ask questions about your landscape plans. Take a sketch of your yard to the nursery with you to get the most out of your visit. For major purchases, a nursery representative may even visit your property to discuss your planting options.

Local landscapers are always proud of their work, and should be happy to provide references or the locations of some of their completed jobs. Their field experience is valuable for answering specific questions about site planning and microclimate. Landscapers may be knowledgeable about hastening plant growth, landscape maintenance, and disease prevention, too. These specialists can also offer advice about efficient and convenient watering systems, such as drip irrigation.

Winter Wind Deflection by Windbreaks

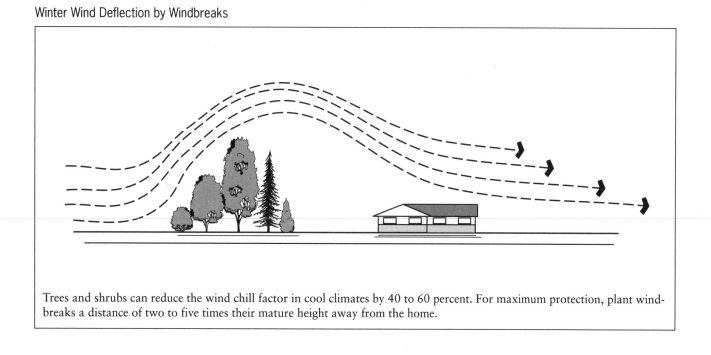

Trees and shrubs can reduce the wind chill factor in cool climates by 40 to 60 percent. For maximum protection, plant windbreaks a distance of two to five times their mature height away from the home.

Although there are exceptions, chain stores or temporary nurseries in hardware or grocery stores are generally not your best source for hardy plant stock and accurate information. Through no fault of their own, the staff of these businesses is frequently ill-prepared to accurately answer the questions of a conscientious home landscaper. The plants sold by these mass retailers often come from far-flung nurseries in climatic regions that are vastly different than yours. This may be harmless if you are buying annuals such as vegetables. But the trees and shrubs you purchase from most nurseries and other providers will be 2 to 10 years old, and they will have adapted to the climate in which they were raised. They may be short-lived at your site, and they may even be of a variety that is completely inappropriate in your region. Shop locally for healthy and hardy nursery stock.

SELECTING TREES AND SHRUBS

Trees and shrubs have a life span of many years. Ideally, your landscape improvements become more attractive and functional with age. But poorly planned landscaping can deteriorate over time and cause maintenance problems.

Every species of tree and shrub has its pros and cons. Ask these questions, whether you are interviewing a landscaping professional or doing research to identify the best plants for your application:

- *Where is this plant from? Is it hardy in my area's climate? During what season should I plant it?*
- *Will this plant grow well in the soils around my house?*
- *How much shading will this plant provide? How well will it shelter the house from winter winds?*
- *What is this plant's growth rate and life expectancy? Is it the right size and shape for the space I have? What is its mature crown size or root ball size?*

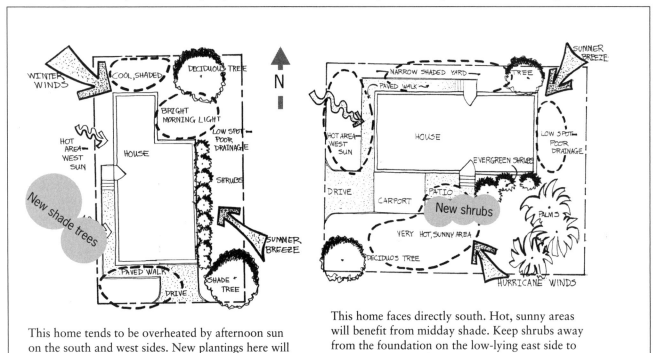

Sample Site Analysis for Hot Dry Region

This home tends to be overheated by afternoon sun on the south and west sides. New plantings here will reduce air conditioning costs.

Sample Site Analysis for Hot Humid Region

This home faces directly south. Hot, sunny areas will benefit from midday shade. Keep shrubs away from the foundation on the low-lying east side to encourage air circulation.

- *Will this plant infringe on nearby structures and walks? Could it interfere with overhead lines, underground pipes, or traffic visibility?*
- *Does this plant offer edible nuts, berries or fruits? Will it attract desirable birds and wildlife?*
- *How much maintenance and watering does this plant require? Does it have any specialized pruning needs? How well does it tolerate pests and diseases?*

Localized Landscaping

Your best landscaping options are plants adapted to your particular region. Localized landscaping includes vegetation appropriate to a particular site's climate, moisture, and soils.

Whether the species is a native or an import, the best predictor of performance is the plant's history of success or failure in your region. Locally grown "hardy" stock is your best bet (some nurseries will guarantee the survival of only local species). Imported stock and untested exotic species could create continual demands on your time, money, water, and patience.

In many regions, water shortages are an increasing problem. If you utilize a municipal supply, you may see increasing water costs. Choose your landscaping with water in mind. If water supply is a concern in your area consider xeriscaping, which is landscaping that does not require supplemental irrigation beyond what naturally occurs in your area.

Basic Tree Forms

When selecting shade trees for your property or community, consider how the tree form, density, and mature size will relate to your garden and house. Will the new tree grow tall enough to shade your roof? Will it also shade your garden? How will the trees you plant today affect your view in ten years?

Fastigiate   These are narrow trees that taper to a point, such as the Lombardy poplar or the fastigiate Washington hawthorn. When planted in lines, fastigiate trees are excellent screens or windbreaks. They are usually fast-growing, gaining 3 to 5 feet a year to pro-

vide quick cooling results. Fastigiates also work well closer to buildings, where a spreading tree would require constant pruning.

Columnar   These are extremely narrow trees that lack a pointed tip, such as the sentry maple or columnar red maple. Columnars are good for narrow sites. They provide excellent shading for rooftops when planted close together in a line or grove. They are also good for planting further to the west and southwest, since their height allows them to shade house roof and walls from afar.

Spreading   Spreading trees, such as the sugar maple, tend to grow wider than their height. They require ample space and are especially good for shading walls and roofs. Although a spreading tree works well when planted as a single shade tree, when several are planted in a grove they provide a cool microclimate.

Weeping   These are trees with pendulous branches, such as the weeping willow or the weeping birch. Weeping trees work well where shade is desired close to the ground and where space is not limited. They are also very attractive when silhouetted against a background of evergreen trees.

Open Headed   These are trees with a loose branch structure and an indistinct silhouette, such as the silk tree, the honey locust, or the flowering dogwood. Since they provide scattered shade, open-headed trees may be good for the east side of your house. This placement allows some morning light to reach your windows. Open-headed trees are good lawn trees, since their open foliage allows filtered sunlight to reach grasses and shrubs below.

Round Top   Round-top trees, such as the white oak or the sycamore, have a distinctly round profile. They usually require plenty of room for their crown to grow. A round-top tree is good when you can plant only a single tree. The lower canopy of a round top tree can be pruned to allow cooling breezes, while its upper canopy provides shade to a house's windows, walls, and roof.

Pyramidal   These are trees with an almost conical outline, such as the Douglas fir, the magnolia, or the acacia. Some pyramidals, such as the Douglas fir, can be used for tall hedges or windbreaks.

The Variety of Tree Forms

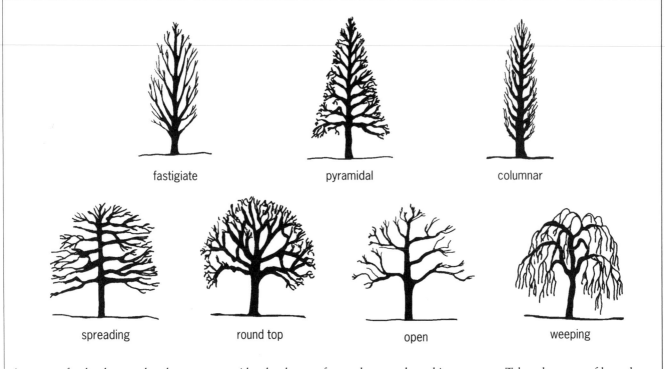

fastigiate   pyramidal   columnar

spreading   round top   open   weeping

As you craft a landscape plan, be sure to consider the shapes of trees that are planted in your area. Take advantage of how they cast shade, control wind, block obstructions, and frame your view in both summer and winter.

Tree and Shrub Growth

A slow-growing variety of tree may require many years of growth before it provides adequate shade for your roof, walls, and garden. Fast-growing species will provide the desired shade in less time. But keep in mind that trees with fast growth rates are generally not as long-lived as trees with moderate to slow growth rates. In addition, trees with fast growth rates may have less rooting depth or less resistance to branch breakage during wind storms or heavy snow loads. These are important considerations when you are choosing trees to place near structures.

Selecting the right shrubs and planting them appropriately is also important. When planting shrubs close to the house, be sure to learn how large the mature shrub will be. Place them with at least a foot of space between the full-grown shrub and the wall of the home. They may look a little lonely at first. But planning ahead will prevent overcrowding in the future.

Buying Trees and Shrubs

Follow these inspection tips at the nursery to be sure you buy healthy, undamaged trees and shrubs:

- Look at the bark to tell if the tree has been handled carefully during growing, digging, and shipping. Scrapes and bruises could provide an entry point for infection or rot.
- If you're buying bare-root plants, look for broken or damaged roots.
- On balled-and-burlap-wrapped plants, check to make sure the ball is well-packed, so the roots are not exposed to air.
- Look for broken or damaged limbs. Minor damage may not be a problem if it can be easily pruned off.
- Look for indications of insects or disease such as cocoons, egg masses, cankers, or lesions.

Keep nursery plants well watered. With bare-root plants, be sure to keep the tiny hair-roots damp at all times. They will not survive if these roots are allowed to dry out.

Balled-and-burlap plants should be handled gently. Don't just drop them out of a truck—use appropriate machinery if necessary to unload and place large balled-and-burlap-wrapped plants.

PLANTING TREES AND SHRUBS

When your plants arrive, store them in a cool, shady place until you can plant them. Do not ever allow them to dry out—keep them well-watered until they go back in the ground.

The process of transplanting causes trauma to the plant, and is best handled carefully. If possible, plant on a cool or overcast day. Hot sun stresses plants by requiring a flow of water and nutrients to the foliage that the traumatized plant may be incapable of providing. If you must plant during hot or sunny weather, try to do so in late afternoon or evening.

Tree-Planting Basics

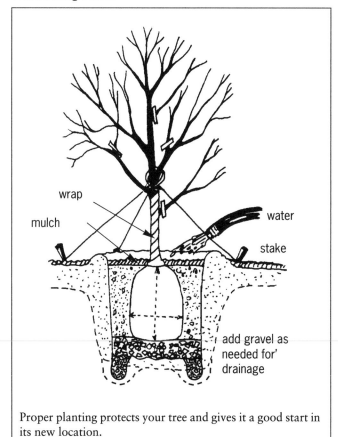

Proper planting protects your tree and gives it a good start in its new location.

Planting

Put a little topsoil in the bottom of the pit. Remove the potted plant from its container, gently freeing its roots. Place the tree or shrub in the hole so its root ball sits evenly. Make sure the plant's original soil line remains at ground level or a little above. Gently fill the area around the root ball to remove air pockets.

If you are planting a bare-root plant, be sure your hole accommodates all the roots without crimping. Build a small cone of soil at the bottom of the hole. Lay the bare roots over the cone and carefully fill around the roots to remove air pockets.

If you are planting balled-and-wrapped stock, leave the burlap around the ball to reduce trauma to the roots. Slit the burlap in a few places to help the roots grow into the surrounding soil as soon as possible. The burlap may be reinforced with twine, which is tied to the trunk. If so, cut the twine when the tree leafs out in the spring.

Fill around the root ball with soil. Flood the hole and root ball with a hose, using a digging bar or crow bar to create holes for the water to penetrate through the fill dirt to the bottom of the filled hole. Gently tamp the tree pit. The water forces air to the surface, ensuring that all roots are in contact with soil.

Build a watering basin around the new tree that is four to six inches high. Make this basin wider than the diameter of the root ball.

After a few initial soakings, most trees and shrubs will need weekly watering during their first growing season. Keep a careful eye on your new plants. If a tree or shrub wilts during the hot part of the day, the root ball is not getting enough water.

Mulching

To help retain root moisture and reduce weed intrusion, cover the ground around the new planting with 4 inches of mulch. Use organic materials such as old leaves, bark, or aged sawdust or wood chips. Don't use peat moss as a mulch since it acts as a sponge instead of letting the water through to the plant. If you use grass clippings, make sure they are brown. Green grass clippings heat up the soil during decomposition and rob it of nitrogen.

Wrapping

With most young trees, it is a good idea to wrap their trunks to prevent sun scalding in summer and, in cold climates, frost damage in winter.

Wrap the trunk with rolled paper wrap available from nurseries. Start at the bottom and wrap upward so each layer will shed moisture rather than trapping it. Remove the wrap the following spring without fail to avoid girdling and to allow the trunk to expand as it grows. Ask your nursery or landscape specialist for more information.

Staking

If the new tree is in an area of high winds or heavy traffic, or if it is top-heavy, you may need to support the tree by staking or guying. Newly established roots may break as an unsupported tree trunk twists in the wind. If the tree is in a public place such as a front yard, staking will also provide some protection against vandalism. Use two stakes opposite each other or three guy wires at equal angles around the tree. Remove the stakes after a year. Otherwise they become a crutch and the tree may not build sufficient trunk strength.

TREE CARE

Once established, trees need only moderate care. But regular watering, fertilizing, and pruning can help keep them in optimal health.

Watering

Consult your local nursery for advice about watering your plants. Don't just spray the surface—shallow watering promotes shallow roots. Occasional deep soakings develop sturdy roots that will better withstand drought. For shrubs planted near the home, be sure to limit watering to just what is needed since excess water can damage the home's foundation. For the most efficient watering, consider installing a drip irrigation system.

Fertilizing

Spring is the best time to fertilize your trees. Trees in dire need of fertilizer have small leaves or slightly discolored leaves. If you fertilize your lawn, trees located there may need no fertilizer.

The best fertilizing method is to create holes ten- to twenty-inches deep and an inch wide in concentric rings around the perimeter from three feet away from the trunk to one-and-a-half times the diameter of the crown. Pour liquid or granular fertilizer into the holes. In sandy soils, apply half as much fertilizer twice as often to reduce loss of fertilizer to run-off.

It's best to fertilize when the soil is relatively dry because spring rains or deep watering can then carry the fertilizer downward.

Pruning

Your new tree or shrub was probably pruned at the nursery and most likely does not need pruning for the first year or two. In general, newly transplanted trees and shrubs need all their existing foliage to support the establishment of new roots.

After the first year or two, you can prune for shaping. Pruning unproductive branches may also help a tree or shrub establish its root system by redirecting the flow of nutrients. Although you can prune most species any time of the year, some species are harmed by spring pruning. Ask your nursery or landscape specialist.

Be careful when pruning. Do some research first, and don't start pruning away at a plant until you understand the principles involved. When cutting large branches, don't just cut downward on the branch because this could tear the bark off the bottom of the branch when the limb falls. The best way is to make an undercut a foot or so out from where you want the final cut. Complete the cut from the top and let the limb fall. Then go back to make a clean cut at the final location.

Don't cut branches off flush to the trunk. Instead, leave the healing collar where the branch meets the trunk. Cut just a little outside of that collar. On smaller branches, cut just ahead of a bud so the new growth which will emerge from that bud doesn't leave a stub.

Disinfect your pruning tools between cuts by dipping them in a solution of one part bleach to four or five parts water. This will help prevent the spread of diseases such as fire blight.

THE BOTTOM LINE

Your attention to landscaping will produce benefits that go beyond energy efficiency. It's worth your efforts to craft a landscape that is both beautiful and bestows long-term energy benefits.

- Identify the rooms in your home that tend to overheat in summer. Consider whether your yard could accommodate plantings that would cast shade on the walls and windows of these rooms.
- Identify the rooms in your home that tend to be the most drafty when the wind blows in winter. Consider whether your yard could accommodate plantings that would buffer winter winds on this side of your home.
- Look over your current landscaping and determine how your existing plantings improve your home's efficiency in summer and winter. Develop a landscape plan that integrates these existing plantings.
- Schedule maintenance for your existing plantings that includes pruning, fertilizing, and watering.

6 Finding and Sealing Air Leaks

Air leaks in the walls, ceilings, and floors of your home can waste up to 30 percent of the energy consumed by your heating and cooling equipment. Holes and gaps in your home's shell also allow moisture, insects, dust, and pollutants to enter your home. Sealing air leaks reduces this energy loss and helps keep these environmental contaminants under control. A properly sealed home is also more comfortable.

In this chapter we'll show you how to evaluate the air leakage between your home and the outdoors. We'll describe some simple projects so you can get started on reducing you home's air leakage right away, and we'll identify some big projects that are best left to professionals. Taken together, these air-sealing tasks can reduce your utility consumption by several hundred dollars a year. The improved comfort and cleanliness of your home will be an added benefit.

EVALUATE YOUR HOME'S AIR LEAKAGE

Do you notice drafts in your home? Drafts indicate that air is moving through your home's shell. This air leakage is expensive. It carries heated air out of your home in winter, and carries cool air out in summer.

If you live in a cold dry climate, do you notice a lot of static electricity in the winter? Excess air leakage in these climates tends to dry out your home and encourage the production of static electricity.

Do you hear a lot of outdoor noise when inside your home? Cracks and holes in your home's shell allow both outdoor air and sound to pass into your home. Well-sealed homes are quieter.

AIR LEAKAGE BASICS

Every home has some drafts. It's just the nature of building construction that gaps and holes will be left in the walls, ceilings, floors, doors, and windows where outdoor air can make its way into the home and indoor air can escape to outdoors. During mild weather, air leakage through these openings is harmless—on any day when you might open a door or window for ventilation, air leakage through the building shell incurs no energy penalty. But air leakage is costly and uncomfortable when you are running your heating or cooling system. During these times, any air leaking through your home's shell is carrying valuable energy with it. Air-sealing controls this expensive loss.

Your home will ideally be surrounded by a continuous layer of insulation that has a continuous air barrier installed immediately adjacent to it. This air barrier may be the drywall, exterior sheathing such as plywood, or building paper that is properly sealed at its seams. In retrofit work you will probably need to seal air leaks at some combination of these locations. For example, you might seal the drywall by caulking around recessed light fixtures, and seal the sheathing and building paper when installing new windows or doors.

In some climates, infiltrating air also carries unwanted moisture. In hot and humid climates, your air conditioner works hard to remove moisture from your home. When moist outdoor air gets into your home, your cooling system must work overtime, at extra expense, to remove this moisture. In cold climates, moist outdoor air can condense in your walls and attic in winter and cause moisture damage. Air-sealing allows you to control where the heat and moisture go in your home.

You may notice air leaks in the form of wintertime drafts. A drafty home is never comfortable, because moving air always feels cool. With proper air-sealing, you can set your thermostat lower and save on your heating bills without sacrificing comfort.

A well-sealed home is quieter inside. This side effect of air-sealing often surprises homeowners after they finish performing major air-sealing work. In areas near airports where residents tire of the sound of aircraft, noise abatement programs always include home air-sealing.

The Driving Forces of Air Leakage

Air moves through openings in your building's shell. Air leakage is driven by pressure differences between indoors and outdoors. Ideally there should be little or no pressure difference between indoors and outdoors. Several things cause pressure differences between the indoors and outdoors.

Wind creates pressure and suction on different sides of the home. You perceive this as drafts on a windy day.

Stack effect takes place when warm air rises toward your ceilings and dense cold air sinks to the floors. This drives air leakage during cold weather more than it does when it's warm outside. When leaks are driven by the stack effect, you tend to notice them low on the ground floor. You don't usually notice air leaks higher in your home, where warm air exits, unless you go up into your attic and feel warm air emerging from around recessed light fixtures and through cracks in the ceiling. But these high leaks in the shell are important because they drive air leakage elsewhere in your home. A draft coming under your front door is driven, in part, by airflow up into your attic.

Exhaust appliances such as exhaust fans, conventional furnaces, fireplace chimneys, and clothes dryers all depressurize the home. These mechanical influences can also compete with one another. This is a potential concern when open-combustion furnaces or water heaters are installed that could be prone to backdrafting, since this can spill carbon monoxide and other gases into your home. To learn more about the potential hazards of backdrafting, see *Combustion Safety on page 130.*

Sealing Air Leaks in Your Attic

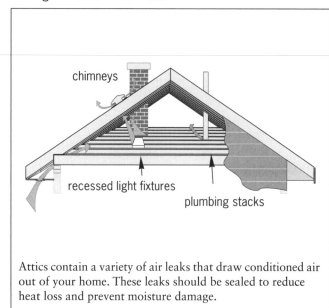

Attics contain a variety of air leaks that draw conditioned air out of your home. These leaks should be sealed to reduce heat loss and prevent moisture damage.

What Drives Air Movement

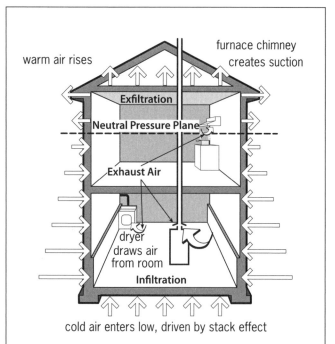

Air is driven through your home by several sources of pressure. The goal of air-sealing is to reduce air movement through the shell, while allowing your appliances and heating equipment the airflow they require.

BLOWER DOOR TESTING

To seal up leaks in your building shell, you must first find out where they are. You may already have some ideas about where air leaks into your home. But the best way to find air leaks is by performing a blower door test. This analysis is often used by energy auditors when evaluating a home. It's also used by home performance contractors to test the airflow among house zones such as attics, crawl spaces, or garages in conjunction with energy retrofit projects. Most importantly, the results of the blower door test will help you or your contractor find air leaks that have been costing you money.

During a blower door test, the energy auditor installs a fan that temporarily blocks one of your main exterior doorways. The fan depressurizes your home, causing exaggerated air leakage that the auditor can measure and convert to natural air leakage.

The energy auditor will report your home's air leakage in either cubic feet per minute (CFM) or air changes per hour (ACH), and will compare your home's leakage to industry standards. From this measurement, you can evaluate the potential for energy savings from air-sealing your home.

A blower door test can also yield important information about the safety of combustion appliances and whether mechanical ventilation is needed to protect your home's indoor air quality.

Doing a Blower Door Test

We recommend that you have an energy audit performed on your home that includes a blower door test. It's the best way to determine what level of savings are available from air-sealing projects. Because blower door testing requires specialized equipment and training, this is a job for professionals.

Energy auditors work generally within three distinct fields.

Utility company auditors who provide services for rate-payers. Some utility energy audits include blower door tests. Many utilities offer these audits for no cost or low cost. Contact the utility company that provides your heating fuel.

Blower-Door Principle

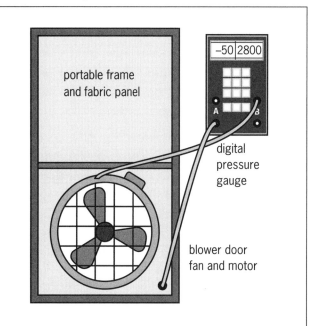

portable frame and fabric panel

−50 2800

digital pressure gauge

blower door fan and motor

The blower door is installed in a doorway. A powerful fan draws air out of your home, and helps the energy auditor find places where air can leak through cracks and holes in the building shell. A pressure gauge is used to estimate the size of those leaks.

Blower-Door Testing

An energy auditor uses a blower door to measure air leakage through a home's shell. Home performance contractors and insulators use this information to guide air-sealing efforts.

Home performance consultants who provide fee-for-service audits. These professionals usually offer a range of services that include blower door tests and more extensive energy evaluations. See the *Resources* on page 173 for information about finding home performance professionals, or check your Yellow Pages under Energy Services.

Home performance contractors who offer consulting and construction services. These professionals may be able to do both analysis and repair. See the *Resources* on page 173 for information about the Home Performance with ENERGY STAR program.

Ask your energy auditor to perform a blower door test of your home, and to provide this information:

- A measurement of your home's airtightness
- A comparison of your home to industry standards for airtightness
- An evaluation of your home's need for mechanical ventilation
- An evaluation of the combustion safety of your heating system and water-heating system
- Recommendations for air-sealing projects that could improve your home's airtightness and reduce your energy consumption.

Have your energy auditor walk through your home with you while the blower door is running. If the blower door is set to depressurize the home (create suction), you can often feel air being drawn through leaks in the building shell. If you plan to perform some of the air-sealing tasks yourself, work with the energy auditor to find the largest leaks. Make a checklist of these locations, and ask your auditor to prioritize them in order of importance.

Indoor Air Quality

It's wise to examine the issue of indoor air quality while you're evaluating air leakage. Air leakage does help dilute pollutants such as carbon dioxide from respiration, formaldehyde from building materials, and combustion by-products. But air leakage isn't very reliable at providing this ventilation. Since air leakage is largely driven by wind, air leakage tends to provide too much fresh air during cold, windy weather and too little during mild weather. You can have a very drafty home in windy weather, and still have air quality problems at other times. Mechanical ventilation systems such as exhaust fans solve this problem.

All well-designed homes should have exhaust fans installed in the kitchen and bathrooms to remove moisture, odors, and pollutants. The most efficient homes utilize whole-house ventilation systems to provide measured amounts of fresh air to every room. Experts agree that it is far more economical and comfortable to build an airtight home and install a whole-house ventilation system than to rely on random ventilation to control pollutants. A blower door test can tell you whether your home needs additional ventilation. You can learn more in *Ventilation Systems* on page 156.

Some houses lack an adequate air supply for combustion appliances like furnaces and water heaters. Too little air available for combustion can lead furnaces to produce carbon monoxide and cause chimneys to backdraft. A combustion safety test can confirm that your heating appliances receive sufficient air to operate properly. Combustion testing is an essential part of a comprehensive energy audit and heating-system evaluation.

MATERIALS FOR AIR-SEALING

Home air-sealing requires a variety of materials in order to create a continuous, airtight, and strong air barrier around your home.

Caulking

You can start with caulking to seal some small leaks, but it won't be your main weapon against air leakage. Caulking works well for cracks less than $3/8$ inch width. Caulking helps establish a continuous air barrier around window trim, baseboards, light fixtures, and electrical boxes. You can purchase caulking at any hardware store. The easiest caulking for simple air-sealing is acrylic or acrylic-latex, since it seals well and washes up with water. Caulking costs $1 to $4 per tube.

Liquid Foams

These are messy and bond well to almost everything including your skin and clothing—wear gloves and safety glasses while applying liquid foam. Plan your application so that you seal all the places requiring this foam at one time. Start foaming and don't stop until you're done or the cans are empty.

One-part foam works well for holes, gaps and cracks that are too big for caulking. This stuff expands a lot, so don't fill a crack with the un-expanded foam; partially fill the crack and wait for the foam to expand. One-part foam comes in canisters that hold about one quart, and cost $5 to $10 each.

Two-part foam can bridge large gaps or be sprayed onto a broad surface. Two-part foam seals and insulates in a single application, creating customized pieces of airtight insulating foam. Two-part foam is furnished with two types of applicator nozzles: for either spraying on a surface or into a wide gap. Two-part foam is harder to find—try a local lumber yard that caters to contractors. An average kit costs $100 to $200, so you'll need to set up several small projects to justify buying a kit.

Rigid Sealing Materials

Seal the largest openings, as around plumbing chases in the attic or crawl space, with pieces of plywood, drywall, or rigid-foam insulation. Use fasteners and adhesive to secure it permanently, or seal the edges down with two-part foam. Thin wood paneling can be cut easily and fastened with construction adhesive and small nails or staples. These materials can all be purchased at your home improvement store. A sheet of drywall costs less than $10. Thin plywood or rigid foamboard insulation costs $10 to $20 per sheet.

Air-Sealing Using Foam Insulation

One-part foam is used to seal gaps around windows that are too large for caulking. Liquid foams provide a permanent seal.

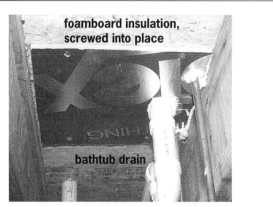

Foam board can be attached over openings created by drains and plumbing fixtures. If necessary, the board can be removed for plumbing maintenance.

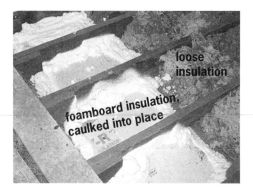

Rigid foamboard is used to fill large openings such as joist spaces and other building cavities. Two-part foam can be sprayed around the edges of the foamboard to seal and fasten it.

Combinations of one-part foam, two-part foam, and rigid foamboard are used to air-seal and insulate tricky areas.

AIR-SEALING STRATEGIES

You can make great improvements in your home's efficiency if you focus your air-sealing efforts on the biggest holes in the building shell. Caulking small cracks and installing door weatherstripping, for example, may improve your comfort somewhat by reducing minor drafts. But the reduction in air leakage you'll achieve with this incremental approach is a small part of the overall air leakage of your home.

Most air leakage in standard frame homes comes through large openings of these types:

- Utility penetrations where pipes and wires connect the living space with attics, under-floor crawl spaces, and the outdoors.
- Light fixtures and plumbing fixtures.
- Integral framing defects that connect building cavities such as floors, walls, and ceilings.

Sealing attic air leaks is a reasonable do-it-yourself task. If you hire a professional insulator or home performance contractor to do the work, the guidelines here will help you know what to ask for.

How to Find and Seal Attic Air Leaks

You can probably find more important air leaks in your attic than in any other part of your home. You aren't normally aware of these leaks because rising warm air leaking out of your home and up into the attic doesn't create obvious drafts down on the main floor. But air exiting into your attic will exert a strong negative pressure on air leaks elsewhere in your home.

You should always find and seal air leaks in the attic before installing insulation. Loose-fill fiberglass and cellulose do not create air barriers when installed in attics. Air leaks reduce the thermal resistance of these fibrous insulations. And your new insulation only makes it more difficult to seal attic air leaks later.

The first step in finding and sealing attic air leaks is to locate access to the space. Your home may have a ceiling attic hatch located in a hallway or closet. Some homes have an exterior hatch located up in the gable end of the roof structure. Find your home's hatch, set a ladder securely, and gather your tools.

Top-of-Wall Air Leaks in Attic

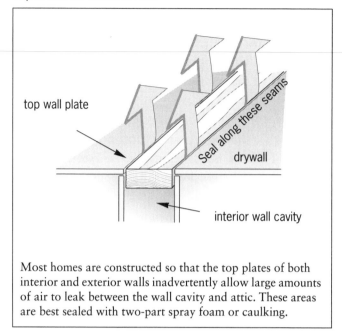

top wall plate

Seal along these seams

drywall

interior wall cavity

Most homes are constructed so that the top plates of both interior and exterior walls inadvertently allow large amounts of air to leak between the wall cavity and attic. These areas are best sealed with two-part spray foam or caulking.

Bring a bright light, a good respirator, and a small board to lay across the top of the ceiling joists. While in the attic, always step on the wooden framing members. Do NOT step between them on the drywall or plaster, or you may do a lot of damage to yourself or to your home. *Always use proper protective gear. Be aware that live electrical wiring is installed in your attic and is always potentially dangerous. Be careful when climbing ladders. Don't attempt this type of work if you are unsure of what you are doing.*

Climb into your attic, adjust your lights, and make yourself as comfortable as you can. There is a lot to see in most attics, and to a trained eye there is no better place to learn how a structure is built.

Search out the areas described here, and try to determine if air leakage pathways connect the attic with the living space. Search out hints such as noise, odors, or dust that transmit up from your living space. Once you've located any likely openings, you can return with air-sealing materials and tools, or ask a contractor to do so.

Attic Hatches or Scuttle   Install weatherstrip around the perimeter of the hatch. Caulk the edges of the frame to the drywall as needed.

Two-Level Attics in Split-Level Houses   Seal the tops of the wall cavities with a rigid material cut as a plug to fit within the stud bays. Caulk or foam the edges.

Sealing Around Masonry Chimneys

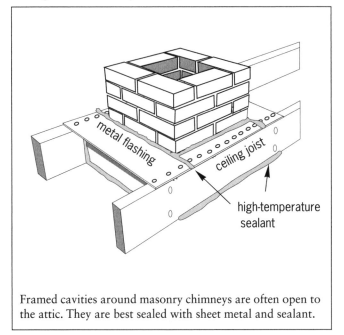

Framed cavities around masonry chimneys are often open to the attic. They are best sealed with sheet metal and sealant.

Tops of Interior Partition Walls   You can see these if you move the insulation away from the top of interior partition walls. Use one-part foam or caulking to seal the holes where pipes and wires pass through. Or do a more thorough job by moving the insulation aside, sweeping the area clean, and spraying two-part foam over the top-plate area in a 4- or 5-inch band.

Wiring and Plumbing Penetrations   Seal around wires and pipes where they emerge from the tops of walls. Look for dedicated chases (boxed-in utility corridors for pipes and wires), since these often lead to a basement or crawl space. Use caulk or foam. If the hole is too large for foam or caulk, cover it with plywood or foamboard, glued and screwed into place. Professionals often spray two-part foam over the top to seal the surface of this rigid patch.

Masonry Chimneys   Seal openings around chimneys with sheet metal. Seal the chimney to the ceiling structure with a high-temperature silicone sealant or chimney cement.

Recessed Light Housings   Recessed lights can create a serious break in the thermal integrity of your attic insulation (the one exception is where they are installed in ceilings under a second floor). The best solution for those that do penetrate the attic insulation is to replace them with a surface-mounted fixture. Recessed lights may also be enclosed from the attic side by building a drywall box or stovepipe cylinder that can be sealed down to the ceiling. This type of enclosure should be large enough to allow 3 inches of space between the enclosure and the fixture to prevent overheating.

Dropped Soffits in Kitchens and Bathrooms   You can often see these openings from the attic, though access can be tricky. Seal the opening in the top of the soffit with rigid foamboard, plywood, or drywall fastened and sealed to ceiling joists and soffit framing.

Bathtubs and Shower Stalls   Seal large openings with securely fastened rigid patches such as drywall that are caulked or foamed at their edges. Use one-part foam for holes that are less than two inches across.

Knee Walls in Finished Attic Areas   Knee walls are short walls built between the second floor and the rafters of finished attics. You should seal the joist cavities under the floor below by creating a rigid seal under the knee wall. Two-part foam may also be used to seal this area.

Duct Chases   These utility pathways may also contain wiring or plumbing. If the opening is large, seal with a rigid barrier such as plywood or drywall, and seal the new barrier to ducts with caulk or foam. Smaller cracks between the air barrier and surrounding materials may be foamed or caulked.

Sealing Split-Level Wall Cavities

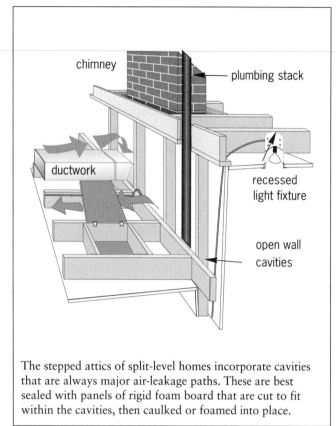

The stepped attics of split-level homes incorporate cavities that are always major air-leakage paths. These are best sealed with panels of rigid foam board that are cut to fit within the cavities, then caulked or foamed into place.

Sealing Around Dropped Soffits

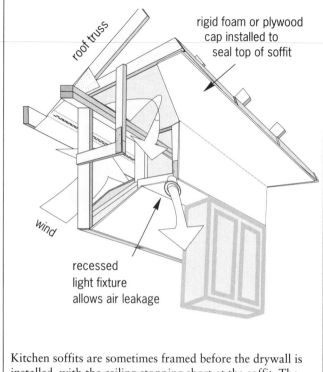

Kitchen soffits are sometimes framed before the drywall is installed, with the ceiling stopping short at the soffit. The resulting cavity is open to the attic. These should be sealed from the attic to slow air infiltration.

Sealing Above Dropped Ceilings

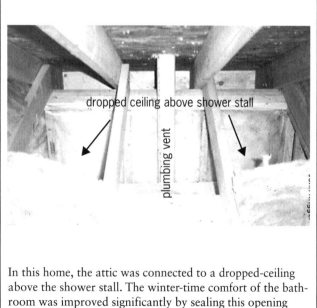

In this home, the attic was connected to a dropped-ceiling above the shower stall. The winter-time comfort of the bathroom was improved significantly by sealing this opening with a sheet of rigid foam insulation.

Sealing Knee Walls and Sloped Ceilings

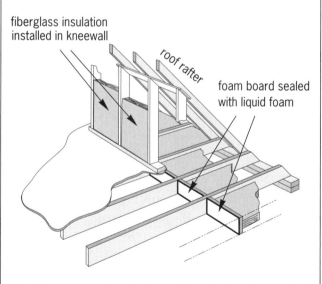

The joist spaces under this kneewall cavity have been sealed to slow air flow between the ventilated attic and the second-floor joist cavity.

THE BOTTOM LINE

The most comfortable homes have a continuous thermal boundary made up of an effective air barrier and abundant insulation. Once you have implemented the recommendations in this chapter, your subsequent efficiency improvements, especially insulation upgrades, will be all the more effective.

The effort you put into finding and sealing air leaks in your home will be well-rewarded. We suggest an investment of between a few hundred and a few thousand dollars on air-sealing projects. Investments in air-sealing will typically return your investment within five years.

- Schedule an energy audit for your home. Be sure the auditor performs a blower door test to assess air leakage, identify air leakage sites, and evaluate the need for mechanical ventilation. Ask to be shown the location of any major air-leakage sites that are identified in your home.

- Find and seal the major air leaks in your home, or have a contractor do so. Focus on areas around chimneys, recessed light fixtures, framing defects, and pipes and wires.

7 Insulation

The comfort and energy efficiency of your home are more dependent on insulation than any other component. Without sufficient insulation, many tasks we recommend for trimming heating and cooling loads are less effective. When you install more insulation, your heating and cooling equipment runs less and your utility bills are lower.

In this chapter, we show you why properly installed insulation is the best way to reduce heating and cooling costs. We also describe how to install insulation so it is effective and long-lived, and which types of insulation work best for each application.

EVALUATE YOUR HOME'S INSULATION

How thick is the insulation in your attic? Your attic insulation should be your first line of defense against energy waste whether you live in a hot or cold climate. Thicker insulation is better.

How thick is the insulation in your walls? Whatever the thickness of your walls, they should be full of insulation in every climate.

Do you have insulation under your floors or around your foundation? Floor and foundation insulation is mandatory for efficient homes in cold climates, and a worthwhile addition to super-efficient homes in warm climates.

INSULATION BASICS

Attic and wall insulation are the best energy investments for many homes. In hot climates, attic insulation gains importance because of the high temperatures attics reach in summer. The greater the temperature difference between outdoors and indoors, the more you need effective insulation. If you live in a climate with hot summers, your attic may be 150°F in summer,

or 70°F hotter than your home's living space. It's worth installing lots of attic insulation to slow the flow of heat into your home. Wall insulation is important during hot summers, too, but it's not as critical since the temperature difference between the two sides of the wall on a hot day may be only 30°F.

In cold climates, wall insulation is just as valuable as attic insulation. This benefit is again driven by temperature difference. When the outdoor temperature is 0°F, the temperature difference across your home's walls is 70°F. You want all the wall insulation you can get. Floor and foundation insulation are more cost-effective in cold climates, too.

But these comparisons must be taken in perspective. So we make one simple recommendation with complete certainty. *Install the maximum amount of insulation possible in your home's walls, ceilings, and floors.*

The Meaning of R-Value

Insulation is rated by R-value, which is a measure of thermal resistance, or resistance to heat flow. Each type of insulation has a particular R-value for an inch of thickness. Hence a 6-inch fiberglass blanket may be valued at R-19, or about R-3 per inch, while a 6-inch sheet of polystyrene foam board has a value of R-30, or about R-5 per inch. Foam board is a better insulator than fiberglass, inch for inch. But that doesn't mean that foam board is always a preferable material.

We often use fiberglass and cellulose loose-fill insulation in attics, for example, because we have enough room there to install 16 to 24 inches of insulation. The lower R-value of these materials is not an issue when there is plenty of space. Fiberglass and cellulose are inexpensive, relatively nontoxic, and easy to install. When choosing insulation, we consider the R-value per inch, the overall cost, the ease of installation, and other factors.

Typical R-Values Versus Recommended R-Values

Type of home	Attic	Walls	Floor	Bsmt. walls
Typical existing older home	15	9	2	0
Recommended in cold climate	50	30	30	20
Recommended in moderate climate	50	21	30	12
Recommended in warm climate	50	21	19	12
The ideal home with super-insulated details	60	40	40	40

R-values represent the whole-wall R-value, and account for the thermal resistance of the entire building assembly, including framing.

Thermal Bridging

The R-value of the insulation itself doesn't describe the overall thermal resistance of an assembly such as a wall or ceiling. The R-value for a wall accounts for both the insulated areas and the areas occupied by framing lumber. Since lumber has a relatively poor R-value per inch, the overall R-value of the assembly is lower than the R-value of the insulation itself. This overall measurement is known as the whole-wall R-value.

The whole-wall R-value of a building assembly can be considerably lower than the R-value of the insulation itself. In typical frame walls, for example, lumber occupies 15 to 25 percent of the surface area. Because wood has an insulating value of only about R-1 per inch, these framed areas create thermal bridges in the insulated wall. The interior wall areas over the framing are cold in winter and hot in summer because heat conducts through wood more rapidly than through the insulated space between the framing. If metal framing is used, the reduction in whole-wall-R-value is even greater.

For a wall with a common two-by-four wood frame and R-11 $3\frac{1}{2}$-inch fiberglass insulation, the whole-wall R-value will be R-9 to R-10. For a similar two-by-six wall with $5\frac{1}{2}$-inch fiberglass insulation, the whole-wall R-value will be R-11 to R-13.

How Much Insulation Is Enough?

Most of our homes have too little insulation. This has happened because energy prices have been low for many years, allowing our building codes to neglect energy conservation. Some of our homes have adequate attic insulation, because it is fairly inexpensive to install. But our walls, floors, and foundations are often the weakest energy detail in our homes.

We recommend that you make a substantial investment in improving your home's insulation. Your attic should be insulated to at least R-50. Your wall cavities should be completely filled—which isn't always the case in homes more than a few decades old—and consider adding two to four inches of foam insulation to the outside of your exterior walls. In cold climates, your foundation or floor should be insulated to at least R-30. The total cost of these projects will range from $2000 to $10,000, and the payback will range from 5 to 15 years. Fortunately, you needn't commit to a complete insulation retrofit—every project you complete will improve your home's efficiency. You can learn more about all these procedures later in this chapter.

The table shown here lists the R-values that we recommend for existing homes.

HOW TO MEASURE YOUR INSULATION

To complete this inspection, you'll need a flashlight, a screwdriver, a tape measure, and pencil and paper. You may need a ladder.

Start by walking around your home and identifying all the parts of the building that could have different insulation details. New additions, for example, often have a framing structure that allows more insulation than in the original building. Your home will have, at minimum, different insulation details at the walls, ceiling, and floor, and it could have several different details for each. Create a list to keep track of your findings.

Inspecting Open Attics

If your home has a pitched roof and an open attic, you'll need to find the hatch. It may be outdoors, in a hallway, or in a closet. If it is in a closet, you may find it troublesome to clear things out of the way to gain access, but this inspection is well worth your time:

- If necessary, find a ladder, set it up securely, climb up and open the hatch. You may be able to inspect the attic from the ladder, or you may need to climb all the way in. Bring a flashlight and tape measure. Wear a respirator. Step only on the framing so you don't damage the ceiling or hurt yourself. *Stop now if you're not comfortable with the risk involved.*

- Inspect the insulation, and identify the type. Fiberglass batts are pink or yellow and come in rolls. Loose-fill fiberglass is white, pink, or yellow, and looks like chopped-up batts. Cellulose looks like, and is in fact made from, chopped-up newspapers. If you don't recognize the type of insulation, take a sample to your local home improvement store and ask an experienced employee.

- If you're evaluating batt insulation that came in rolls, it is probably marked with an R-value printed either on a paper or foil face, or on the batt itself. Note the R-value.

- If you're evaluating loose-fill insulation, measure the thickness all the way down to the top of the ceiling surface. If it varies in depth, take an average of thicknesses. Calculate and record the R-value according to the procedure shown here.

How To Calculate R-Value of Insulation

Once you know the type and thickness of your insulation, you can calculate its R-value:

- **Identify** the type of insulation. Determine the R-value per inch from the table *R-Value of Common Building Materials* on page 85. Use the average R-value from the table.
- **Measure** the thickness in inches.
- **Multiply** the R-value per inch times the number of inches.

Examples of R-Value Calculations

$3\frac{1}{2}$ inches fiberglass loose-fill in attic

Average R-value of 2.3 per inch

3.5 x 2.3 = R-8

$3\frac{1}{2}$ inches cellulose loose-fill in attic

Average R-value of 3.4 per inch

3.5 x 3.4 = R-12

24 inches fiberglass loose-fill in attic

Average R-value of 2.3 per inch

4 x 2.3 = R-55

$3\frac{1}{2}$ inches fiberglass dense-pack in wall

Average R-value of 4.0 per inch

3.5 x 4.0 = R-14

Inspecting Closed Cavities

The most common closed cavities are within standard vertical walls. In North American frame homes, the typical wall is assembled from wooden two-by-fours ($3\frac{1}{2}$ inches in actual thickness), or two-by-sixes ($5\frac{1}{2}$ inches in actual thickness).

Vaulted or cathedral ceilings have closed cavities above their ceilings instead of attics. These roof cavities vary in depth depending on the roof framing, but are usually 8 to 14 inches thick. Some homes are built with a combination of open and closed attic cavities.

Oftentimes the re-insulation of a poorly insulated ceiling vault can solve comfort problems and produce annual savings on the order of three to seven cents per square foot of ceiling.

Closed cavities are also sometimes constructed over garages or above unheated basements. These floor vaults vary in thickness depending on the framing, but are usually 6 to 12 inches thick.

The trick to inspecting vaults is in finding access to look inside. You may be tempted to skip this inspection on the assumption that the cavity was completely and correctly filled during construction. Our experience has shown this is rarely the case.

To complete this inspection, you'll need a flashlight, a screwdriver, a tape measure, and pencil and paper. You may need a drill and small bit for drilling drywall. You'll also need some type of thin probe that doesn't conduct electricity and can slip past a plumbing drain or electrical box and into the wall cavity. The ideal tool is a pointed bamboo skewer like those used for grilling teriyaki. *Do NOT use a piece of wire if you expect to probe around electrical boxes. If you do probe around electrical boxes, identify the proper circuit and shut the power off at the electrical panel. Stop now if you're not comfortable working around electrical equipment.*

- To inspect wall insulation, look first for an opening around plumbing or electrical penetrations. Look under your kitchen or bathroom sink, if they are on exterior walls, to see if there is a space around a drain line that goes through the wall. Try in the laundry room, where the washer or dryer pipes and vents may pass through exterior walls. You can also use a drill to cut a small hole (½ to 1 inch in diameter) through the drywall in an inconspicuous place. This is the method usually chosen by professionals. The ideal location is in the back of a closet in an exterior wall and near the floor, or in the wall under the kitchen sink. Avoid drilling into studs, and be careful not to cut any wires or pipes.

- Once you have created an access hole, peer into the cavity with your flashlight to see what type of insulation is installed. If you don't recognize it, take a sample so you can ask your expert at the home improvement store. Try to determine how thick it is, and don't assume the cavity is full. Push your wooden probe all the way to the outside of the wall, up against the exterior sheathing. You can often discern the thickness of the insulation, and the presence of any paper facing or plastic air barrier, as your probe penetrates the layers.

- Measure and record the depth of the insulation, and of the wall cavity itself.

- Walk around your home again, and determine if the cavity you inspected is representative of the wall framing throughout the structure. Have

additions been added to the building? Is there a second story that has a different framing design? Perform additional inspections as needed.

With this information, you've reached a critical decision point. Are the closed cavities completely full of insulation? If you have found cavities that are empty or only partly full, you have an excellent opportunity to improve the thermal efficiency of your home. The procedure for adding insulation to existing wall cavities is described in *Retrofit Wall Insulation* on page 94.

If the cavities are full of insulation, then you'll need to direct your insulation improvement efforts elsewhere. You would still benefit, for example, from adding exterior insulation, outside of the existing cavity, in conjunction with the installation of new siding and windows. That large retrofit is one of our primary recommendations for homeowners who are committed to creating the ultimate in efficient homes, and is described in *Insulated Thermal Sheathing* on page 95.

TYPES OF INSULATION

If you tour the insulation section in a large home improvement store, you'll see many types of insulation. But they are manufactured from only a few basic materials. Fiberglass, cellulose, mineral wool, and plastic foams make up the majority of products. The remaining variations are mostly in shape, size, and density.

Fiberglass Batts

Fiberglass batts and blankets are the most common and widely available American insulation products. Mineral wool, or rock wool, is a similar material that is made of mineral sand rather than glass. It holds only a small market share in the United States but is more common in Canada and Europe.

Batts and blankets are composed of glass fibers, held together by an adhesive binder. Most batts have a facing of kraft paper or foil-kraft composite to facilitate fastening and to act as a vapor barrier. Fiberglass and mineral wool absorb very little water and are not organic.

Newer medium-density batts have twice the density of standard batts, and high-density batts have three times the standard density. The higher density gives better R-values per inch, a distinct advantage in fixed-thickness cavities such as walls. The medium-density batts are rated at about R-3.8 per inch, and high-density batts are rated at about R-4.3 per inch. The 3½-inch standard batts achieve R-11, medium-density batts achieve R-13, and high-density achieves R-15. For 5½-inch batts, the standard batts achieve R-19, and high-density batts achieve R-21.

Batts are most commonly installed into building cavities during construction, and are sized to fit between framing members that are spaced on 16-inch or 24-inch centers. As a retrofit, batts are applied most often to ceilings and floors. Fiberglass blankets have a variety of special uses, including as metal building insulation, duct and tank insulation, and sound insulation. Blankets are commonly available in rolls 3 to 6 feet wide.

R-Value of Common Building Materials

Building material	R-Value per inch
Concrete	0.1 or less
Wood	1.0 to 1.5
Fiberglass batts (standard)	2.6 to 3.4 (avg. 3.0)
Fiberglass batts (high density)	3.8 to 4.3 (avg. 4.0)
Fiberglass (loose-fill in open attic)	2.2 to 2.4 (avg. 2.3)*
Fiberglass (dense-pack in cavity)	3.6 to 4.4 (avg. 4.0)*
Cellulose (dense-pack in cavity)	3.0 to 3.4 (avg. 3.2)*
Cellulose (loose-fill in open attic)	3.2 to 3.6 (avg. 3.4)*
Mineral wool batts	3.0 to 3.6 (avg. 3.3)*
Expanded polystyrene foam board (white beadboard)	3.9 to 4.3 (avg. 4.1)*
Extruded polystyrene foam board (usually blue, yellow, or pink)	4.5 to 5.5 (avg. 5.0)
Polyurethane spray foam (low density)	3.5 to 3.8 (avg. 3.7)**
Polyurethane spray foam (high density)	6.0 to 7.0 (avg. 6.5)**
Polyisocyanurate foam board (foil-faced)	6.0 to 7.0 (avg. 6.5)**

* Varies according to installed density.
** Varies according to age and formulation.

The thermal performance of batts is highly dependent on proper installation. To attain maximum R-value, the batts should be in continuous contact with all the surrounding cavity surfaces where they are installed. They should be cut exactly to length. If they are too long, they bunch up; if they are too short, the spaces at the top and bottom promote convection, which reduces the R-value. Indentations or compressions of the batt can create air pockets, decreasing the R-value.

Proper Installation of Fiberglass Batts

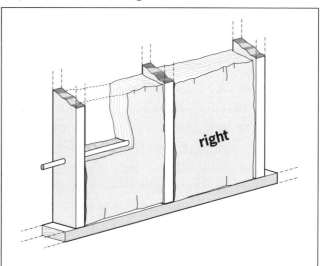

This batt was split and pulled apart to fit around the electrical cable. It fills the cavity completely from top to bottom. This eliminates air pockets and allows the batt to achieve its full potential R-value.

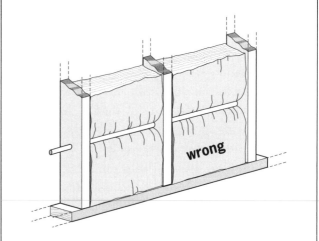

Here the electrical cable compresses the batt, creating an air pocket that reduces the wall's thermal resistance. Poor attention to detail can reduce the performance of batts by up to 30 percent.

Blown Loose-Fill Insulation

Loose-fill insulation is sold in densely packed bags. It is broken up and fed into a blowing machine to fill attics or closed cavities such as walls or vaulted ceilings. Loose-fill comes in two common varieties: fiberglass and cellulose. If installed properly, it forms a seamless blanket with few voids or edge gaps. It tends to have a better R-value per inch than fiberglass batts.

Both cellulose and fiberglass loose-fill settle after they are installed. Cellulose settles 15 to 20 percent, while fiberglass settles only 3 to 5 percent. Settling isn't a problem in attics as long as you plan for it by adding more insulation in the first place. But settling can be a serious problem in walls, so loose-fill insulation should be packed to the maximum density possible.

Adding loose-fill insulation to an attic is a reasonable weekend project for a dedicated homeowner. This project is covered later in this chapter. Blowing loose-fill into wall cavities, however, is a difficult job best saved for professionals. A professional insulator would charge $.50 to $1.00 per square foot for attic insulation and $.80 to $1.75 per square foot for wall insulation.

Fiberglass Loose-Fill Blown fiberglass is manufactured in two types: chopped-up batt waste and virgin short fibers. The batt-waste type has longer fibers and binder, so its R-value per inch is slightly lower than the virgin fibers, which are thinner and shorter. The shorter, thinner fibers create smaller and more numerous air spaces, which improve thermal resistance.

Fiberglass for blowing is packed in compressed 24- to 40-pound bales. The compressed fiberglass requires a blowing machine with an agitator that tears it up into small pieces that fly fluidly through the blower hose without plugging up.

It is easy to over-fluff fiberglass in attics, leading to low density and excessive air permeability. If you have loose-fill insulation installed by an insulation contractor, ask to have the material installed at its maximum density.

Cellulose Loose-Fill Blown cellulose is usually made of ground-up newspapers or wood wastes that are treated with fire retardants. This insulation blows quickly and easily, achieving a high density when installed into closed building cavities with a fill tube. Cellulose usually contains a lot of small fibers that pack into the cracks and crevices of closed building cavities, retarding airflow through these cavities. This characteristic of cellulose is used extensively for air-sealing older homes. Cellulose has better resistance to air convection than fiberglass at its commonly installed density. Cellulose is slightly less expensive than fiberglass but both are very inexpensive for the benefits they provide.

The major disadvantage of cellulose is that it absorbs and holds water—cellulose can hold moisture water totaling 50 to 100 percent of its weight. This becomes a problem in attics if roof leaks aren't repaired, or in walls if the siding is damaged enough to admit rain. Water absorption is also a problem in coastal climates with high, constant relative humidity.

Water can also carry fire retardants out of the cellulose, causing a reduction in fire resistance and possibly corrosion of metal siding and roofing.

Cellulose is a good insulating material used by many expert insulators and building performance contractors, but it should only be installed where it can be kept dry.

Sprayed Fibrous Insulation

Fiberglass and cellulose blowing wool can be sprayed directly onto vertical surfaces through a system referred to as wet spray. This material must be blown into open cavities, and is usually used in new construction or major remodel projects.

The fibrous material is fed dry into an insulation blower and travels through the blower hose to a hose and spray nozzle. Here a thin solution of glue and water meets the insulation and propels it toward the building cavity. This water-glue mixture binds the loose-fill together and adheres it to the surface. Wet spray dries within a few days. Wet spray requires specialized equipment, and so requires professional application. The cost for blowing wet-spray fibrous insulation into a two-by-four cavity is about $1 per square foot.

Once dry, this type of sprayed insulation has a fragile surface. It shouldn't be installed in places where it may be bumped or abraded. In humid locations, such as extremely wet crawl spaces, fibrous sprayed insulation may absorb large quantities of water, reducing its thermal resistance, and weakening its adhesion. Fiberglass is the preferred material in these areas. In any location, wet spray insulation should be allowed adequate time to dry before it is covered.

Plastic Foam Panels

Plastic foam panels, such as expanded and extruded polystyrene, are available in four-by-eight or two-by-eight-foot sheets of various thicknesses. Plastic foam panels create an air barrier, unlike fibrous insulation. If you seal the panels at their seams you are creating a continuous air barrier on the home's exterior.

Foam sheathing reduces thermal bridging through thermally conductive structural elements like wood and steel studs. It is often used to insulate over masonry walls or frame walls to reduce the heat transferred through the framing. These four-by-eight panels also have many retrofit insulation uses. Foam insulation panels should be installed whenever a building undergoes interior or exterior renovation—for example, when replacing siding. Projects of this nature are golden opportunities to improve your home's thermal integrity.

Molded or expanded polystyrene (R-3.2 to R-4.0 per inch) is widely used to insulate exterior doors, garage doors, and masonry walls. Molded polystyrene is manufactured in many small factories throughout North America, and is made by expanding polystyrene in a mold.

Only a few manufacturers make extruded polystyrene, and it is slightly more expensive than expanded polystyrene. The manufacturing process is like pressing cookie dough through a cookie press. Extruded polystyrene has good strength, a thermal resistance of about R-5 per inch, and excellent moisture resistance due to its smooth water-repellent surface. These qualities make it a good choice for underground foundation insulation.

When space limitations are a consideration, rigid polyisocyanurate (polyiso) board gives excellent service, because of its superior R-value of R-6 to R-7 per inch. You can recognize polyiso board by the aluminum foil that is adhered to both faces. This protects its fragile surface, and also provides a barrier to the flow of radiant energy if the foil faces an air space. The R-value of polyiso board deteriorates slightly over a period of years as its chlorofluorocarbon intercellular gas is replaced by air, but this slight deterioration does not seriously affect its utility.

Insulated Sheathing Installation

In this home, four inches of polystyrene foam sheathing have been fastened to the exterior walls with one-by-four strips and long screws. Conventional siding such as wood, vinyl, or steel will be fastened to the wood strips.

Foamboard Rim-Joist Insulation

Foil-faced polyisocyanurate foamboard can be cut to fit between floor joists and up against the hard-to-insulate rim joist. The cracks around the perimeter are sealed with caulk.

All plastic foam insulation requires a covering when installed outside, as on a foundation. This is to protect it from degradation caused by sunlight, and from mechanical damage as from lawnmowers. This covering can be metal, plastic, or stucco.

When installed on an interior surface, as in a crawl space, plastic foams must be protected from heat and fire. A layer of drywall is often installed for this purpose.

Sprayed or Injected Foam Insulation

Sprayed foam insulation comes in several formulations. It is among the most expensive of insulation materials, but often worth its higher price when adhesion, moisture resistance, air-sealing ability, and structural strength are important. It is used for walls, foundations, and roofs, and is usually applied by professional crews with truck-mounted equipment.

The most common types of sprayed foam insulation are high-density and low-density polyurethane. During installation, polyurethane resin combines with a blowing agent, such as hydrochlorofluorocarbon gas (HCFC) or carbon dioxide and expands into a foam, encapsulating millions of tiny gas cavities.

Sprayed Polyurethane Wall Insulation

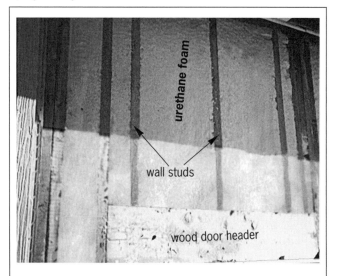

Spraying polyurethane foam into wall cavities after the siding and sheathing are removed is an excellent way to achieve a high R-value. Adding an inch or two of foam sheathing over the studs would be the next step in creating a truly efficient wall.

High-density sprayed polyurethane insulation has excellent adhesion, structural strength, air-sealing capacity, and thermal resistance. The HCFC gas is the reason for polyurethane's superior R-value of R-6 to R-7 per inch. The initial high R-value of high-density foam does diminish somewhat as air replaces the gas over a period of years, but this is not great enough to affect its utility.

Low-density polyurethane foam can be either sprayed or injected into closed cavities, making it versatile for residential use. It has an R-value of about 3.7 per inch and is slightly less expensive than the high-density urethane product. These sprayed and injected plastic foams must all be protected from heat and fire by drywall when installed toward the inside of the home.

Air Krete® is a proprietary foam, composed of expanded Portland cement and sand, that is the only noncombustible foam in common usage. It is normally used to fill closed cavities but can also be applied to open cavities. It has an R-value of around 3.9 per inch and is comparable in price to other liquid-applied foams.

Spray foams range in price from $.50 to $1.50 per square foot for each inch of thickness.

ATTIC AND ROOF INSULATION

Fibrous insulation is relatively inexpensive and easy to install. If your ceiling or roof has less than 6 inches of insulation (a resistance level of R-19 or below), adding insulation to a total of 14 to 16 inches (or about R-45) is an excellent investment. If your attic is tall enough, there is no reason not to add enough to total as much as 24 inches (R-60). The payback on this investment will only get better as the price of fuel rises.

Loose-fill insulation is blown into attics and roof cavities using an insulation-blowing machine. Many lumber yards will loan small insulation-blowing machines to customers who buy insulation. Insulating an attic this way is a strenuous and dirty job that involves climbing ladders and working in a confined space where sharp objects poke out and live electrical wires could be exposed. Nonetheless, if you are comfortable with this level of home improvement task, you can install attic insulation yourself.

To upgrade the attic insulation in a simple 2000-square-foot home from R-19 to R-40, the cost of the materials should be about 25 to 35 cents a square foot, or about $500 to $700. For professional installation, expect to pay 60 to 90 cents a square foot for labor and materials, or $1200 to $1800 total.

PREPARING TO INSTALL INSULATION IN OPEN ATTICS

Preparing to increase attic insulation is often more work than installing the insulation itself. This is your last opportunity to seal the many important air leaks through the ceiling before insulating. Spend whatever time and money you need to do a good job. Air leaks through the attic are among your home's most costly energy problems.

For this project, bring a bright light, a good respirator, and a board to lay across the top of the ceiling joists.

Always step on the wooden framing members. Do NOT step between them on the drywall or plaster, since you could do a lot of damage to yourself or your house. Wear a respirator and other protective gear. Don't attempt this type of work if you are not willing to assume some risks.

Roof Repair

Repair roof leaks and other attic-related moisture problems before insulating your attic. If attic-related moisture problems can't be repaired, don't insulate the attic.

Attic Hatch

If your home has an attic hatch, it should have an insulation dam installed around it. An insulation dam allows the installation of a thick blanket of loose-fill insulation right up to the hatch, and prevents the insulation from spilling through the hatch into the living space when you next open the hatch. The best materials for building a dam around the hatch are plywood or other rigid building board. The hatch itself should be insulated with fiberglass batts or foamboard.

Heat-Producing Devices

The next step in your preparation is to note the locations of all heat-producing devices. These include recessed light fixtures, bathroom fans, chimneys, and exhaust fans. Build an open-topped drywall box or metal tube around each fixture to protect the insulation from heat. Many fixtures have an IC rating (rated for insulation coverage), which means that they can be covered with fibrous insulation. This traditional approach often leaves the fixture as a significant air leak into the attic since they are fireproof but still leaky. A better strategy is to build a closed-top box or cylinder out of metal or drywall around the fixture to allow 3 inches of clearance on all sides and on top. Place the enclosure over the fixture and use two-part foam to seal the enclosure to the ceiling and also to seal its joints. The material cost of these protective coverings is negligible. The labor can be difficult, but the air leakage and safety benefits are substantial.

Insulating the Attic Hatch

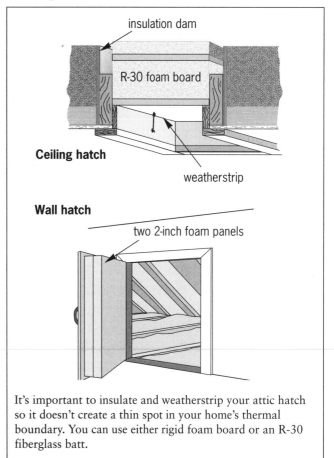

It's important to insulate and weatherstrip your attic hatch so it doesn't create a thin spot in your home's thermal boundary. You can use either rigid foam board or an R-30 fiberglass batt.

Enclosure Protects Heat-Producing Fixtures

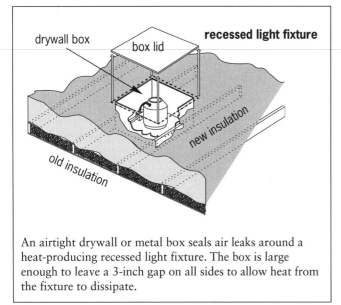

An airtight drywall or metal box seals air leaks around a heat-producing recessed light fixture. The box is large enough to leave a 3-inch gap on all sides to allow heat from the fixture to dissipate.

Attic Ventilation

Attic vents will also require special attention. These vents are intended to remove heat from the attic in summer, and moisture in winter. Baffles, which are cardboard dams, should be installed at the eaves (overhang) to prevent insulation from spilling out into the overhang and blocking the attic vents. Baffles also prevent wind-washing, which takes place when wind blows through soffit vents and circulates through the insulation. In an attic that lacks baffles, wind can even blow insulation away from the outside walls.

If your attic is partly insulated, it may already have baffles installed. Inspect your attic by looking at your eaves from outdoors to see if attic vents are installed. If so, memorize or measure their position, then climb into the attic to see if baffles are installed in the corresponding locations. You don't need baffles along the entire edge of the roof—just at the vent locations.

In the past, attic ventilation was considered necessary for keeping attic insulation dry. Now most experts believe that keeping moisture out of the attic is far more important than ventilating the attic—indeed, some believe that attic ventilation is irrelevant to moisture management. We recommend that you stop moisture movement into your attic by sealing all air leaks between the attic and the living space before you install insulation. You should also repair any roof leaks as soon as you detect them.

Baffles Protect Attic Vents

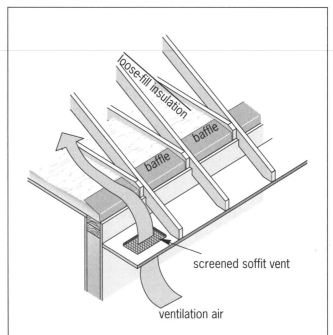

Baffles made of cardboard, plastic, or plywood are often installed at the eaves to prevent insulation from plugging the attic vents. They also shield the insulation from "wind-washing" that can reduce the effectiveness of the insulation.

Attic Vents Remove Heat and Moisture

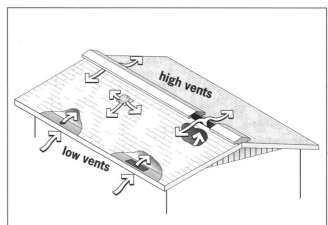

A moderate amount of ventilation in the attic will control overheating in summer and moisture accumulation in winter. But attic vents cannot not be relied upon as the sole method of controlling either overheating caused by dark roofs, or excess moisture that has migrated into the attic from elsewhere in the building.

Electrical Wiring

Warning: Don't work on electrical equipment unless you are familiar with its hazards. Get professional help if you need it.

Your attic probably houses hundreds of feet of electrical wiring, junction boxes, and fixtures that are part of your electrical system. In the course of inspecting your attic, you will have an opportunity to inspect this equipment. Confirm that there are no bare wires present, that all electrical boxes have covers, and that everything is properly installed. Get help if you need it. Once you install attic insulation, any further work you need to do in your attic will be more difficult because of the insulation. If you need to perform electrical upgrades, do not insulate your attic until the work is completed.

Exhaust Fan Ducting

Vent all kitchen and bath fans outdoors through roof or soffit fittings. Use aluminum or galvanized steel vent pipe. Insulate the pipe to prevent condensation during cold weather, or use pre-insulated flexible ductwork. Avoid using flexible plastic or aluminum duct because it is short-lived and its corrugated surface inhibits airflow. Check all fans for proper backdraft damper operation while you are working on them. The damper should close automatically when the fan is off and open when it is on. Repair or replace the damper or the entire fan assembly if the damper doesn't operate freely.

Attic Rulers

Most manufacturers of insulation make cardboard rulers which you can staple to the roof framing so you can judge the depth of your new insulation. Once you're installing insulation, this saves you the trouble of stopping the machine to check your progress. It also gives future inspectors or homeowners a way to gauge how much material is installed. Attic rulers are usually marked both in inches and R-value for a particular product. Hence a ruler for one popular brand of fiberglass is marked: 9 inches = R-19 and 17 inches = R-40. Before you insulate your attic, staple rulers to the roof framing at a rate of one every 250 square feet. If you don't have pre-made attic rulers, make marks on the roof framing to show the depth of insulation you expect to install.

INSTALLING INSULATION IN OPEN ATTICS

Once you have prepared your attic for insulation, the task of installing insulation can usually be performed by two people within a day's time. You will need a truck, ladders, lights, and common hand tools. Always use proper protective gear, including gloves, a respirator, and knee pads.

Visit the home improvement store where you'll buy the insulation. Ask to see a bag of the insulation you'll install. It will include a chart that allows you to calculate how many bags you'll need. The supplier may also have a brochure with the same information.

How to Calculate Amount of Attic Insulation Needed

To upgrade a 2000-square-foot attic: R-19 to R-40.

A typical bag of fiberglass insulation will cover about 60 square feet if you are upgrading from R-19 to R-40.

2000 square feet ÷ 60 square feet per bag = 33 bags.

Calculate and order the bags you need. Reserve the insulation blower for the day of your job. Arrange delivery of both, or make plans to haul them yourself.

Set-Up Tasks

On the job, identify the best way to access your attic. If you have an outside access hatch, use this to avoid creating a mess inside. If you're working inside, clear furniture and valuable belongings out of the way. You are going to make a mess.

- Set up a ladder to reach the attic. Be sure it is secure. *Stop now if you aren't comfortable with heights.*
- Set up lots of bright lights in the attic. Place a board across the ceiling joists near the hatch where you can stage your tools. Don't step any-

where besides on top of the framing. If you do, you could fall through the ceiling.

- Stack the insulation outdoors as close to the hatch as you can. Set up the insulation blower nearby.
- The blower will have either one or two electrical cords. If it has two, plug them into two separate circuits so the large motors don't trip a circuit breaker.
- Stretch the hose out from the machine and up into the attic. Give the hose enough slack to reach within ten feet of the far end of the attic. Use the minimum length of hose possible to minimize friction and speed the process.
- You need two people to install the insulation, one to feed the machine on the ground and one to deploy it in the attic. The machine should have a remote control so the person in the attic can control the machine as he or she sees fit.

Loading the Insulation Machine

This crew member is loading the hopper of an insulation machine with loose-fill cellulose. The contractor added thirty 24-pound bags to the attic of an existing home, raising the R-value from R-19 to R-50.

Working the Machine

These are instructions for the person on the ground, who will be feeding the machine and controlling the insulation-to-air ratio:

- Look down into the machine and identify the chopper and paddles that break up the insulation. Remember that these will be moving once you start the machine, and that you could lose a hand if you reach down there when the machine is running. *Stop now if you're not comfortable with this risk.*
- Put on your gloves, respirator, and safety glasses as needed.
- Feed the first bale of insulation into the machine's hopper. Signal to the attic person that you are ready to go. Remember that the machine is run by remote control, and can start at any time.
- Once the machine starts, adjust the speed at which insulation flows. Insulation blowing machines allow you to throttle the airflow and to control the flow of insulation. The goal of these adjustments is to move the insulation down the hose with a minimum of air and maximum amount of insulation. If you feed too much air, the job will take longer, and the insulation will be too fluffy. If you feed too little air, you run the risk of clogging the hose. This will become obvious once you start blowing.
- Once the machine is running, your task is to keep the hopper full.

Working in the Attic

These are instructions for the attic installer who will be applying insulation and controlling the machine:

- Put on your gloves, respirator, knee pads, and safety glasses as needed.
- Inspect the attic to determine where you will sit or crouch while working. You'll need to get within ten feet of every corner of the attic. Consider cutting a piece of plywood a few feet square to place across the joists so you'll be more com-

fortable and be less apt to inadvertently step off the framing.

- Stretch the hose out to the far end of the attic. You'll start here and work your way back toward the hatch. Identify obstructions such as chimneys and skylights and determine where you'll work from to get insulation behind them.

- Measure out one-quarter of the attic's area, and mark this point for later reference.

- Start the machine when you are ready. Start at the far corners and work your way back. Lay out an even layer of insulation up to your marks on the attic rulers. Work back and forth, then back up as needed. It's all right to use a stick if you need to level uneven spots.

- When you get to the one-quarter mark, shut the machine off. Confer with the machine operator to learn how many bags you have installed. Confirm that this is roughly the number shown by your calculations. This will tell you if your thickness and density is correct.

- Restart the machine and continue. Adjust your thickness as needed according to your calculation at the one-quarter mark. Finish the installation by backing up to and out of the hatch.

The task of actually installing the insulation should take an hour or two, though it can vary widely depending on the speed of the machine you're using. When you're done, you can rest easy knowing little of your home's energy will be lost through your attic.

ROOF CAVITY INSULATION

Some homes don't have an open attic to insulate. Homes with flat roofs, and homes with vaulted or cathedral ceilings, often have an attic cavity no more than a foot deep which has a finished surface such as drywall on the bottom, and roofing material applied directly to the top. Insulation may fill some or all of the cavity, but the total insulation thickness will always be less than can be installed in an open attic.

It is possible to add insulation to these types of cavities, but it is a complicated job best left to professionals. Hence the description here is only detailed enough to help you in planning a job with an insulation contractor.

The question of how to insulate closed cavities, and whether to leave an airspace for ventilation, is fraught with controversy. Experts don't agree about whether it's proper to completely fill a roof cavity with blown insulation. We believe that filling closed roof cavities completely full with blown fiberglass is acceptable if accompanied by meticulous air sealing between the insulation and living space, and a careful evaluation of the roofing. The issue is that the insulation must not get wet. Water reduces insulation's thermal resistance and can damage the insulation. Fiberglass is preferred for closed cavities since it doesn't absorb as much water as cellulose insulation. Meticulous air sealing is needed to keep house air out of the roof cavity during winter, when condensation can occur as warm, moist indoor air leaks into building cavities and encounters cold surfaces. The roof should be absolutely waterproof.

Even if ventilation is provided in these closed cavities, it may not help to control moisture problems. To prevent moisture problems, you must prevent moisture from getting into the cavity. Experience has shown that leaving a gap above the insulation for "attic ventilation" is ineffective at best, and a contributor to moisture problems at worst, since moist outdoor air can be channeled into the insulation.

Installing Attic Insulation

Your job will be easiest if you have good lighting, a small board to kneel on, and proper protective gear.

Improving Closed Roof Cavities

A closed roof cavity, whether created by a flat roof or by a vaulted cathedral ceiling, is a poor design in most climates. The R-value will always be far inferior to what is possible in an open attic, and the ceiling will be too warm in summer and too cold in winter. The difficulty of effectively managing ventilation and moisture causes many of these closed attics to succumb to moisture damage and rot over the life of the buildings. If you own a home with a flat roof, or one with vaulted ceilings that have the roofing applied directly to the top of the roof framing, we recommend that you consider one of two retrofits to improve its thermal performance and moisture management.

- For flat or nearly flat roofs, you can add a new pitched roof over the top of the existing structure to create a new attic that can be well insulated. You'll also benefit from a sloped roof that will be less prone to leaks than the flat roof. Choose a light-colored roofing material with good reflectivity for an added reduction in summer cooling costs.
- For vaulted ceilings, you can add 4 to 8 inches of foam insulation on the top surface and above the current roofing. This could be rigid foamboard, or a sprayed application. You'll then need to re-roof. This is often the preferred option because the work is all performed outdoors, avoiding the mess of interior work. Choose a light-colored roofing material when you re-roof to help deflect solar energy during summer. You can also install a similar layer of foam from the interior up against the drywall or other interior finish. You'll then have to install new interior finish. But this could be preferable if the roof is inaccessible, or if major interior work is already planned so the indoor disruption is less of an issue.

RETROFIT WALL INSULATION

Wall insulation is one of the most underestimated and neglected energy savers for homes. Most new homes are built with too little wall insulation, and many older homes languish with inadequate thermal resistance in walls because the owners haven't installed retrofit wall insulation. We believe that new and existing homes need both insulation within the wall cavities *and* insulated sheathing (two to four inches of foam board) installed on the wall's exterior.

Consider the thermal integrity of the walls in a typical 2000-square-foot frame home as compared to its standard open attic. The walls are often ignored in favor of adding easier-to-install attic insulation, but the walls are in fact more significant.

- The walls have a total area of 1440 square feet.

40' wide by 50' long = 180 linear feet of perimeter

The walls have an assumed height of 8 feet

180' x 8' = 1440 square feet

- The average R-value of the wall insulation will be R-19 for two-by-six framing (even less for two-by-four walls). But that doesn't account for the poor insulating value of the wood framing that makes up 15 to 25 percent of the wall area. If you include these thermal bypasses, this R-19 wall will actually perform at about R-12.

1440 square feet of R-12 insulation

- The attic in the same home would total 2000 square feet.

40 feet x 50 feet = 2000 square feet

- The attic would typically be insulated to R-40. The ceiling framing is mostly covered with insulation, and so doesn't diminish the R-value very much. The R-40 attic performs at about R-39.

2000 square feet of R-39 insulation

- You can now make a comparison: 1440 square feet at R-12 versus 2000 square feet at R-39. The end result is that the walls in this home will lose two-and-a-half times more heat in a cold climate than the ceiling.

For this reason, the most efficient homes today have wall insulation that exceeds the inadequate minimum levels specified by the building codes. The walls of superinsulated homes being constructed to Passive

House standards have walls insulated to at least R-40. This level of insulation will probably become standard in North America in the next twenty-five years. If you're ready to pursue the benefits of super-insulation, you have several options for retrofitting your home.

Tube-Fill Wall Insulation

Wall insulation for existing homes is usually blown in through a hole in the exterior or interior wall surface. Wall cavity insulation must be installed at a density sufficient to avoid settling, since voids in the insulation significantly reduce its thermal resistance. Better insulation contractors blow insulation through a tube that is inserted into the wall, rather than through a short nozzle, to ensure that density is uniformly high throughout the wall cavity. If a fill tube isn't used, the insulation will probably contain voids and will usually settle, leaving empty spaces inside the wall. Filling an empty wall cavity costs from $.50 to $1.50 per square foot depending on how difficult it is to drill holes and repair the interior or exterior wall after the insulation is installed.

If you plan to install new siding on your house, or to paint the interior or exterior, you'll have a good opportunity to blow insulation into uninsulated or partially insulated wall cavities. It costs less to patch the holes necessary to blow in the insulation while these cosmetic improvements are being made.

Insulated Thermal Sheathing

You can also attach foam sheets or sheathing to your exterior walls after the existing siding is removed and before a home is re-sided, adding valuable extra thermal resistance. Insulated thermal sheathing is the best way of improving the R-value of walls that already have cavity insulation installed. Insulated sheathing vastly improves the performance of frame walls by providing continuous insulation over the thermal bridges created by the underlying framing. As a result, the whole-wall R-value of walls with insulated sheathing is considerably higher than walls with only cavity insulation. Installing two to four inches of foam with new siding costs between $3 and $6 per square foot.

Dense-Packed Wall Insulation

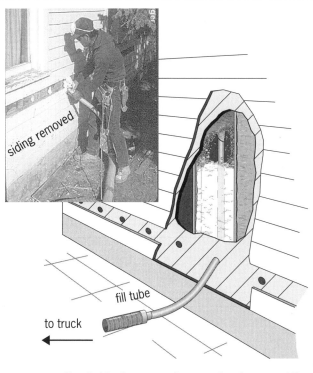

Exterior walls of older homes are best insulated using a fill tube inserted into the wall cavity. The tube helps achieve the high density needed to prevent settling by packing the insulation throughout the height of the wall.

A weather-resistant barrier is often incorporated into insulated sheathing, adding an additional measure of durability to the building. In framed houses, it's common that rain occasionally penetrates the siding during severe weather. That's why most builders install a weather-resistant barrier like tar paper, or the white house-wrap you see on new homes under construction.

The rainwater stops at the weather-resistant barrier and drains down and out of the wall. Some foam sheathings are covered with aluminum foil. Extruded polystyrene (usually blue or pink) functions as a weather-resistant barrier by itself.

The ideal thermal retrofit for walls is to install insulated sheathing, replace siding, and replace windows at the same time. This way the insulated sheathing could be one to four inches thick and the contractor could extend the exterior window frame to accommodate the insulated sheathing, and install the window properly. The window jambs may need to be extended on the inside also. Or the windows can be installed from the outside against the interior trim. See *Weathertight Window Installation* on page 110.

Insulated sheathing can also be installed on the surface of the interior wall. This is a good option for historical homes, or for buildings where exterior retrofits aren't practical.

Retrofit Foam Sheathing

This builder created a superinsulated wall detail by installing four inches of foam insulation over the exterior of the existing two-by-six wood frame wall. The foam is attached by screwing through strips of one-by-four lumber. One-by-fours also frame the new windows.

This builder installed four inches of foam, equipped with wood strips embedded in each foam sheet. The strips help to fasten the foam to the exterior wall, and they also serve as fastening strips for the new siding. Each existing window is framed with a new four-inch-deep frame. This foam product is called Styro-Stud®, Strip-It®, or drywall backer by its manufacturers.

Exterior Insulation and Finish System

Exterior insulation finish system (EIFS) is a good wall-insulation choice. EIFS provides both a durable weather-resistant surface, and 1 to 4 inches of polystyrene foam that adds R-4 to R-16 to your exterior walls. The stucco-like surface of EIFS contains acrylic adhesive applied in multiple layers. A plastic mesh is applied under the first coat to provide reinforcement.

EIFS is one of the few practical options for exterior insulation of solid masonry walls. Exterior insulation avoids disturbing the building's interior. Unlike interior insulation, it effectively covers all the building's thermal bridges.

It must be carefully sealed around windows to avoid water intrusion. It works reliably in dry climates and buildings with generous overhangs. Wet-climate buildings with little or no overhang are poor candidates for the EIFS system.

EIFS is comparatively expensive at an installed price of $6 to $16 dollars per square foot. But it provides the best insulation improvement available for the walls of many homes, and so can provide a good payback.

Exterior Insulation and Finish Systems

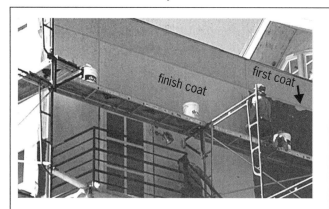

Exterior insulation and finish system (EIFS) combines polystyrene insulation with a lightweight stucco. The first coat of stucco is applied directly to the foam insulation. Reinforcing plastic mesh is embedded in the first coat. The finish coats provide texture and color.

Insulated Lightweight Frames

Another increasingly viable option for insulating walls is the insulated lightweight frame which many builders are now adapting. With this method, you attach a lightweight wood frame to the outside of the existing exterior wall and fill it with insulation. This method allows the use of less-expensive fibrous insulation in place of using multiple inches of foam sheathing.

The most important details of this system are sealing to protect against water around windows and achieving an adequate density of insulation to prevent settling. The correct window details aren't much different from installing windows in new wood walls.

Retrofit Wood Frame Wall Filled with Low-Density Foam

Retrofitted exterior wall attached to existing wall

Workers attach a new wood-frame wall to the home's exterior. The new wall stands off the existing wall by one inch so that the sprayed foam will fill in behind each stud, preventing thermal bridging between the existing wood wall and the new one.

Retrofitted wall filled with Icynene® foam insulation

Icynene foam is sprayed into the new cavities and planed off even with the face of the studs. Workers next cut the new window openings, then install the new windows, and finally install the new siding.

Installing an Exterior Lightweight Frame

cross-section of new exterior frame

outside   inside

A lightweight wood frame has been attached to the exterior of this existing home. It allows for the installation of six or more inches of fibrous insulation such as fiberglass. Its lightweight construction improves whole-wall R-values by minimizing thermal bridging through the assembly.

Managing Moisture in Basement Walls

Unfaced batts are the most common way of insulating basements. Unfortunately, moisture can accumulate in these walls when it migrates from outdoors through the foundation wall. Foam insulation, whether applied in sheets or by spray application, provides much better resistance to both moisture and air leakage.

FOUNDATION AND FLOOR INSULATION

Many houses have no floor or foundation insulation at all. While this is not as important in hot climates, homes in cold climates need foundation insulation, floor insulation, or both in order to be energy efficient. Since floor insulation tends to be relatively inexpensive it is cost-effective in all but the warmest North American climates.

Basement Wall Insulation   When a house has a heated basement, the basement walls are usually insulated and the floor above the basement is not. Unfortunately, many insulated basement walls become moisture traps. Moisture can usually find some path into the wall, where it will condense on the coolest surfaces inside this assembly. Condensation encourages the growth of mold and mildew.

For these reasons, moisture is an important concern when it comes to basement insulation. Don't insulate your basement wall unless you know that the basement is dry. If you have drainage problems outdoors, your foundation isn't waterproofed correctly, or water is seeping through your foundation wall, don't insulate.

The most common way to insulate basement walls is to build a framed wall against the concrete or masonry wall and fill it with fiberglass batts. The frame is then covered with drywall. Unfaced batts are probably the best choice of fiberglass insulation since they contain no vapor barrier to trap moisture. Moisture may travel in either direction: from outdoors in or from indoors out. Eliminate the vapor barrier when insulating basements with fiberglass to give moisture a chance to escape.

The best choice for insulating flat basement walls is sheets of polystyrene foam at least two inches thick. If you install them at the exterior, as during new construction, use a durable and water-resistant insulation, such as blue or pink extruded polystyrene. You'll also need to provide damage protection for portions that are exposed above ground level. Sheet metal, fiberglass panels, or troweled-on stucco work well. If foam board is installed at the interior, as is typical in retrofit applications, the foam must usually be covered with drywall to provide a finished surface and a fire barrier.

Insulating Rubble Foundation Walls

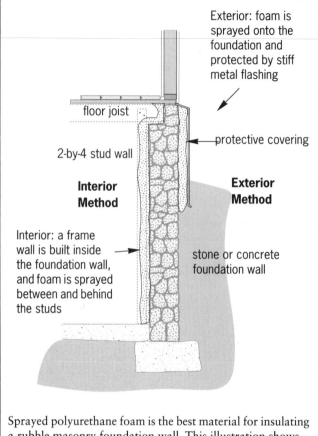

Sprayed polyurethane foam is the best material for insulating a rubble masonry foundation wall. This illustration shows both interior and exterior methods. The choice of one method over another usually depends upon which area has easiest access.

Foam Board Foundation Insulation

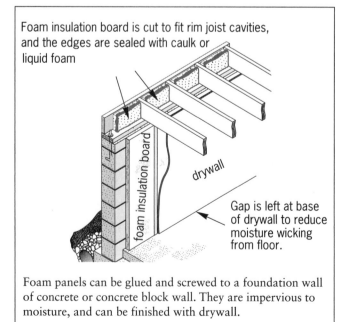

Foam panels can be glued and screwed to a foundation wall of concrete or concrete block wall. They are impervious to moisture, and can be finished with drywall.

Crawl Space Wall Insulation In crawl spaces you'll need to choose between insulating the foundation walls or the floor. This choice will often be driven by practical considerations such as the type of foundation (avoid trying to attach insulation to stone walls), the presence of ground water (don't insulate the foundation wall if water drains through it), and the presence of heating and cooling ducts (insulate the foundation wall, not the floor, so the ducts remain within the heated and cooled boundary of the home).

The ground is wet in many crawl spaces, even in crawl spaces that seem dry. If moisture is allowed to accumulate in the crawl space or elsewhere in the home, it will encourage rot and the growth of mold and mildew. Insulation should never be installed in a wet crawl space. All crawl spaces should have a polyethylene ground-moisture barrier on the soil. It should be lapped and sealed with tape or construction adhesive at the seams, and should run vertically up the foundation walls at least six inches and be adhered to the clean masonry wall with polyurethane construction adhesive.

If you insulate the floor from inside the crawl space, and have a central heating or cooling system, be sure to seal and insulate any ductwork that is located in the crawl space.

You'll face complex choices when choosing how to insulate your crawl-space walls. Many builders use vinyl-faced fiberglass batts. Unfortunately, the vinyl facing on the batt is a vapor barrier that can trap moisture in the insulation. A good alternative is two-inch foam panels, but some building departments want the walls covered for fire protection by drywall, even when it is installed in the crawl space. Even foam rim-joist insulation may be subject to this requirement in some states and regions.

You'll need two or three feet of headroom in a crawl space to comfortably install insulation. If the crawl space is much shorter, then it may not be practical to install crawl-space insulation, unless you or your contractor are both tough and resistant to claustrophobia.

Rim Joist Insulation Whether you insulate the floor or foundation wall, you should insulate the rim joist at the same time. Although using pieces of fiberglass is most common, this can encourage mold or rot when moisture migrates behind the fiberglass and condenses on the cold rim joist. Sprayed polyurethane foam in the rim-joist area is a better practice. Or you can install rigid foam by cutting rectangles to roughly fit each rim pocket and sealing them in place with one-part foam.

Insulation Under Floors Floors are usually insulated with unfaced batts. They should fill the entire floor cavity from top to bottom, or at least touch the floor above to avoid creating a void.

Air leaks through the floor should be sealed before floor insulation is installed. In crawl spaces where the floor is insulated, any crawl-space ducts should be carefully air-sealed and insulated.

If you live in a cold region, and have plumbing installed in your crawl space, installing floor insulation may increase the probability of pipes freezing in winter since waste heat from your home will no longer inadvertently heat the crawl space. The most common locations for pipe freezing are where pipes travel near the foundation wall and foundation vents. If the pipes are installed near the floor framing, you can drop the floor insulation in this area to insulate under and around the pipes. You can also insulate the pipes themselves to prevent freezing.

Spray-Foam Crawl-Space Insulation

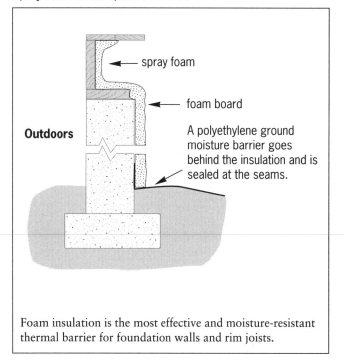

Foam insulation is the most effective and moisture-resistant thermal barrier for foundation walls and rim joists.

Insulating the Floor Above a Crawl Space

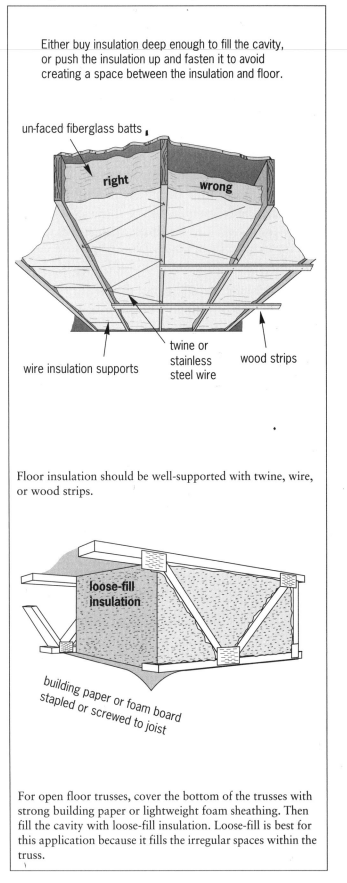

Either buy insulation deep enough to fill the cavity, or push the insulation up and fasten it to avoid creating a space between the insulation and floor.

un-faced fiberglass batts

right

wrong

wire insulation supports

twine or stainless steel wire

wood strips

Floor insulation should be well-supported with twine, wire, or wood strips.

loose-fill insulation

building paper or foam board stapled or screwed to joist

For open floor trusses, cover the bottom of the trusses with strong building paper or lightweight foam sheathing. Then fill the cavity with loose-fill insulation. Loose-fill is best for this application because it fills the irregular spaces within the truss.

THE BOTTOM LINE

Your choice of insulation systems will largely determine the efficiency and durability of your home. We recognize that the projects we describe here are among the most expensive in this book, but there is no better way to trim utility expenses than slowing the flow of heat through your home. Upgrades to your home's insulation are solid investments that will reduce your energy costs for as long as you own your home.

- Determine the insulation levels of your home.
- If your wall cavities are not already full, have a professional insulator install dense-packed insulation to fill the cavities.
- Install attic insulation to a level of R-40 or more.
- If you live in a cold climate and have a crawl space, install insulation at either the foundation wall or floor. Install a ground-moisture barrier if your crawl space is damp.
- If you live in a cold climate and have a basement, install insulation at the foundation walls if possible.

To achieve the ultimate in energy efficiency, add two to four inches of foam insulation to the outside of your walls, install new siding, and replace your windows with the best units available.

8 Windows and Doors

We all want to have ample windows in our homes. Windows provide light, ventilation, fire escape, and a view. Yet they create a weak link in your home's thermal boundary, because they can't be insulated as well as the walls in which they are installed. Windows also allow some air leakage into your home.

Fortunately, you can have plenty of windows and still have an efficient home. You just need to choose the right types and install them properly. And your existing windows may be better than you think. Window replacement is not the only answer to window inefficiency.

In this chapter, we show you how to evaluate the energy performance of your existing windows and decide whether to improve them or replace them. If you choose to replace them, we show how to decide which windows are best for your home. We also include important installation details to assure that your new windows perform as well as possible.

At the end of the chapter we show how to weatherstrip doors to slow air leakage, and how to choose doors for replacement.

EVALUATE YOUR WINDOWS AND DOORS

Do you have at least two panes of glass on all your windows? Windows are always the weakest point in your home's thermal boundary. If you have single-pane windows, you can cut your window energy loss in half by installing either storm windows or insulated double-pane glass.

Are your windows watertight at the exterior? The cost of window replacement is often difficult to justify based solely upon energy savings. But if they are in such poor condition that water leaks into your home, replacement or repair should be a top priority in order to protect your home from water damage.

Do have you heavy blinds or drapes that can be drawn in cold weather? Insulated window coverings can cut the heat loss through your windows by half or more. Light curtains, mini-blinds, and roller shades are less effective.

Do you have some way to keep the sun off your windows in summer? If your home overheats during hot weather, you can trim the cost of air-conditioning substantially by shading your windows with curtains, roller shades, awnings, or trees.

Do your doors allow drafts into your home? You may be able to slow air leakage by simply installing high-quality weatherstripping. If you choose to replace an existing door, you should upgrade to an insulated unit. If you have a sliding glass door, consider replacing it with a hinged unit that has insulated glass.

Do you plan to replace the siding on your home in the near future? The cost of installing windows will be less if you are already replacing the siding on your home. You'll also have the opportunity to perform an integrated super-insulation retrofit that includes additional insulation under your siding.

WINDOW BASICS

The average home has twenty to thirty windows, totaling some 12 to 25 percent of the wall area. Since even the most advanced windows have an R-value of between R-3 and R-6, windows are by far the weakest link in your home's thermal boundary. It is for this reason that window improvement is so worthwhile.

During winter, windows probably account for 15 to 40 percent of the heat loss from your home. In summer, windows allow the sun to overheat your home, and can be responsible for up to 75 percent of the heat gain on hot days. Efficient windows can slow this heat flow and reduce your heating and cooling costs.

Window Terminology

You'll find it helpful to understand the terminology as you do research and make decisions about your home's windows:

- Glass assembly—One or more glass panes with spacers and/or gaskets.
- Sash—Frames the glass assembly. Sashes are often openable for ventilation and fire escape. Sashes can also be fixed so they don't open.
- Frame—Surrounds the sash and attaches to the building.
- Rough opening—Structural framing of the building to which the window frame is attached.
- Sill—Lowermost horizontal surface at the base of the window.
- Jamb—Trim that wraps the sides and top of the window.

Types of Window Operation

Double-hung windows are the oldest window design still in use. They include two sashes that slide vertically past one another. Single-hung windows are similar, with a fixed sash at the top. Horizontal sliders usually include one sliding sash and one fixed sash. Hinged windows include casements, which are hinged on the side, and awning windows which are hinged on the top. Casement windows tend to have the lowest infiltration rates of all opening windows because their hinged swing compresses the weatherstrip most effectively when closed. They also have an advantage in hot climates because they tend to direct breezes into the home when open.

Fixed windows don't open. Though you wouldn't want them throughout your home, they do have the advantage of lower cost (no mechanism needed) and low infiltration rates (they are permanently sealed).

Types of Window Operation

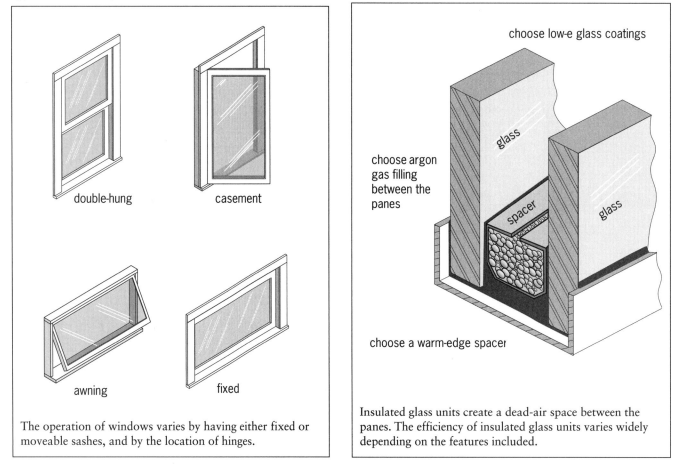

The operation of windows varies by having either fixed or moveable sashes, and by the location of hinges.

Insulated Glass Unit

Insulated glass units create a dead-air space between the panes. The efficiency of insulated glass units varies widely depending on the features included.

UNDERSTANDING WINDOW RATINGS

If you're purchasing new windows, pay close attention to the ratings published by the National Fenestration Rating Council (NFRC). Most windows carry labels with the NFRC ratings on them. Don't buy windows unless they display this label.

Thermal Transmittance (U-Factor)

A window U-factor measures heat loss and is the most important information for window comparisons in cold climates. The lower the U-factor, the better the window will reduce heat loss and minimize moisture condensation on the glass during cold weather. The U-factor is the reciprocal or inverse of the R-value ($U = 1 \div R$).

Single-pane glass has a U-factor of 1.10 (about R-1). A simple insulated glass unit with no coatings or gas fill will have a U-factor of approximately 0.50 (R-2). A U-factor of 0.35 (about R-3) is the minimum acceptable rating for modern energy-efficient homes.

Achieving a U-factor of less than 0.30 requires advanced details, including some or all of these features:

- Double-pane or triple-pane glass: more panes of glass help slow heat *transmission* through the window. Some manufacturers use plastic films as interior panes for these multi-pane windows.

- Low-e coating on one or more of the panes: low emissivity (low-e) coatings reduce heat flow by slowing the rate at which heat is *emitted* from the glass. A low-e coating is made up of a transparent layer of metal just a few molecules thick that is applied to one of the inside layers of double- or triple-pane glass.

- Argon gas filling: argon gas is installed between the panes of insulated glass units. It is a slightly better insulator than air.

- Warm edge spacers: these reduce thermal bridging at the edge of the insulated glass unit.

- Insulated frames: these slow heat flow through the edges of the sash.

Window Rating Labels

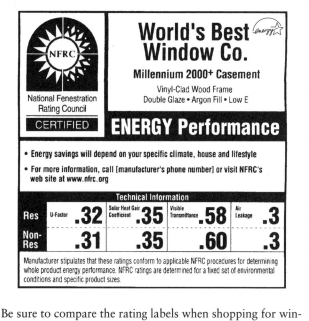

Be sure to compare the rating labels when shopping for windows. The most energy-efficient windows will display the ENERGY STAR logo.

Solar Heat-Gain Coefficient (SHGC)

Solar heat gain through windows can account for up to 40 percent of the total heat removed by an air conditioner. SHGC is the fraction of solar heat passing through the glass compared to solar heat falling on the glass. Single-pane glass has an SHGC of 0.87.

A recent glass innovation is a special low-e coating that blocks solar heat while admitting visible light (a low SHGC and a high Visible Transmittance, in technical terminology). This innovation, called spectral selectivity, is widely chosen by window buyers in the South, where air-conditioning is a major expense. The heat-blocking low-e glass is sold under brand names such as Sungate 2 and Low-e². Ask about this feature if you spend more money on air conditioning than you do on heating.

Visible Transmittance (VT)

Visible transmittance is the measure of how much visible light is admitted by window glass. Visible transmittance is important because one of a window's main functions is to admit visible light. On the north side of a home, we want as much visible transmittance as possible. However, on the east and west sides, low morning and afternoon sun may cause uncomfortable glare. In these cases, window glass with a low VT and low SHGC is the best choice for controlling both heat and glare.

Air Leakage (AL)

Window air leakage is usually a less important energy consideration than thermal transmittance during the heating season or solar heat gain during the cooling season.

Air-leakage ratings are measured in CFM (cubic feet per minute) per square foot of window surface area. The NFRC's CFM-per-square-foot ratings range from about 1.0 all the way down to 0.06. Lower is better.

Window air leakage varies according to the window's type of operation. Casement and awning windows have compression weatherstripping, which is more effective than the felt or pile weatherstripping of sliding windows. For this reason casement and awning windows have lower air leakage rates than sliding windows.

Characteristics of Window Glass

Glass Type	U-factor	R-value
Single-pane clear glass	1.10	0.9
Insulated glass unit (IGU) clear glass, $1/2$" space	0.50	2.0
Low-e IGU with $1/4$" space	0.44	2.3
Low-e IGU with $1/4$" space and argon gas filling	0.38	2.6
Low-e IGU with $1/2$" space	0.33	3.0
Low-e IGU with $1/2$" space and argon gas fill	0.29	3.4
Triple-pane with 2 low-e surfaces	0.23	4.3

WINDOWS: IMPROVE OR REPLACE?

Before you make the decision to replace your windows, be sure to do some research so you know about the entire range of choices. New windows include many convenient features and choices of styles, but if you're interested in improving the efficiency of your home, you should do some careful analysis before committing your money to buying new windows.

Advantages of Old Windows

Existing windows are usually made of either aluminum or knot-free softwood lumber. These materials are hard to beat in terms of functionality and durability. It's true that aluminum is very conductive and not the most attractive of materials. Wood must be painted faithfully to preserve it. But if your existing windows work properly and don't leak water into the building, count your blessings and think carefully before deciding to replace them.

Though your home's thermal resistance could be increased by replacing existing windows with more energy-efficient windows, it is difficult to justify the expense for the energy savings the new windows would provide. The cost of installing windows runs from $30 to $80 per square foot, or perhaps $400 to $1200 each, including installation. New windows definitely improve the efficiency of your home, but it will take many years to recover your investment.

You may have other reasons for replacing your windows: they may be deteriorated, you are about to replace your siding, or you are just tired of repainting the old windows. But if energy savings is your main motivation, consider replacing windows only after you have performed all the more cost-effective energy improvements.

THE VALUE OF STORM WINDOWS

Installing storm windows is often more cost-effective than installing new windows. The simple reason is cost. Storm windows can be installed on either the inside or outside of the home. Storm windows can usually be purchased and installed for $8 to $15 per square foot, less than one-quarter the cost of new windows.

A storm window adds a layer of glass, which creates an insulating air space, approximately halves heat loss, and increases comfort.

The most familiar type of storm window has an aluminum frame and sashes. An aluminum storm window permanently mounts to the exterior of a wood double-hung window. These storm windows have sliding mechanisms and built-in insect screens for summer ventilation.

The sliding sashes of an exterior storm window should be removable from the inside to allow easy cleaning and access for fire escape. A little silicon lubricant occasionally sprayed in the track helps the sashes slide freely.

Aluminum Double-Hung Storm Window

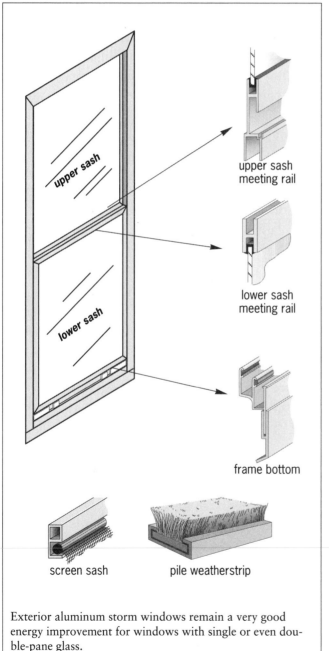

upper sash

lower sash

upper sash meeting rail

lower sash meeting rail

frame bottom

screen sash

pile weatherstrip

Exterior aluminum storm windows remain a very good energy improvement for windows with single or even double-pane glass.

Types of Interior Storm Windows

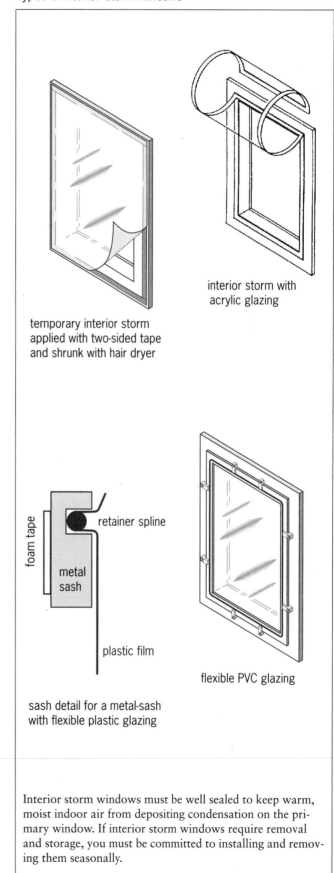

temporary interior storm applied with two-sided tape and shrunk with hair dryer

interior storm with acrylic glazing

foam tape

retainer spline

metal sash

plastic film

sash detail for a metal-sash with flexible plastic glazing

flexible PVC glazing

Interior storm windows must be well sealed to keep warm, moist indoor air from depositing condensation on the primary window. If interior storm windows require removal and storage, you must be committed to installing and removing them seasonally.

Optimal Wood Double-Hung Retrofit

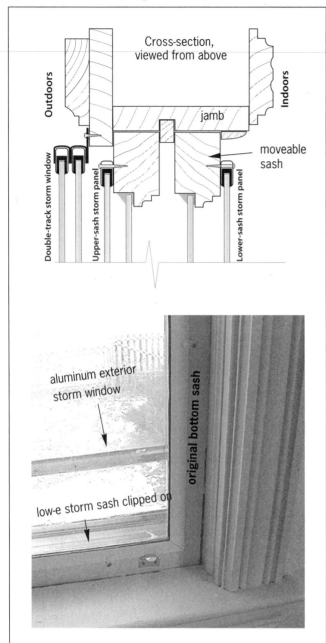

A good cold-climate retrofit for old double-hung windows is adding a storm panel to the inside of the bottom sash and to the outside of top sash. Outdoors, the window is protected and insulated by a double-track storm window, for a total of three layers of glazing.

Fixed Storm Windows

Primary window sashes can sometimes be fitted with a fixed exterior or interior storm window. Non-movable storm windows can be clipped or screwed to existing window frames or sashes. You can order storm win-

dows with high-efficiency low-e glass for an added boost in efficiency. In this case, the low-e surface should face the space between the glass panes to protect the low-e coating from being scratched.

Interior Storm Windows

Interior storm windows with plastic frames and plastic glazing aren't as permanent as exterior metal-and-glass storm windows. However, they are usually more airtight than metal storm windows. The airtight seal of indoor storm windows is created by closed cell foam tape, Velcro, or magnetic tape. The glazing material is usually clear plastic, which loses transparency with exposure to ultraviolet sunlight over the years. In some temporary applications, plastic film is applied directly to the window frame. Whether a movable or fixed storm window is installed on the interior or exterior of the primary window, glass is the best glazing choice. The best choice of interior storm-window design for a sliding prime window is a sliding storm window that operates in the same direction as the prime window. Storm windows that you have to remove for ventilation are usually a temporary solution because the panels get lost or broken.

WINDOW REPAIR AND RETROFIT

If you're considering spending $500 to $1200 per window for the installation of replacement windows, why not consider instead spending $100 to $500 repairing or improving your existing windows? You'll often get almost the same results in energy savings, and with much less expense.

Weatherstripping Double-Hung Windows

Common wooden double-hung windows are fairly easy to weatherstrip. Weatherstripping is the gasket material that resists air leakage and is installed between the sashes and window jambs.

Paint is an obstacle when weatherstripping double-hung windows. Sometimes the upper sash has slipped down, and is locked in place by layers of paint, producing leaking gaps at the top and at the meeting rails. To solve this problem, break the paint seal and push the upper sash up. Block, screw, or nail the repositioned upper sash in place.

To weatherstrip the window, you must remove the lower sash. Cut the paint where the window stop meets the jamb so the paint doesn't flake off. Removing one stop is sufficient to remove the bottom sash.

Scrape excess paint from the sashes and the window sill. Apply vinyl V-strip to the side jambs, and bronze V-strip to the meeting rail on the top sash. The point of the bronze V faces upward. Caulk the weatherstrip on its back side and staple it in place, as shown in the illustration.

Replacing Parts on Modern Windows

If a window is in good condition except for broken or worn parts that are available, it is often worth replacing these parts to rehabilitate the window.

A number of suppliers carry parts for wood and aluminum windows. Window parts are also available by special order through local glass companies.

Common parts replaced by glaziers are cranks and hinges for casement windows, pile weatherstrip for sliding windows, and sash cords, balancing springs, and sash locks for wooden double-hung windows.

INSULATING SHADES AND DRAPERIES

Whether you have your ideal windows in place yet or not, you can make changes to the window treatment that will affect your energy consumption. Insulating shades and draperies can be effective for insulating windows and improving comfort indoors if the residents open and close them at the appropriate time. Shades and draperies are expensive and require many years to return the investment, but they cost considerably less per square foot than a new window.

The shades, draperies, or shutters are far more effective if they are airtight, because this creates a dead air space between the treatment and the glass. The airtight seal also prevents warm, moist indoor air from depositing condensation on the glass, which can deteriorate window surfaces. For more information on window treatments, see *Shading Windows for Summer Comfort* on page 48.

Weatherstripping Double-hung Windows

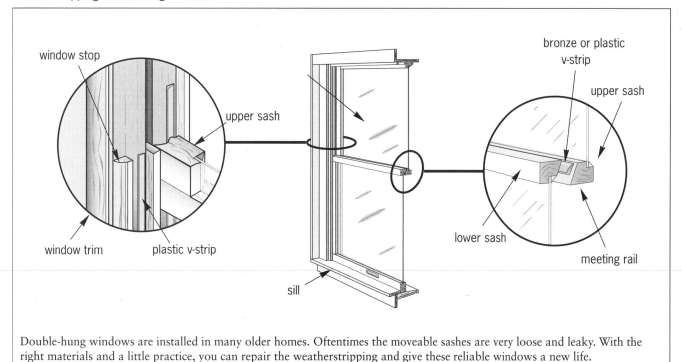

Double-hung windows are installed in many older homes. Oftentimes the moveable sashes are very loose and leaky. With the right materials and a little practice, you can repair the weatherstripping and give these reliable windows a new life.

REPLACEMENT WINDOW CHOICES

If you're going to replace your windows, it pays to study your options and make the right choices to maximize the benefits of the investment. All-new replacement windows commonly cost between $30 and $80 per square foot of window area, including installation.

The modern approach to window replacement is to create a low-maintenance window exterior. Vinyl, aluminum, or fiberglass qualify as low-maintenance materials. If your house already has siding in a low-maintenance material like steel, vinyl, or stucco, you might want to encase the remaining wood exterior trim in colored steel flashing to completely eliminate future painting chores. A variety of glass and frame options are available.

Window Frame Materials

Aluminum conducts heat better than any other building material, making them the most inefficient window frames in terms of heat transfer. Some manufacturers build an aluminum-frame window that is thermally improved by splitting the frames in half and joining them back together with an insulating gasket called a thermal break. But in cold climates, even the best aluminum frames are cold in winter and prone to condensation problems. Condensation is less of an issue in warm regions. The fact remains that aluminum-framed windows are among the most durable and least expensive windows available, so they will always have some market share.

Wood-frame window manufacturers have improved exterior maintenance with metal cladding on the frame's exterior. This means less painting. Metal-clad wood windows are among the most expensive options, and are popular for new custom homes.

Vinyl-frame windows are the best-selling window type. Low cost and freedom from maintenance are the key benefits of vinyl windows. Manufacturers vary in the quality of their vinyl formulation and assembly. Expected window lifespans also vary between about 20 to 40 years because of differences in strength and ultraviolet resistance.

New fiberglass-frame windows are energy efficient, strong, and low maintenance. Fiberglass is stronger than vinyl and expands and contracts much less with temperature change than aluminum or vinyl. Fiberglass comes with baked-on finishes or can be painted. Some window frames combine fiberglass with a wood interior frame. Many manufacturers offer insulated fiberglass frames and we highly recommend this design, which significantly reduces thermal bridging around windows.

Thermal Characteristics of Window Frames

Frame Material	U-factor	R-value
Aluminum	1.20 to 2.50	0.4 to 0.8
Aluminum (with thermal break)	0.70 to 1.50	0.7 to 1.4
Wood, vinyl, or combination	0.25 to 0.50	2.0 to 4.0
Vinyl	0.25 to 0.45	2.2 to 4.0
Insulated vinyl	0.15 to 0.30	3.3 to 6.7
Insulated fiberglass	0.15 to 0.25	4.0 to 6.7

Choosing the Right Window

You should consider a variety of criteria when choosing new windows, including the coldness of the weather, the amount of sunshine in winter and summer, the window's orientation, the ventilation needs of the room, your expectations for energy consumption, and your interest in performing maintenance.

U-factor is the most important criterion for cold climates. Don't replace windows in northern climates without making a significant reduction in U-factor. The U-factors for windows range from 1.0 to about 0.15. A U-factor of 0.40 is often given as a minimum for cold climates, but lower U-factors are available. Lower U-factors will decrease heat transmission and the occurrence of condensation during cold weather.

In the warmest U.S. climates, windows should have window shading coefficients of less than 0.25 including exterior and interior shading devices. A solar heat-gain coefficient (SHGC) of 0.50 or less for the window glass would be a good start.

Low-e double-pane glass returns the investment in all but the very hottest U.S. climates. The exterior pane's interior surface is the best place for the low-e coating for cooling-dominated climates. In heating-dominated climates, the low-e coating should be on the exterior surface of the interior pane.

WINDOW REPLACEMENT

Once you've chosen the right window, you still have to ensure installation is done carefully to avoid future problems. The most important consideration for window replacement is making the installation watertight. Preventing air leakage around the frame and sizing the windows correctly are also essential.

Window replacement is not the kind of job you can economize on without serious consequences. If you decide to replace windows, don't use the low-bid approach to choosing windows or the contractor who installs them. If you can't spend the money to do it right, you're probably better off rehabilitating the windows you have.

Weather Barrier and Thermal Resistance

The best option for installing new windows is to install them at the same time as new siding and exterior insulation. This allows you to add foam sheathing or a lightweight, insulated frame to the exterior walls. The new windows can then be installed into the wall assembly in an energy-optimized way.

Wood-frame houses should have a weather barrier between the window and the wall. This might be perforated asphalt felt paper or woven waterproof vapor-permeable polyethylene such as Tyvek® or equivalent. It is not uncommon that a small amount of rain water penetrates through or around the siding over the years. This barrier keeps the underlying wood building materials dry. The weather-resistant barrier should be sealed at the edges and overlapped at the seams to direct water down and out of the wall.

Windows are a weak point in this weather-resistant barrier. A lot of moisture damage results from poor original installation of windows or botched window replacement. If the weather barrier isn't completely water-tight around the window perimeter, water leakage can lead to mold, rot, paint failure, and other problems. Moisture problems are most serious in wood-frame buildings. The potential for water damage

caused by less-than-perfect window installation depends on several factors:

- Your annual rainfall, and whether rain tends to be accompanied by wind.
- The depth of the building's roof overhangs.
- The vertical distance from the overhang to the top of the window.

The risk of water damage is greatest at the window sill and when the weather-resistant barrier is disturbed by removing the old window. Hiring an installer who is trained to install windows correctly to prevent water damage may not be easy. Ask your installer about professional certifications. The American Architectural Manufacturers' Association (AAMA) publishes the window installation guidelines *Installation Masters* that specify details to assure a quality installation. See the *Resources* on page 173 for more information.

Installation Options

Window replacement should be carefully planned, especially in severe climates.

The first installation decision is whether to install the new window inside the old window frame or to tear out the old frame. Using the old window frame is cheaper and often used when the existing frame has a beautiful interior and exterior finish. This may be the best approach if the windows are worn beyond repair and the siding can't be replaced at the same time as the windows.

But it is always best to strip the entire unit down to the wall framing. If the new windows are installed inside old window jambs, the thermal problem isn't adequately resolved. The new window frame, old window frame, perhaps old sash weight pockets, and the extra wall framing around the window create thermal bridges in the exterior wall that significantly reduce the wall's overall R-value. If the old window jambs are removed all the way down to the studs, these areas can be sealed and insulated properly. If you replace windows without addressing the thermal bridging around them, you will have given up some possible efficiency gains.

Weathertight Window Installation

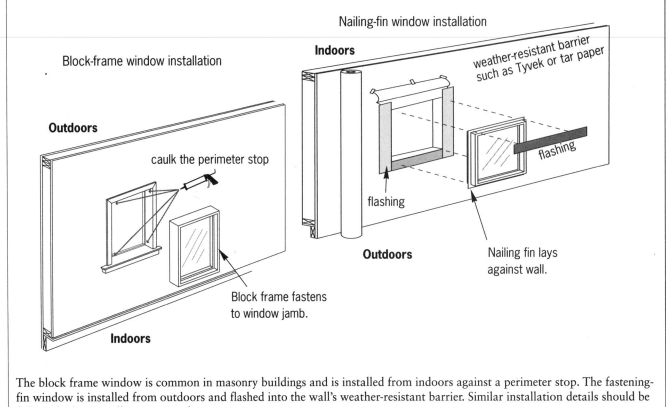

Block-frame window installation

Nailing-fin window installation

Indoors

weather-resistant barrier such as Tyvek or tar paper

Outdoors

caulk the perimeter stop

flashing

flashing

Block frame fastens to window jamb.

Indoors

Outdoors

Nailing fin lays against wall.

The block frame window is common in masonry buildings and is installed from indoors against a perimeter stop. The fastening-fin window is installed from outdoors and flashed into the wall's weather-resistant barrier. Similar installation details should be followed when installing exterior doors.

Installing a replacement window in the existing rough opening provides the opportunity for better waterproofing, better thermal performance, and better-looking interior and exterior finish, compared to installing the new window in the old window frame. This is the best method when the windows and siding are replaced at the same time.

Flange Installation

If you have a wood fastening surface, you will probably use the flange-installation method, in which the replacement window has a fastening flange. The flange is a fin that protrudes from the frame and is used to attach the wood sheathing and framing around the rough opening. For wood windows the traditional flange is brick mold, a standard type of window trim that is used by the installer to nail the window into place.

Flange installation is the preferred method because it provides the best weather-seal. This method works best when both the windows and siding are replaced.

If you don't replace the siding, be sure your installer protects the weather barrier from damage during removal, and integrates new paper window flashing into the weather barrier to prevent moisture penetration into the window and wall.

The rough opening in the frame of the building is typically $1\frac{1}{2}$ to 2 inches larger than the window frame itself. This allowance gives the installer room to plumb and square the window in what may be an irregular opening. But the gap remaining between window and frame is often poorly sealed, allowing excessive air leakage into the home. Poor air-sealing in this area often causes what homeowners think of as "leaky windows," when in fact the windows are relatively airtight. Window installers should fill the gap between the window frame and rough opening with one-part polyurethane foam. Because the gap is several inches deep the foam should be applied in subsequent layers. The low-expansion type of foam is appropriate in this case to avoid deforming the window frame during installation.

Replacing the window often involves repairing water damage to the siding or interior finish around the rough opening. Protecting the new window from moisture damage outdoors involves flashing the window's bottom, sides, and top to prevent water intrusion into the wall framing. The flashing that works best for this purpose is a flexible membrane or sheet metal. The flashing installs under the flange on the bottom and over the flange on the sides and top. On the window sill, install a sill pan that reliably deflects water to the outside of the siding.

Block-Frame Installation

Block-frame installation is an installation method where the window is installed in a surrounding wood frame and without a flange. Block-frame installation is used in three common ways:

- Installing a new window in the old window frame
- Installing the window in a masonry wall
- Installing the window in an energy-optimized way

There is no flange used in block-frame installation. Installing a new window in the old window frame is a satisfactory option when the exterior siding and window trim are in good condition and the window frame is also in good condition. Block-frame installation is also employed when installing windows in masonry walls.

The block-frame method can be employed from indoors or outdoors. The most common practice is to place the face of the new window frame against the existing wood, metal, or plastic stop (the strip that held the original sash in place). Sealant should be applied between the two surfaces just before the window is put in place.

Energy Optimization of Window Installation

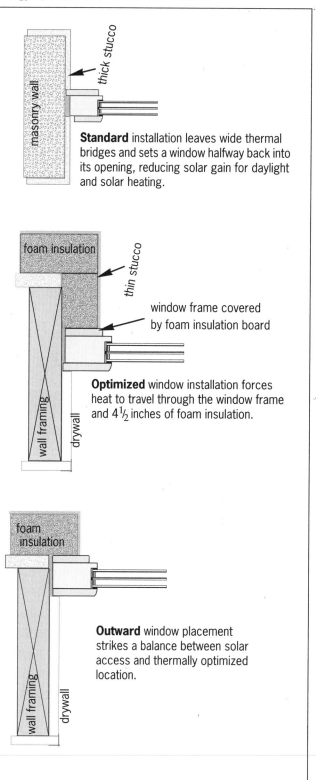

Standard installation leaves wide thermal bridges and sets a window halfway back into its opening, reducing solar gain for daylight and solar heating.

window frame covered by foam insulation board

Optimized window installation forces heat to travel through the window frame and $4\frac{1}{2}$ inches of foam insulation.

Outward window placement strikes a balance between solar access and thermally optimized location.

If you install windows as part of a major exterior renovation, you can integrate the new windows into the exterior insulation and weather-resistant barrier.

European Superwindows

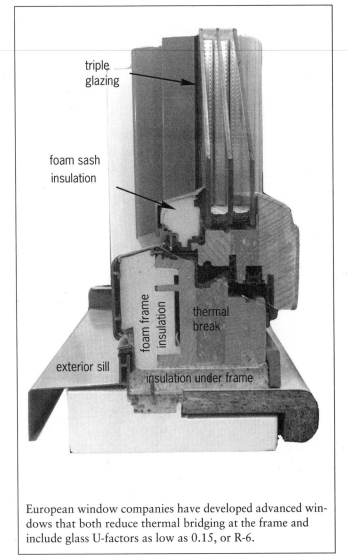

triple glazing

foam sash insulation

foam frame insulation

thermal break

exterior sill

insulation under frame

European window companies have developed advanced windows that both reduce thermal bridging at the frame and include glass U-factors as low as 0.15, or R-6.

Optimized Window Installation

Leaking windows wreck buildings. Metal or composite sill pans should be installed under the window to protect the wall from water damage. When a weather-resistant barrier like Tyvek or asphalt-impregnated felt is installed at the exterior of the building, the window should be flashed into that barrier using paper flashing or tape.

It's easier to install windows properly when the siding is replaced at the same time. When windows are installed as part of an exterior insulation and siding project, the installation can be optimized for water-proofing, solar transmittance, and the minimization of thermal bridges.

Exterior insulation can be used to improve the performance of windows. If the window is installed using the block-frame method, the exterior insulation should be run over the edge of the window to minimize its thermal bridging. The window should be located as close to the outer surface of the wall as practical if you want to get the maximum solar heating and daylight through the window.

Double Windows

Another good option is to install new sliding windows on the *interior* of existing double-hung or other sliding windows that are in good condition.

Many aluminum single-pane windows, for example, will last many years despite their poor energy efficiency. The upgrade we recommend is to install a complete new single-pane or double-pane primary window (metal or vinyl frame) at the interior and inside the existing jamb. This way the old window will continue to take the weather while your new interior window provides slows heat flow and reduces infiltration. You should choose windows with the same type of operation so that you can still open both windows.

IMPROVING THE EFFICIENCY OF DOORS

Doors are expensive to replace, and they have a long payback compared to the other energy conservation measures. But since doors offer many non-energy benefits such as security, weatherproofing, and aesthetics, they are often included in energy retrofit plans.

Improving Sliding Glass Doors

A sliding glass door's large expanse of glass transmits a large amount of heat into and out of the home. This heat flow takes three forms: heat that conducts directly through the glass in winter, solar heat that transmits through the glass in summer, and air that leaks around the edges of the door year-round.

Heat travels rapidly through glass when there is a large temperature difference between indoors and outdoors. In winter, the glass surface radiates coldness, pulling heat directly out of objects in the room, including your body if you are nearby. Cold glass also creates drafts by cooling nearby indoor air. This denser air sinks toward the floor, pulling more air into the area next to the glass. This air movement creates apparent drafts near the sliding glass door, even though the drafts don't include air leaking into the house. This combination of convective air movement and actual air leakage makes sliding glass doors a huge energy drain.

Sliding Door Winter Solutions Insulating quilted shades, though fairly expensive, can greatly improve winter comfort and energy efficiency. The best of these products have vertical tracks that seal the edges of the shade, and a roller system fastened to the wall above the door. Insulated or quilted fabric can also be fastened to the frame with velcro, and removed for storage in summer. The fabric for either is available in both light-transmitting or room-darkening design.

Sliding Door Summer Solutions For blocking glare and solar heat, exterior solutions are best. These include exterior reflective rolling shades and exterior solar screens. The solar screens are fastened to the frame of the sliding glass door and can be removed during cool weather. Interior shades and curtains are less effective because the solar heat has entered the home already.

Sliding Door Repair A less serious energy problem for sliding glass doors is air leakage, though this is a common cause of comfort complaints. This air leakage takes place around the perimeter of the door panel. Older sliding glass doors often have operating problems. These are usually caused by dirt in the tracks and worn rollers that contribute to air leakage by keeping the door from shutting properly. Replace worn and leaking weatherstrip, and dirty and broken rollers, to improve the seal and operation of the door. You can find replacement weatherstrip and rollers at a local glass shop in their window hardware catalogs.

Sliding Door Replacement If you choose to replace your older sliding glass door, be sure to buy one with advanced insulated glass, improved rollers, and high-quality weatherstripping. A hinged patio-door unit may be an even better option because hinged doors leak less air around their weatherstripping than sliding doors.

Your choice of glass will be particularly important when buying a sliding glass door. The most efficient glass in cool climates will have a low U-factor (more resistance to heat flow). In hot climates, glass should have a lower solar heat gain coefficient (blocks solar heat more effectively).

Weatherstripping Doors

Weatherstripping a door reduces drafts, dust entry, and noise travel through exterior doors.

Before beginning to weatherstrip a door, examine the door to ensure that it is operating properly. Tighten the screws in the hinges, door knob, and strike plate, if necessary. The hinges shouldn't move when you grab the handle and move the door up and down in the open position. If they are loose, you should tighten the hinges before installing weatherstrip.

The door stop, which is the strip that the door closes against, should be snug against the door on the sides and the top.

The strike plate is the metal plate in which the latch is inserted to keep the door closed. If the door moves back and forth, adjust the strike plate so that the door remains tight against the stop when pulled.

The door frame should have a threshold on the bottom. The threshold sits above the floor covering, sealing the bottom of the door and allowing the door to swing inward without scraping on the carpet or door mat. Avoid thresholds with imbedded weatherstrip, because the weatherstrip will be damaged by foot traffic.

The gap at the bottom of the door is usually the door's biggest air leak. Install a vinyl sweep or a metal door bottom with a built-in sweep to seal the door to its threshold. A sweep is easier to install since it is simply screwed to the face of the door, but it hangs below the door and may drag on the floor covering. A door bottom is attached to the door and closes the gap between the door and threshold. A door bottom doesn't hang down as far, and so is less likely to drag on the floor.

Types of Weatherstrip

The most common types of door weatherstrip mount to the door stop, and seal the face of the door to the stop. The best stop-mounted weatherstrips are very flexible. They allow the door to move slightly with temperature and humidity changes without losing the seal. Weatherstrip that attaches to the stop is easiest to install, but is somewhat prone to damage.

Jamb-mounted weatherstrip seals to the edge of the door. Weatherstrip that installs to the jamb is a little more difficult to install but lasts longer because it is protected from abrasion behind the door stop. Wooden doors expand and contract considerably as they absorb and shed moisture with weather changes. Make sure that you choose a weatherstrip that is flexible enough to mold to the door as it moves.

The best jamb-mount weatherstrip is probably bronze V-seal, because it lasts a long time and allows the door to warp slightly without losing its seal. It does take some skill to install—since it requires at least $1/8$ inch of space between the door and the door jamb, you may need to plane the door to provide clearance.

Flap weatherstrips, silicone bulb weatherstrips, and fabric-covered foam weatherstrip are easiest to install, and do good job of slowing drafts.

Avoid foam tape, felt tape, and most self-adhering plastic weatherstrips because their adhesive tends to fail. The cheaper types of weatherstrip are sometimes easier to install, but they are temporary and may never seal well.

The time you take to weatherstrip and adjust your doors will be paid back both in the improved operation of your doors and in the slowing of drafts. You may need to renew your weatherstrip occasionally because it will always be prone to damage, but that is more economical than replacing doors that are still functional.

Door Replacement

If you choose to replace an exterior door, choose a model that has built-in insulation and weatherstrip. The insulation in doors is measured in R-value, rather than U-factor like windows. Choose a door with insulation of R-5 to R-10.

Install doors to the same rigorous standards as windows. Be sure that the door is integrated in the home's weather-resistant barrier so water can't enter the wall cavity, and seal the gap between the new door jamb and the rough wall frame with liquid one-part foam. See *Weathertight Window Installation* on page 110.

Door Weatherstripping Choices

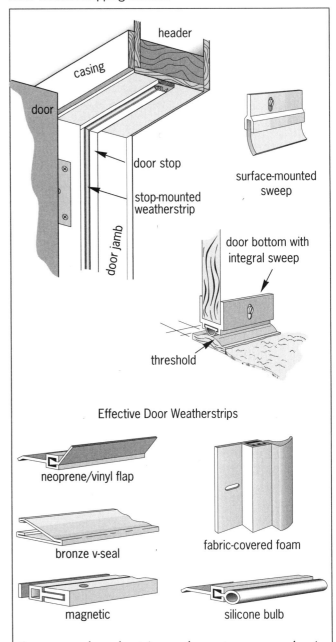

header
casing
door
door stop
stop-mounted weatherstrip
door jamb
surface-mounted sweep
door bottom with integral sweep
threshold

Effective Door Weatherstrips

neoprene/vinyl flap
bronze v-seal
fabric-covered foam
magnetic
silicone bulb

Stop-mounted weatherstrips are the most common and easiest to install. To seal against the threshold, sweeps are the easiest solution. A one-piece door bottom, though more difficult to install, is superior to a sweep because the door bottom is more durable.

THE BOTTOM LINE

Windows and doors are critical components in your home's thermal boundary. They are expensive, and replacement can consume a large part of your home improvement budget. Yet some of the simplest repairs and upgrades are the most effective energy conservation measures.

- Inspect your windows to ensure that each has at least two layers of glass. If you have any single-pane windows, install an exterior storm window. Make sure your storm windows remain closed tightly during the heating season.
- Consider repairs and window treatments to improve comfort and energy efficiency before deciding to replace windows.
- If you do replace windows, spend the extra money to buy premium windows that bear the ENERGY STAR label.

- When replacing windows, choose thermally advanced windows with glass that is customized to your climate and the direction that your windows face. Choose a low U-factor if you live in a cool or cold climate. Choose a low solar heat-gain coefficient (SHGC) if you want to save money on air-conditioning and a high SHGC if you want solar heating from your new windows.
- To achieve the longest lasting, most efficient window installation, integrate new windows with exterior foam insulation and new siding.
- If your doors allow drafts into your home, consider rejuvenating them by installing new weatherstripping.
- If you choose to install a new exterior door, buy one with built-in insulation and weatherstripping. Install it so water and air can't leak into your home.

9 Cooling Systems

The cost of running an air conditioner can be exorbitant, accounting for the largest electrical expense for many households in hot regions. The U.S. Environmental Protection Agency estimates that one-seventh of all electricity generated in the U.S. is used to air-condition buildings. It's a huge burden on all of us.

The good news is that you can reduce or eliminate your use of air-conditioning by implementing the alternate low-energy cooling methods described here. And you can do so with little reduction in your comfort.

If you don't already use air-conditioning, the low-energy cooling methods we describe can keep you comfortable without having to resort to using an air conditioner. Low-energy cooling is particularly important if you live in an area that is experiencing increasingly hot summer weather.

If you do use air-conditioning, the low-energy cooling methods we describe are still relevant. If you improve your home's efficiency, your air-conditioner will run less in summer, and you may be able to shorten your air-conditioning season by a few weeks in spring and fall.

We also show you how to perform maintenance on your air-conditioning equipment that will improve its performance, and we describe the most important guidelines for installing new air conditioners.

EVALUATE YOUR COOLING EFFICIENCY

If you use a central air conditioner, has it been professionally serviced in the last year? No home energy system is more prone to poor efficiency than air conditioners that go without professional maintenance.

If you use a central air conditioner, have you cleaned the filters in the last year? You can reduce the frequency of professional service visits by performing this simple do-it-yourself maintenance task.

Is your home a consistent temperature when your air conditioner is running? If the temperature in your home swings widely when your cooling system is running, it may indicate that the system is oversized, or has other problems that can be solved with a service call.

If you have a room air conditioner, do you ever use it in place of central air conditioning? Room air conditioners are considerably cheaper to operate than central systems because they cool only selected areas of your home. If you can run a room air conditioner or two, rather than your central system, you'll reap big savings.

If you live in a hot and dry region, do you use an evaporative cooler? Evaporative coolers (swamp coolers) provide sufficient summer comfort where summer humidity is low. They are a very effective substitute for air-conditioning at about one-third the electrical cost.

COOLING SYSTEM BASICS

Cooling is the most variable type of energy consumption. Two similar homes in the same neighborhood can vary widely in cooling costs, with an inefficient air-conditioned home consuming $500 worth of electricity in a hot month, while a neighbor in a well-designed home might spend only $20 per month to operate room fans and an evaporative cooler.

Air-conditioning systems are expensive and environmentally destructive to operate. The environmental problem is that everyone who has an air conditioner needs it at precisely the same time, creating a summer peak load for utilities. This peak is the driving force for the construction of new power plants.

Fortunately, we have proven low-cost cooling strategies that can trim home cooling costs substantially:

- Install and use window shading when possible to minimize solar heat gain. See *Shading Windows for Summer Comfort* on page 48.
- Install the maximum amount of attic insulation. See *Attic and Roof Insulation* on page 88.
- Install a reflective cool roof, or cool-roof coating. See *Improving Roof Reflectivity* on page 51.
- Run indoor fans in occupied rooms to create a wind chill. See *Circulating Air for Summer Comfort* on page 44.
- Run ventilation fans at night to remove accumulated solar heat (if the air isn't too humid). See *Ventilating with Outdoor Air* on page 45.
- Install an evaporative cooler if you live in a dry climate. See *Evaporative Coolers* on page 125.

Many of the measures described in this book will reduce your reliance on air conditioning. But if you do need to use your air conditioner, you'll save money by assuring that it is properly installed and maintained.

How Air Conditioners Work

Air conditioners employ the same principles as your home refrigerator. An air conditioner cools your home with a cold indoor coil, called the evaporator. A hot outdoor coil, called the condenser, releases the collected heat outdoors. The evaporator and condenser coils are actually serpentine copper pipes surrounded by aluminum fins, similar to a car radiator. Fans move air through these coils.

A fluid, called the refrigerant, collects heat at the evaporator coil and releases it at the condenser coil. The compressor forces the refrigerant through the circuit of coils and pipes.

Air-Conditioning Creates an Electric Peak Load

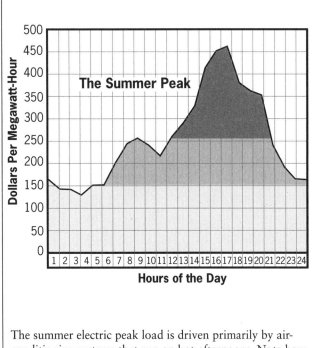

The summer electric peak load is driven primarily by air-conditioning systems that run on hot afternoons. Note how the cost of electricity rises with daily demand. Providing this most expensive electricity incurs great economic and environmental burdens.

Air Conditioner Operating Principles

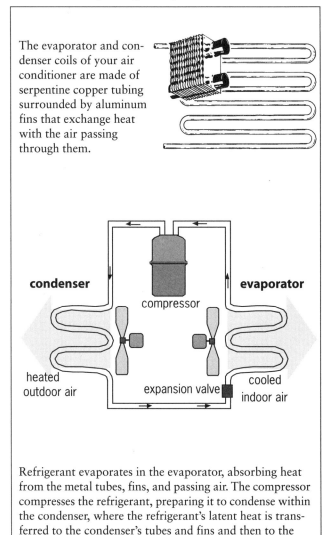

The evaporator and condenser coils of your air conditioner are made of serpentine copper tubing surrounded by aluminum fins that exchange heat with the air passing through them.

Refrigerant evaporates in the evaporator, absorbing heat from the metal tubes, fins, and passing air. The compressor compresses the refrigerant, preparing it to condense within the condenser, where the refrigerant's latent heat is transferred to the condenser's tubes and fins and then to the outdoor air passing through.

The refrigerant absorbs heat from indoor air as it changes from a liquid to a gas in the evaporator. You've felt this evaporator effect if your index finger has ever felt numbed with cold while using aerosol spray. When the liquid evaporates at the spray nozzle, it absorbs heat from the surrounding air and cools your finger. Using this same effect, the air conditioner's refrigerant evaporates inside the evaporator coil and removes heat from the house air moving through the evaporator's fins.

Heat pumps and air conditioners are almost identical in operation except that heat pumps are reversible for winter heating.

Types of Air Conditioners

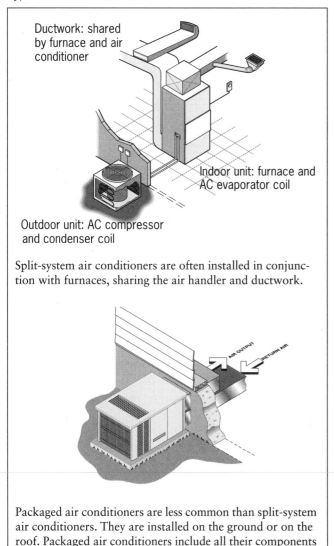

Split-system air conditioners are often installed in conjunction with furnaces, sharing the air handler and ductwork.

Packaged air conditioners are less common than split-system air conditioners. They are installed on the ground or on the roof. Packaged air conditioners include all their components in a single cabinet.

Types of Central Air-Conditioning

Central air conditioners are designed in two basic configurations: split-system units and packaged units. The difference between these is the location of the air handler. Split systems have indoor air handlers and the less common packaged units have outdoor air handlers.

The air handler is a steel cabinet containing the blower and the evaporator coil. It is connected to supply and return ducts. The supply ducts carry air from the air handler to the living spaces. The return ducts bring air from the house back to the air handler. For a more thorough discussion about duct systems, see *Inadequate Ducted Airflow* on page 133.

Split-system air conditioners are often installed in conjunction with a gas or oil furnace, and share the ductwork and air handler. The evaporator coil is located indoors in the air handler. The condenser, condenser fan, and compressor are located outdoors in a separate cabinet.

Packaged air-conditioners (also called unitary air conditioners) have the compressor, condenser, evaporator, and two fans all contained in a single cabinet located outdoors. Packaged air-conditioning systems may also contain a gas furnace or some electric resistance heating coils. Packaged air conditioners are usually horizontal-flow units, mounted on the roof or on a concrete slab outdoors.

Controlling Your Air Conditioner

One of the best ways to reduce air-conditioning costs is to manage your thermostat carefully. Move the temperature setting up a degree at a time until your family's temperature limit is reached. For every degree that your cooling thermostat setting is raised, your air conditioning costs will be reduced about 3 percent.

Your cooling system will use less energy if you turn it down while you are gone. When you leave, turn the thermostat up 5 to 10°F. Your air conditioner will run very little or not at all while you are gone, then will run longer than usual when you return. But the net effect will be lower energy consumption. You can also use a programmable thermostat to do the same thing. Try programming your thermostat with a higher energy-saving temperature during most of the day, then set it to lower the temperature a half-hour before your first family member returns home. *There is no reason to cool your house excessively when no one is home.*

For best results use a programmable thermostat to set temperatures higher during the day if your family is typically gone during the day.

PROFESSIONAL AIR-CONDITIONING SERVICE

Many of us assume that our air conditioners are installed correctly and that they will function indefinitely with no thought or action from us. Nothing could be further from the truth.

Central air conditioners are intended to cool an entire home. Central air conditioners typically consume much more electricity than necessary because of installation-related problems and maintenance problems.

The most common installation problems found in central air conditioners are leaky ducts, low airflow, incorrect refrigerant charge, and oversizing of the system:

- Leaky ducts are a widespread problem that affects most central air-conditioning systems. Allowing cool air to escape into attics, garages or crawl spaces is expensive and can lead to moisture condensation. Sealing the leaks improves efficiency, saves energy, and improves building durability.
- Low airflow stems from ducts that are typically too small or restricted, as well as other problems. Low airflow reduces air-conditioning efficiency and cooling capacity. Airflow problems can be fixed by a trained technician who can install larger ducts, install less restrictive duct fittings, or take other actions to improve return airflow.
- Incorrect refrigerant charge—either too high or too low—can make an air-conditioning system perform inefficiently. A trained technician should measure the refrigerant charge to determine whether or not the charge is correct and then adjust the charge if necessary.

- Most central air conditioners are oversized by 50 to 150 percent. For both comfort and environmental sustainability, a smaller air conditioner is better. Be sure to insulate, air seal, and improve shading before buying a new air conditioner. A smaller air conditioner is more efficient, quieter, and more appropriate to your home's existing ducts, which are probably too small for your current air conditioner, especially if it is oversized.

The most common air conditioner maintenance problems are related to dirt on filters, coils, and fan blades. This debris is deposited by the large quantity of air that travels through them during normal operation. The most basic service tasks include cleaning.

The service tasks described here are usually performed by professional technicians since they require specialized tools and training. You may choose to perform these tasks if you have the experience to do so. If not, we still recommend that you review these procedures so that you are better able to specify the proper procedures when working with heating and cooling contractors.

These tasks are often performed as a group by a service technician, with the cost ranging from $100 to $300 total. Air-conditioning service is well worth the money, especially considering the electrical cost of operating poorly-tuned equipment.

Common Causes of Poor AC Performance

Installation problem	How often found	Potential savings
Duct air leakage	70%	17%
Inadequate airflow	70%	7%
Incorrect charge	74%	12%
Oversized by 50% or more	47%	2–10%
Findings compiled from multiple studies.		

Why AC Coils Should Be Cleaned

Air-conditioning coils collect dirt from the air that travels through them. This reduces airflow and efficiency. Air-conditioning coils must be cleaned as often as they get dirty or performance will deteriorate and the air conditioner will eventually fail.

Coils have a dirty side facing into the airstream, and a clean side facing away from the airstream. The first step in cleaning a coil is to gain access to the coil's dirty side and to brush away the loose dirt and debris. The second step is to use water and cleansers to remove the more entrained dirt.

Cleaning Outdoor Coils

Probably 90 percent of all condenser coils are dirty and need cleaning. These outdoor coils collect vast quantities of dirt. Assume that your coil is dirty unless a service technician has cleaned it within the past year. If the coil is very dirty, you can usually see dirt, grass clippings, and other debris on the outside of the aluminum fins, a sure sign that dirt has penetrated the coil.

The procedure for cleaning an outdoor coil is relatively straightforward. *Note: Before beginning this type of work, the power should always be shut off at the equipment's main disconnect switch.*

- Remove the grillwork or louvers from around the coil. The top panel of the outdoor unit contains the fan. This panel can be lifted out of the way for access to the inside of the coil.
- Remove all the surface dirt from the coil with a stiff brush. Wetting the dirt with water or spraying it with biodegradable outdoor coil cleaner helps to soften it up, making brushing more effective and less dusty.
- Spray biodegradable outdoor-coil cleaner on both sides of the coil and wait five minutes for trapped dirt to soften. Then spray cold water from the inside through to the outside. The idea is to wash the dirt out the same way it came in rather than trying to push it all the way through the coil.
- Replace all the sheet metal shrouds. Turn the power back on.

Even with care, you can't prevent dirt from eventually clogging the outdoor condenser coil. How long should you wait between cleanings? The answer depends on how much dirt is in the outdoor air around the condenser. If the air is relatively free of particulates, the condenser might go three years or more without needing to be cleaned. If your outdoor air contains a lot of pollen, dust, or smoke, you should clean your condenser every year.

Cleaning Outdoor Air Conditioner Coils

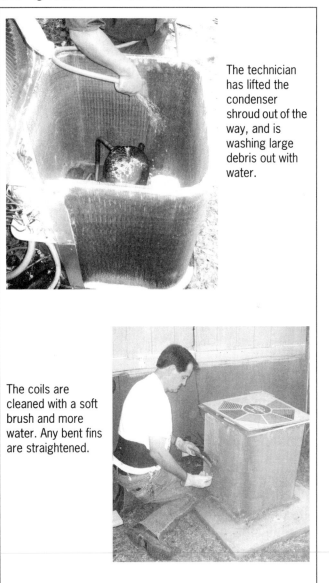

The technician has lifted the condenser shroud out of the way, and is washing large debris out with water.

The coils are cleaned with a soft brush and more water. Any bent fins are straightened.

Cleaning the outdoor condenser coils is an important maintenance task for all air conditioners and heat pumps. You can perform a simple visual inspection to see if your system's condenser needs to be cleaned.

Cleaning Indoor Coils

The air filter in your furnace or air conditioner is designed to catch dirt before it can lodge on the indoor evaporator coil. But even with periodic filter maintenance, the evaporator coil will collect dirt and lose efficiency over time. If you neglect to have your indoor coil cleaned, it will shorten the life of your air conditioner, and lead to excessive cooling costs.

The evaporator coils in packaged air conditioners (a single unit) are usually reached by removing an access panel. Evaporators in split-system air-conditioning systems are typically more difficult to reach, sometimes requiring a technician to cut a hole in the main supply duct to make access. In either case, have your evaporator coil professionally cleaned every three to six years as needed.

While cleaning the evaporator, your technician should check the drain line in the evaporator drain pan to make sure that it is open. When water is applied to the coil, water should flow out of the drain. If the drain is plugged, clean it so water from the evaporator will flow out. A plugged drain can hold excess water in the pan and encourage mold growth. You should know the location of the small plastic drain hose that drains your air conditioner's pan. During air conditioner operation, there should be some water dripping or running out of this tube.

Cleaning indoor coils is tricky because of the difficulty of obtaining access. Cleaning indoor coils is usually performed by a professional technician.

Cleaning the Blower

The blower is a squirrel cage fan that moves air through the cooling system's ductwork. The blower and ductwork may be shared with the heating system. Dirt on the blower will greatly reduce its ability to move air over the cooling coils and into your home. The amount of airflow over the cooling coils directly affects cooling efficiency.

For thorough cleaning, the blower is usually removed from the air handler. Pressurized air or water is the quickest way to clean it, though you can do a sufficient job with a brush and vacuum if the debris isn't too greasy. If pressurized water or air is used, the blower's motor should be protected from damage by taping plastic over the motor's ventilation openings and controls. The blower cabinet and nearby ductwork should be cleaned at the same time.

Cleaning a blower is a professional task owing to the proximity of line voltage.

Checking Refrigerant Charge

It is common for central air conditioners to run at a poor efficiency because of incorrect refrigerant charge. The ideal amount of refrigerant is specific to each air conditioner and installation. Incorrect charge reduces the equipment's efficiency, impairs its cooling capacity, and shortens the life of the compressor.

Many air-conditioning technicians don't regularly check refrigerant charge. Be sure that your contractor checks the refrigerant charge during a maintenance call, and corrects the charge if necessary. Note that a specialized certification is required for technicians who work with refrigerant since some refrigerants are potentially damaging to the ozone layer.

Checking refrigerant charge is a professional task owing to the specialized tools and training required.

REPLACING CENTRAL AIR CONDITIONERS

The energy efficiency of today's air conditioners is twice that of models built even a few decades ago. This improvement in efficiency has resulted from several technical advances:

- Blower motors are more efficient, and run on multiple speeds.
- Compressors run at dual speeds.
- Time-delay relays control evaporator fans.
- Tubing that makes up the coils is grooved inside to increase surface area.
- Heat-dissipating fins are spaced closer together and are perforated to improve heat transfer.

Rating the Efficiency of Air Conditioners

For central air conditioners, the efficiency rating is called the *Seasonal Energy Efficiency Ratio (SEER)*. For room air conditioners, a similar rating called *Energy Efficiency Ratio* (EER) is used. For both scales, higher is better. Air conditioners with higher ratings generally cost more, but during the air conditioner's life span the energy savings will be far greater than the initial cost.

SEER or EER describes how much heat the unit can remove from your home for each watt of energy it consumes.

The Energy Guide Label always lists the EER or SEER. Central air conditioners in the U.S. have had a minimum legally required SEER of 13 since 2006. Units with a SEER of 14 qualify for the ENERGY STAR label. We recommend buying a unit with a SEER rating of at least 15 or higher, especially if you live in a dry climate.

To determine the approximate SEER of an existing central air conditioner, find the model number and manufacturer from the nameplate on the outdoor unit. Contact a local dealer of that manufacturer's equipment and ask them to look up the efficiency rating for you. This will help you evaluate the payback from a potential replacement.

Before 1979, the efficiency of central air conditioners ranged from SEER 4.5 to 8.0. If you replace a vintage 1970s SEER 7 central air conditioner with a new SEER 14 unit, you will cut your air-conditioning costs in half.

Removing Humidity

The sensible heat factor (SHF) is an important sizing consideration that rates the air conditioner on its ability to remove moisture. The SHF is a decimal number between 0.5 and 1.0. The lower the SHF, the more moisture the unit will remove from the air. The SHF depends on the type of the evaporator coil and on the speed of the blower.

Homeowners in dry and moderate climates should purchase a unit with high SHF, because they need less moisture removal and air conditioners with high SHF are more efficient. However, homeowners in humid climates will probably want an SHF of between 0.67 and 0.77 to reduce humidity and the accompanying mold, mildew, and microscopic pests. Be sure your contractor understands and considers moisture removal when sizing your central air-conditioning system. Air conditioners control humidity, and a relative humidity of less than 40 percent will suppress mold, mildew, and other microscopic pests that are linked to respiratory problems.

Proper sizing and equipment selection are especially important with new high-efficiency air conditioners. These new energy-efficient units must have a low enough SHF to provide adequate moisture removal.

A damp location and home can cause high air-conditioning costs. Air-conditioning is a very expensive way to dry a home. In many homes, the least expensive way to control indoor moisture is to install a ground moisture barrier and sump pump if necessary. For more information, see *Moisture Basics* on page 153.

ROOM AIR CONDITIONERS

Room air conditioners cool one room at a time. They are usually less expensive to operate than central air-conditioning because they don't cool the entire house, and because they don't have duct systems that incur energy losses. Since they are manufactured as a sealed unit, room units also have fewer installation problems than central units.

Room air conditioner sizes range from 5500 to 20,000 British thermal units per hour (BTUH). This measures how much heat the unit can remove from your home for each hour of operation.

The legal standards for room air conditioners sold in the U.S. require a range of EER ratings that varies from EER 8.5 to EER 10.5 depending on the output of the unit.

Units with an ENERGY STAR label must have an EER that is at least 10 percent higher than the federal minimum, or a range of about EER 9.0 to EER 10.5. To get the most efficient model available, look for the ENERGY STAR label, and for a unit with the highest EER possible.

Several manufacturers make portable room air conditioners that sit completely inside the room rather than being installed in a window. They do not remove heat from the home. Instead, they cool one part of a room while heating another. You should avoid this technology. Efficient portable air conditioners must be installed in a window or through the wall.

Cleaning Room Air Conditioners

Cleaning your portable air conditioner's filter and coils helps it perform better while using less electricity. The need for cleaning depends on how much you use your room air conditioner and how much dust is suspended in the indoor and outdoor air. If you wash the filter in your room AC periodically, it will keep dirt from accumulating in the indoor coil. This is a reasonable task for a motivated homeowner. *Caution: Unplug the air conditioner before servicing it.*

- You may be able to clean the indoor coil without removing the unit. But if you plan to clean the outdoor coil, you'll need to remove the unit. In either case, remove the panel(s) and grilles necessary so you can get to both coils.

- If this coil is dirty, clean it with an old hairbrush to remove surface dirt and lint. Brush in the same direction as the fins, being careful to avoid bending them. Straighten any damaged fins with an old comb.

- The outdoor condenser coil is accessible from the outdoor side of your room air conditioner, so you'll need to remove the entire unit for this task. To determine if it needs cleaning, inspect it from outdoors through the louvered openings on its housing. If it is dirty, remove the unit.

- Once you have the unit out, remove the exterior housing by removing its screws. Cover the electric controls with plastic bags and secure them with rubber bands. Clean the coil by spraying a strong household cleanser into the coil, waiting a few minutes, and rinsing with water. The excess water should run into the pan that forms the bottom of the air conditioner and out the drain to the outdoors.

- Often you can loosen the condenser coil and turn it carefully outward just enough to work on the

dirty inside surface of the aluminum fins. Use your brush, water, and household cleanser or outdoor coil cleaner. Let your room air conditioner dry in the sun before replacing the housing and reinstalling it.

During the heating season, remove the room air conditioner so you can close and latch the window. Or cover the indoor side of the air conditioner with either plastic sheeting or an insulated removable box. Do not cover the unit on the outside, unless you also have an indoor cover, because warm, moist, indoor air leaking into the unit can form condensation that encourages condensation.

Cleaning Room Air Conditioners

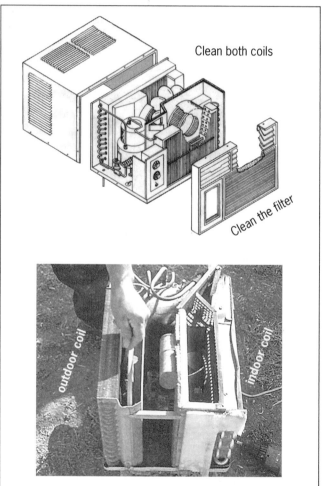

The best way to clean a portable air conditioner is to remove it from the window or wall so you can work on it easily. The sheet metal cover is removed to provide access to both coils. Periodic cleaning will help this equipment run at peak efficiency.

EVAPORATIVE COOLERS

Evaporative coolers (also called swamp coolers) are a highly efficient alternative to air conditioners. They are a popular and energy-efficient cooling strategy in the warm, dry climates of the western U.S.

Evaporative coolers work well when the dew point is below 55°F. It is in this dry air that evaporation takes place most quickly, and it is evaporation that provides the cooling effect. When the dew point is above 55°F, the moisture that evaporative coolers introduce to your house can cause condensation to take place. The lower your summertime relative humidity, the more an evaporative cooler can drop the temperature of your home.

Unlike central air conditioning systems, evaporative coolers provide a steady stream of fresh air to the home. This can be a problem if your home is located in a dusty or polluted environment, but for many homeowners the fresh air is a bonus.

Traditional Evaporative Cooler

Traditional steel coolers need faithful maintenance to provide good service. Their installed cost is $800 to $1500, making them a extremely good investment in hot and dry climates.

Evaporative cooler fans move air through absorbent pads that are saturated with water. The absorbent pads are made of aspen wood fibers, glass fibers, or specially formulated cardboard. Some of that water evaporates, reducing the temperature of the hot outdoor air. As this cooler air is forced into the house by the fan, it pushes warmer air out through slightly open windows or out through dedicated vents in the ceiling or walls.

A water pump in the reservoir pushes water through tubes into a drip trough, which then drips water onto the pads. A float valve connected to the home's water supply keeps the reservoir supplied with fresh water to replace the evaporated water. The reservoir is flushed periodically to remove debris, and the drain water can be directed to nearby landscaping.

Evaporative coolers operate much more cheaply than air conditioners. They do not have a SEER rating, but if they did, it would be between SEER 30 and 40, or 2 to 3 times the SEER of the most efficient air conditioners. Recent studies show that the typical savings from using evaporative cooling rather than air-conditioning is 3000 to 4000 kilowatt-hours of electricity per year, or $450 to $600 at current rates.

Unlike air conditioners, evaporative coolers do consume water. But the cost of this additional water is minimal when compared to the electrical savings, accounting for only $10 to $20 in increased annual water costs for most homeowners. The issue of water consumption for evaporative coolers is even less of an issue when viewed on a regional basis, since most of the electrical generating plants that support air conditioners consume vast quantities of water themselves.

Sizing and Selection

Evaporative coolers are rated by the volume of air they deliver. Most models range from 3,000 to 25,000 cubic feet of air per minute (CFM). Manufacturers recommend providing enough air-moving capacity to change the entire volume of the home every $1\frac{1}{2}$ to 3 minutes, depending on the climate.

Cooler Options and Features

Evaporative coolers can be controlled with thermostats to minimize energy use, water use, and maintenance. Thermostats also reduce the chance of overcooling with unnecessary nighttime operation.

An evaporative cooler should have at least two speeds in the cooling mode. It should also have a vent-only option to allow use of the cooler as a whole-house fan during mild weather. When using the vent-only option, the water pump does not operate and the outdoor air is not humidified. A pump-only option is also useful since it can be run at the beginning of the cycle to wet the pads and wash out dust before the circulating fan is started.

Filters can be fitted on the cooler during or after installation. They increase the need for regular maintenance, but they also remove most of the dust from incoming air—an attractive option for homeowners concerned about allergies. Filters can also reduce the tendency of some coolers to pull water droplets from the pads into the blades of the fan. Most evaporative coolers do not include air filters as original equipment.

Modern Evaporative Cooler

Modern evaporative coolers include mostly plastic and stainless steel components. Their initial cost is high, at $1000 to $2000 installed, but their lifespan tends to be longer than that of traditional steel coolers.

Room Evaporative Coolers

Room evaporative coolers are becoming more popular in areas of the western U.S. with milder summer weather. These portable coolers don't mount in a window or wall, and so don't move outdoor air into the home. Since they aren't tied into your plumbing system, they must be filled with water manually. They work well enough in moderate climates, but may not be able to cool a room adequately in hot climates. They can reduce the temperature in a single room by about 10°F.

Two-Stage Evaporative Coolers

Two-stage evaporative coolers include a pre-cooler, denser and more effective pads, and more efficient motors. Two-stage coolers are one-quarter to one-third more effective at lowering the air temperature than conventional models.

The pre-cooler is a closed heat exchanger that drops the incoming air temperature somewhat without exposing the air to moisture. This precooling provides an extra temperature drop of 3 to 9°F, so the air feels cooler and drier. The principle cooling system, similar to those used in one-stage coolers, utilizes wet pads and drops the temperature farther.

Operation of Evaporative Coolers

Evaporative coolers move cool air into your home. When running an evaporative cooler, you should open windows or vents on the downwind side of your home to provide 1 to 2 square feet of opening for each 1,000 cfm of cooling capacity. Experiment to find the right windows to open and the correct amount to open them. If the windows are open too far, then hot outdoor air will enter. If the windows aren't open far enough, your home's humidity level will rise. You can choose which rooms to cool by opening windows in the areas you want to cool, and closing windows in unoccupied areas. This concentrates the cooling in the rooms you choose.

Specialized ventilation openings called up-ducts are sometimes installed in the ceiling to exhaust warm air that the evaporative cooler pushes out of the home.

Up-ducts are preferred by home owners who do not feel secure leaving windows open. Since they usually exhaust air into the attic, it is important to check that the attic has adequate attic ventilation to allow this moist air to escape.

Evaporative Cooler Installation

Evaporative coolers are installed with two types of distribution. Either the cooler outlet blows air into a central location through a single grille, or the cooler outlet joins ductwork that distributes the cool air to different rooms in the house. Single outlet installations work well for compact homes that are open from room to room. Ducted systems are necessary for more spread-out homes with hallways and closed rooms.

Many people install down-flow evaporative coolers on the roofs of their homes. Others prefer wall-mounted or ground-mounted horizontal units for easier maintenance and decreased risk of roof leaks.

A horizontal-flow evaporative cooler is attached to a wall or sits on a concrete pad. The large supply duct from this unit connects to one or two large, central registers indoors or to ducts in the basement or crawl space. The best place for a horizontal-flow evaporative cooler is in the shade on the windward side of the home. The wind helps circulate cooled air through the unit and into the home. The windward location also discourages recirculating the exhaust air from the house.

Evaporative Cooler Maintenance

Most problems with evaporative coolers are caused by neglecting basic maintenance. The more it runs, the more maintenance it needs. An evaporative cooler will definitely need a major cleaning every season, and may need routine maintenance several times during the cooling season. In very hot climates where the cooler operates much of the time, you may need to look at the pads, filters, reservoir, and pump every few weeks. It is a small price to pay, considering that the monthly cost of running an evaporative cooler may be hundreds of dollars less than running an air conditioner. This is a good task to learn how to perform yourself.

You'll need a simple set of tools for this project: screwdrivers, a scrub brush, and clean rags. *Caution: Before doing this work, always turn the power to your evaporative cooler off by either unplugging the unit, or disconnecting it at your home's main electrical panel. Don't perform this task if you're not comfortable with assuming some risk.*

- Clean or replace the pads at least twice during the cooling season, or as often as monthly during continuous operation. Some paper and synthetic cooler pads can be cleaned with soap and water or a weak acid according to manufacturer's instructions.

- Drain the reservoir. Dust from the air, and minerals and dirt from the water, collect there. All coolers have a drain fitting at the bottom of the unit. To drain the reservoir, shut off the water, connect a garden hose to the fitting on the outside of the cooler cabinet, and then unscrew the overflow tube. Let the water drain out.

- Clean the reservoir. If you have an old-style traditional evaporative cooler, you'll need to drain and clean it at least once a year. Modern evaporative coolers have dump valves or dump pumps that empty the reservoir, so cleaning will be needed less often. Scrub the sump with a stiff brush, then wash the debris out with more water. Most manufacturers of metal coolers recommend painting the reservoir area once a year with a water-resistant coating. Plastic coolers don't need this service.

- Clean the fan. If there is any significant amount of dirt on the blades, clean the fan thoroughly with a brush and household cleaner.

- Clean the cabinet. Brush the dust and dirt off the louvers in the cooler cabinet and clean the holes in the drip trough that distributes the water to the pads.

- Inspect and clean the pump. The pump and the float assembly are the source of many maintenance problems in evaporative coolers. Check the hoses and fittings for leaks while the pump is running.

- Check the blower belt for wear and tightness. The belt shouldn't move more than one inch when you press it firmly. Some newer units don't have a drive belt.
- Check for leaks in the float valve when you turn the water back on. This valve operates like those in toilet tanks, and leaks here will increase water use. Replace any parts as needed.

Once you have performed these service tasks the first time, you'll learn how to gauge the need for service. Keep an eye on your equipment, and you'll learn about its requirements.

THE BOTTOM LINE

The task of reducing cooling energy consumption requires attention to several different areas. Your first efforts should be directed at improving your home's ability to reflect and shed heat, as covered in other chapters in this book. If this isn't sufficient to provide the comfort you need, consider using evaporative cooling or room fans for some relief. Finally, if you need to use air conditioning, install the most efficient equipment you can, and keep it tuned up.

Avoiding the Use of Air-Conditioning

- Before buying a new air conditioner for an existing home, upgrade your home's insulation, air-tightness, shading, and roof reflectivity.
- If you live in a hot and dry climate, consider installing an evaporative cooler rather than a central air conditioner.
- In any hot climate, use room fans to provide a cooling effect.
- In hot climates where it is cool at night, use ventilation fans once the sun goes down to move hot air out of your home.

Do-It-Yourself AC Service

- Clean your air conditioner's air filters. If these are shared with the furnace, this service will also improve your heating efficiency.
- If you have central air conditioning, clean the outdoor coil.

Professional AC Service

- Clean both indoor and outdoor coils. Straighten any bent fins.
- Check the refrigerant charge and adjust if needed.
- Clean the blower so that it moves air more efficiently. Check the airflow and duct leakage. Improve the airflow and seal the ducts if needed. If the duct system is shared with the furnace, this service will also improve your heating efficiency.

Replacing AC Equipment

- If you choose to replace a central air conditioner, ask your contractor to perform a load calculation and to install the smallest air conditioner that will give you acceptable comfort.
- Ask your contractor to provide easy access to the filter and to the indoor coil for maintenance. Order a dozen filters for your new unit.
- If you plan to replace your air conditioner, ask your contractor to measure the duct leakage in your systems, and the amount of airflow through the ducts. Ask your contractor to seal and insulate ducts that are located in attics, attached garages, and crawl spaces. If the duct system is shared with the furnace, this upgrade will also improve your heating efficiency.

# **10** Heating Systems

The cost of heating is the biggest single utility expense for many families. Heating your home has a large environmental impact, too. If you heat with natural gas, propane, or oil, your chimney probably emits 10,000 to 20,000 pounds of carbon dioxide, in addition to other pollutants, each year. Most homeowners can trim this by 10 to 50 percent through a combination of maintenance, repairs, and upgrades.

If you heat with electricity, your emissions are probably two to three times greater than they would be with gas or oil. Even though electric heat releases no emissions at the point of use, the electricity you use is most likely linked to the operation of a very inefficient power plant in a distant location.

Most single-family homes in North America are heated by central combustion heating systems that burn natural gas, propane, or oil. Most of these central systems are furnaces that distribute heat through ductwork that connects to rooms within the home. Combustion space heaters, on the other hand, are installed directly in the room and have no ductwork. Boilers that distribute heat by way of circulating water and other fluids are common in some regions. A few homes are heated by electric resistance heaters, including both furnaces and room heaters, which are also covered here.

The remaining common heating system is the electric heat pump. See "Cooling System Basics" on page 117 for information on heat pumps, since a heat pump is essentially a reversible air conditioner.

You can trim your use of energy for heating in two principle ways. The first is to improve the shell of your home so it loses less heat during cold weather. You can do this by performing air-sealing tasks or by improving your home's insulation. See "Air Leakage Basics" on page 71, and *Insulation Basics* on page 81. The second way to trim heating consumption is by upgrading the efficiency of your heating equipment itself, or by improving the delivery system, such as the ducts. Both equipment and ducts are covered in this chapter. We also describe the basic principles and common designs of heating equipment here, as well as the most important details for new installations.

EVALUATE YOUR HEATING SYSTEM

Have you had your heating system serviced recently? You should have a professional heating technician perform periodic maintenance on your heating system to assure that it operates safely and at peak efficiency. You may also want to learn how to perform the simplest maintenance tasks yourself.

Do you ever notice peculiar odors near your water heater or heating system? If so, you should investigate this right away since these systems can sometimes spill dangerous combustion gases into the home.

If you have a furnace, what is the condition of its ductwork? Energy loss in your ductwork may account for up to 40 percent of your heating expense, especially if it runs through an attic or crawl space. This can be reduced by sealing and insulating your duct system.

Do you have plans to do any major remodel work on your home? If so, you'll have an opportunity to improve the shell of your home. If you first install more insulation, seal air leaks, and improve your doors and windows, you'll be able to install a smaller and more efficient heating system.

How old is your heating system? What is its efficiency? Older furnaces and boilers operate at 60 to 70 percent efficiency, with the remaining 30 to 40 percent of the energy you purchase going up the chimney. If your home is heated by one of these systems, you can reduce your consumption substantially by upgrading to a system that operates at 90 percent efficiency or higher.

HEATING SYSTEM BASICS

In both gas and oil heaters, burners mix and burn fuel in combustion chambers. The heat exchanger surrounds the combustion chamber, and transfers heat from the flame and combustion gases to a heating fluid such as air, water, or steam. Combustion gases leave the combustion chamber and enter a chimney. Chimneys are made of metal, masonry, or other noncombustible material.

The efficiency of a combustion heater depends on the losses of heat up the chimney, losses at the beginning and end of each burn cycle, and losses through the cabinet of the heater itself. The sum of these losses is reflected in the annual fuel utilization efficiency (AFUE), a description of the percentage of available heat actually delivered to the distribution system. The AFUE is always included on the yellow Energy Guide label which is included by law on all new heating equipment.

When comparing the AFUE ratings of heating equipment, higher is better. Older open-combustion heating equipment has an AFUE of 55 to 75 percent. The best modern sealed-combustion heating equipment, which we recommend for all replacements, can achieve an AFUE of 90 to 95 percent. If you replace an older AFUE 60 furnace with a new AFUE 90 furnace, it will reduce your fuel consumption by one-third.

Combustion Safety

Combustion fuels are primarily hydrocarbons—molecules composed of hydrogen and carbon. The process of combustion, or burning, is simply rapid oxidation: oxygen combines with the carbon and hydrogen, splitting the hydrocarbon molecule. Carbon dioxide (CO_2) and water vapor are the main products of this heat-liberating chemical reaction. Carbon monoxide (CO), a poisonous gas produced by incomplete combustion, can also be produced if the equipment isn't operating properly.

If your home has combustion heating equipment such as a furnace, boiler, or water heater, you'll want to know that the chimney system operates effectively to carry these flue gases out of your home. When you next have a technician perform service of your heating equipment, ask them to confirm that the chimney systems for all your combustion appliances are functioning properly.

You should also perform an occasional personal inspection of your heating equipment. There should be no signs of soot or scorching, and you shouldn't notice any odd odors. Call your service technician or power company if you have any concerns.

Gas kitchen stoves present a unique air quality problem since they don't usually have chimneys, and so release all their combustion by-products into the kitchen. The best solution to this low-level pollution is

What's Included in AFUE and Other Types of Efficiency

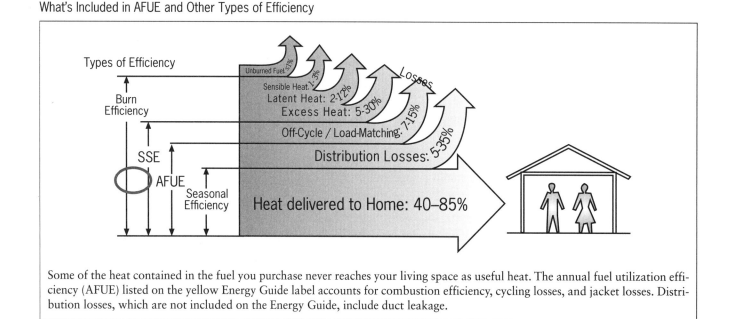

Some of the heat contained in the fuel you purchase never reaches your living space as useful heat. The annual fuel utilization efficiency (AFUE) listed on the yellow Energy Guide label accounts for combustion efficiency, cycling losses, and jacket losses. Distribution losses, which are not included on the Energy Guide, include duct leakage.

to always operate a kitchen fan when using a gas stove. In this case, it's critically important that the kitchen fan is ducted to the outdoors. Many range hoods only filter kitchen air to remove grease, and then return it to the room. This doesn't do anything to control carbon monoxide or other gaseous pollutants.

Finally, one of the best defenses against carbon monoxide and other combustion by-products is to install a carbon monoxide detector ($30 or less) on each level of your home. Be sure to replace the batteries periodically.

Combustion: The Chemical Reaction

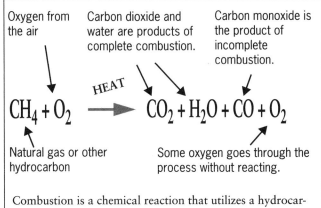

Oxygen from the air | Carbon dioxide and water are products of complete combustion. | Carbon monoxide is the product of incomplete combustion.

$$CH_4 + O_2 \xrightarrow{HEAT} CO_2 + H_2O + CO + O_2$$

Natural gas or other hydrocarbon | Some oxygen goes through the process without reacting.

Combustion is a chemical reaction that utilizes a hydrocarbon and oxygen to produce heat. It releases carbon dioxide (a potent greenhouse gas), water, and other by-products. A properly cleaned and tuned combustion appliance will produce very little or no carbon monoxide.

Components of Conventional Furnaces

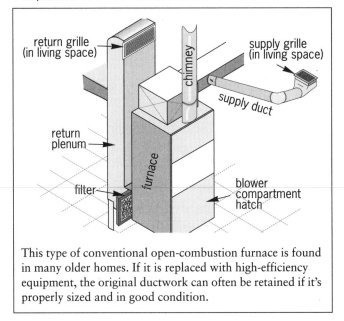

This type of conventional open-combustion furnace is found in many older homes. If it is replaced with high-efficiency equipment, the original ductwork can often be retained if it's properly sized and in good condition.

Open-Combustion Furnace (< 75 AFUE)

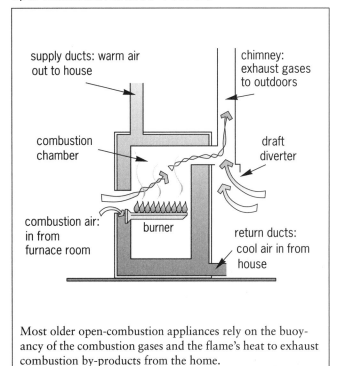

Most older open-combustion appliances rely on the buoyancy of the combustion gases and the flame's heat to exhaust combustion by-products from the home.

Sealed Combustion Furnace (90%+ AFUE)

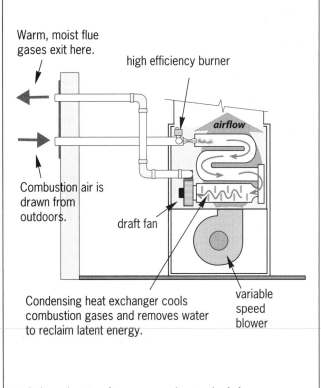

Sealed combustion furnaces use electric draft fans to move combustion gases safely out of the home. The combination of features shown here raises the efficiency of modern furnaces and improves their safety.

DUCT SYSTEM BASICS

Forced air furnaces deliver heated air to the home through ductwork. The same ductwork may also deliver cooled air for a cooling system. Duct systems usually include pressurized supply ducts that move heated air out to the living space, and depressurized return ducts that draw cool room air back to the heating system.

Duct leakage and poor duct insulation are common problems. Air will leak out of the ducts if they are not airtight. Heat will conduct through the walls of the ducts if they are not insulated. Both will incur an energy penalty that varies in cost depending on the location of the ducts. If the ducts are located outside the living space, as in an attic or under-floor crawl space, the loss can total up to one-third the total energy consumption. If the ducts are located within the home's thermal boundary, as in a finished basement, the losses are less severe, though they can still result in comfort problems if heated air never makes it to the intended rooms.

Duct systems must carry sufficient air to heat or cool the home. The size and number of ducts should be calculated at the time a heating or cooling system is installed, but this step is often skipped in favor of an inaccurate rule-of-thumb approach. As a result, many duct systems are undersized, and can't move enough air to properly heat or cool the rooms they serve. This forces the heating system to run overtime, and wastes fuel as a result.

If your furnace and ductwork are located in an attached garage, fumes within the garage could be drawn into leaks in the ductwork when the furnace is running. This could carry carbon monoxide and other garage pollutants into your home. The best solution is to seal any duct leaks that are located in the garage. As a further precaution, always pull your car out of the garage immediately after starting it so that it doesn't contribute carbon monoxide to the house air. Then close the garage door and drive away—modern cars don't need to be warmed up.

PROFESSIONAL HEATING SYSTEM SERVICE

Your furnace's safety and efficiency are closely related to one another. Proper tuning and adjustment of any combustion appliance can improve its efficiency dramatically. An added benefit is that these tasks reduce the production of carbon monoxide and assure that combustion gases are carried safely out of the home.

You can perform the most basic furnace service task yourself: inspecting and replacing your furnace filter periodically. For more information about this task, see *Simple Furnace Maintenance* on page 53.

You'll need to hire a professional to perform the most critical service tasks, such as testing combustion efficiency, cleaning the combustion chamber, and assessing chimney draft. We describe a complete set of service tasks here so you know what sort of work to ask for when hiring service technicians. If your heating contractor is not familiar with the procedures we describe, we recommend that you shop for someone else with more experience. See the *Resources* on page 173 to find certified heating technicians who have the training to test and tune your equipment for maximum efficiency and safety.

Professional Gas Furnace Service Tasks

Gas heating equipment should be inspected and serviced every two to four years. The following specifications apply to gas furnaces, boilers, water heaters, and space heaters. The goal of these measures is to reduce carbon monoxide, optimize combustion efficiency, and verify that safety controls are operating. We include them here to illustrate what types of procedures you should ask for when contracting for service work:

- Look for soot, melted wire insulation, and rust in the burner and manifold area outside the fire box. These signs indicate flame roll-out, combustion gas spillage, and CO production.
- Inspect the burners for dust, debris, misalignment, flame-impingement, and other flame-interference problems. Clean, vacuum, and adjust as needed.
- Inspect the heat exchanger for leaks.

- Determine that the pilot is burning (if equipped) and that main burner ignition is satisfactory.
- Test the pilot-safety control for complete gas-valve shutoff when pilot is extinguished.
- Check the venting system for proper size and pitch, obstructions, blockages, or leaks.
- Test to ensure that the high-limit control is functional.
- Measure gas input and observe flame characteristics if soot, CO, or other combustion problems are present.

The technician should proceed with burner maintenance and adjustment if any of these conditions are noted:

- The CO is greater than 100 ppm.
- Indicators of soot or flame roll-out are visible.
- Burners are visibly dirty.
- Measured draft is inadequate.
- The appliance has not been serviced for two years or more.

Gas-burner maintenance should include these measures:

- Correct causes of CO and soot, such as over-firing, closed primary air intake, flame impingement, and lack of combustion air.
- Remove dirt, rust, and other debris that may be interfering with the burners. Clean the heat exchanger, if necessary.
- Take action to improve draft, if inadequate because of improper venting, obstructed chimney, leaky chimney, or depressurization.
- Seal leaks in vent connectors and chimneys.
- Adjust gas input if combustion testing indicates overfiring or underfiring.

Professional Oil Furnace Service Tasks

Oil furnaces require all of the same maintenance chores as gas furnaces. But oil doesn't burn as cleanly as gas, so oil furnaces need more frequent service, including complete combustion analysis and a thorough cleaning of the burners and heat exchanger.

Have a heating contractor clean and tune your oil-burning furnace at least once a year. A tune-up performed by a qualified technician will usually save 5 to 20 percent on your fuel bills. The heating technician should perform these tasks:

- Measure efficiency, CO, draft, and all other parameters that are relevant to the seasonal efficiency of a furnace or boiler.
- Check the heat exchanger for cracks, corrosion, and soot.
- Test for CO and correct the causes, if found.
- Clean the burner's blower, blast tube, and electrodes.
- Set the gap between electrodes at the correct distance.
- Replace the oil filter, test oil-pump pressure, and repair any oil leaks.
- Adjust spinner and shutter for minimum smoke.
- Test the flame sensor.
- Perform final combustion test.

INADEQUATE DUCTED AIRFLOW

Furnace efficiency suffers when too little air flows through the ducts. Dirty filters, a dirty blower, damaged ducts, a dirty air-conditioning coil, or blocked registers can cause reduced airflow. Another very common cause of low airflow is inadequately sized return air ducts.

Duct blockage has two major effects. The first effect is to reduce airflow through the ducts, which reduces heating and cooling efficiency. The second effect is increased air leakage through the building shell due to house pressures created by the blockage. Both of these defects waste energy. Your heating technician should assess the airflow through your ducts to confirm that it is both adequate and balanced among all the rooms in your house. If airflow is inadequate, it will be worth the effort to add to or replace the existing duct system.

IMPROVING DUCT EFFICIENCY

Duct sealing yields the biggest savings when the ducts are located in a ventilated intermediate zone—such as a crawl space or attic—where ducts exchange air freely with the outdoors. This air exchange between ducts and outdoor air wastes energy in two ways: heated or cooled air is lost to outdoors, and outdoor air enters the home and needs to be heated or cooled.

The best way to evaluate duct leakage is with a portable calibrated fan known as a duct blower. Like a blower door, which is used to test the airtightness of a building shell, a duct blower measures how much leakage is present in the duct system. This indicates how much benefit could be derived from duct sealing, and can also be used to identify the locations of duct leaks.

Duct blower tests are performed either by energy auditors or heating and cooling contractors.

Duct Blower Test

An energy auditor uses a duct blower to measure air leakage in a duct system. The duct leakage test will show technicians how much leakage is present and where those leaks are apt to be located.

If you have a duct leakage test performed, you'll learn about the location and severity of leaks in your duct system. Many home-performance contractors will use the duct blower during the course of duct-sealing jobs to evaluate their progress and refine their efforts.

Sealing Your Duct System

Finding and sealing duct leaks is a reasonable project for a motivated homeowner who doesn't mind getting dirty. The primary difficulty is gaining access to your duct system. This project may require working in your crawl space or attic. But if it does, you will have a lot to gain since leaks in these un-conditioned areas are among the largest energy wasters in many homes.

Gather a basic kit of tools for this project. You should have a long-sleeved shirt, long pants, and sturdy shoes. Choose clothing that can get smeared with duct mastic—mastic sticks to everything and won't wash out. Buy a pair of disposable gloves, and a respirator to protect against dust. You'll need a sharp knife, a one- or two-inch putty knife, and some disposable brushes. *Warning: You may encounter hazards in your crawl space or attic that include live electrical wires, sharp sheet metal, live animals, or hazards not mentioned here. Do not attempt this work unless you are willing to assume some risks.*

Materials for Duct Sealing

Duct mastic is the preferred duct-sealing material because of its superior durability and adhesion. Apply it at least $1/16$ inch thick, and use reinforcing mesh for all joints wider than $1/8$ inch or those that may be subjected to movement. Do not use gray fabric "duct tape" to seal ducts since it fails when exposed to repeated heating and cooling.

Duct joints should be fastened with screws to prevent joint movement or separation. Tape should never be expected to hold a joint together.

Visit your home improvement store to buy duct mastic and fiber tape. A one-gallon bucket of mastic will be enough for most duct systems. If you expect to seal any holes in the air handler or furnace cabinet, buy a roll of self-adhesive metal duct tape. Use this removable tape anywhere that you may need to maintain access for future service.

Duct-Leakage Locations

Because the materials used to build ducts—sheet metal, fiberglass duct board, and insulated plastic flex ducts—are all effective air barriers, air leakage only occurs at joints, seams, and ruptures. This makes the process of discovering duct leaks fairly easy.

If you have had a duct blower test performed, you will have learned where the largest leaks are located. If not, you can still begin sealing your ducts. Oftentimes the gaps in your duct system will be obvious, and there is no harm in sealing any duct leaks, however small they may be.

The following is a list of duct-leak locations in order of their relative importance. The most wasteful duct leaks are the ones near the furnace, because the air pressure is greatest. Start your work there.

Furnace Cabinet Leaks in the air handler or furnace cabinet itself are the top air-sealing priority. Seal these with removable self-adhesive metal duct tape.

Plenum Joints at Air Handler These joints may have been difficult to fasten and seal because of tight access. Go the extra mile to seal them airtight with mastic and fabric mesh tape.

Sealing Ducts with Mastic and Fiber Tape

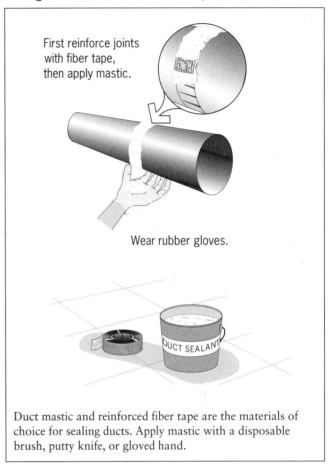

Duct mastic and reinforced fiber tape are the materials of choice for sealing ducts. Apply mastic with a disposable brush, putty knife, or gloved hand.

Fastening and Sealing Flex Duct

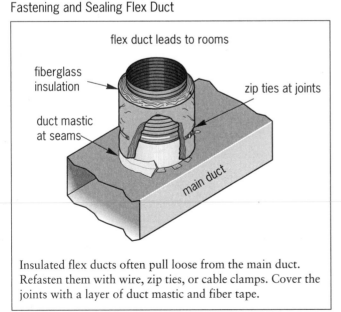

Insulated flex ducts often pull loose from the main duct. Refasten them with wire, zip ties, or cable clamps. Cover the joints with a layer of duct mastic and fiber tape.

Floor and Wall Cavities Used as Ducts

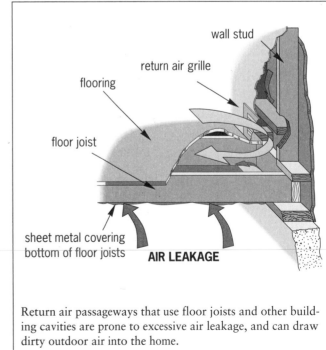

Return air passageways that use floor joists and other building cavities are prone to excessive air leakage, and can draw dirty outdoor air into the home.

Cavity Returns Mechanical contractors sometimes create return-air ducts by installing sheet metal or other materials across floor joists or wall studs. These "cavity returns" are usually quite leaky. If they are connected to the outdoors at the perimeter of the building, a significant percentage of their return air may come from outdoors. If you identify one of these cavity returns, seal the edges of the sheet metal to the wood framing as best you can. Or consider hiring a heating contractor to replace it with metal ductwork.

Joints at Branch Takeoffs These high-leakage joints, where room ducts meet the main duct, should be sealed with a thick layer of mastic.

Joints in Adjustable Elbows Seal these triangular metal sections, known as gores, with duct mastic.

Large Holes Seal holes larger than 1 inch with a metal patch screwed on with sheet metal screws. Cover the patch with mastic.

Tabbed Sleeves Attach the sleeve to the main duct with four to six screws and lay on the mastic.

Joints in Rectangular Main Ducts Run two or three screws into each joint to fasten the sections together. Run mastic and mesh tape around the joint.

Joints Between Flex Duct and Plenums Use wire, or a plastic wire tie, to clamp the flex duct inner liner to the metal boot. Cover the seam with mastic. Clamp the insulation and outer liner with another wire or tie.

Sealing and Insulating Ducts

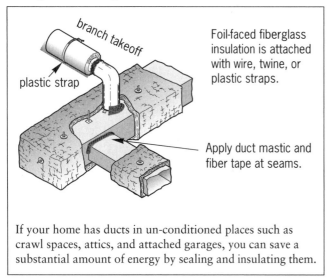

branch takeoff

plastic strap

Foil-faced fiberglass insulation is attached with wire, twine, or plastic straps.

Apply duct mastic and fiber tape at seams.

If your home has ducts in un-conditioned places such as crawl spaces, attics, and attached garages, you can save a substantial amount of energy by sealing and insulating them.

Installing Duct Insulation

Ducts should be well insulated if they are located anywhere outside the heated and cooled areas of the home, such as attics, under-floor crawl spaces, or garages.

Fiberglass duct insulation is the most common material, and is usually sold in R-6 and R-8 thicknesses. It should be stocked at any large home improvement store. Buy the thickest you can find.

Installing duct insulation is a reasonable do-it-yourself job. Follow these guidelines:

- Make each piece as large as possible to avoid seams.
- Cut carefully around obstacles to avoid gaps and voids. This is important to achieve a good overall R-value.
- Overlap the seams.
- Tape the seams with a high-quality tape, like aluminum foil tape or vinyl tape. The end of each piece of tape should point downward; if it faces upward, gravity will eventually pull it off.

Duct insulation that depends entirely on tape to hold it in place will eventually fall off. Fasten the insulation with twine, wire, or plastic cable ties.

HEATING SYSTEM REPLACEMENT

You should ideally improve your home's insulation and airtightness before buying a new heating system. We suggest upgrading your wall insulation to between R-21 and R-30 by installing 2 to 4 inches of foam insulation on your home's exterior, and improving your attic insulation to R-60, before deciding to replace your heating system.

But once you have improved your home's shell, you then have the option of installing a much smaller heating system. It's important to get the sequence correct: spend your money on the shell first, then ask your heating contractor to calculate how small a heating system you can then install to heat your newly improved home. If your current system has the common problem of undersized ductwork—resulting in too little airflow—your present duct system may be correctly sized once you have performed the combination of improving your building shell and installing a smaller heating system.

If you reduce the heat load enough, you may be able to heat your home with a small high-quality space heater that does not require a duct system. This will save energy by reducing the heat loss always associated with duct systems.

Choosing a New Gas Furnace

To estimate how much a new furnace can reduce your heating bills, look at the portion of your utility costs that you typically spend on heating. You can determine your heating cost by following the procedure described in *Analyzing Your Utility Bill* on page 8.

Then compare the efficiency of your existing furnace with that of your proposed new furnace. Your old furnace likely has an efficiency of about 65 percent. We recommend that you install a furnace of at least 90 percent efficiency, for a savings of about 25 percent on your heating costs.

The efficiency of furnaces is rated by their Annual Fuel Utilization Efficiency (AFUE). This information is posted on the furnace's Energy Guide Label.

If your furnace has no draft fan and an old-fashioned pilot light, you should consider replacing it. This type of open combustion furnace usually operates at about 65 percent AFUE. You'll have two efficiency choices when shopping for a new gas furnace:

Advanced Heat Exchangers

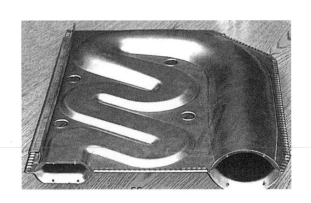

High-efficiency furnaces utilize light-weight stainless steel heat exchangers that extract more heat out of the flame and combustion gases. A fan pulls combustion gases through the restrictive passageways.

- An improved version of your existing furnace that has an AFUE of about 82 percent. This furnace is equipped with electronic ignition and a draft fan. We call this the 80+ furnace here.
- A condensing furnace that has an AFUE of more than 90 percent. This condensing furnace recovers extra heat from combustion gases by extracting water from the combustion gases with a special corrosion-resistant heat exchanger. We call this the 90+ furnace here.

Upgrading an older furnace to an 80+ furnace will save between 10 and 15 percent of your current heating costs. A 90+ furnace will save between 20 and 25 percent. Considering the small cost difference, the more expensive 90+ furnace is the better option at today's fuel prices. That advantage will only increase as fuel prices climb.

The 90+ furnace also offers very important safety advantages because it is normally installed so that it draws combustion air from outdoors. This type of installation is called sealed-combustion or direct-vent. Tell your contractor that you want your new 90+ furnace to be connected so it draws combustion air from outdoors.

Choosing a New Boiler

New high-efficiency gas boilers can save a lot of energy for customers in energy-efficient homes. However, your home must be heavily insulated and airtight to apply this technology successfully. Condensing boilers save energy by circulating lower-temperature water than conventional boilers. To use your existing radiators effectively, you must usually wrap the home in two or more inches of foam and have very efficient windows.

If you can't reinsulate your home but need to replace your current boiler, a condensing boiler might not be your best choice. An 80+ boiler is cheaper and more suitable for delivering water to your existing radiators at the current design water temperature. However, your existing boiler may already be pushing 80 percent AFUE, so the savings available from boiler replacement may not be much.

Radiant Floor Heating

Radiant floors offer unbeatable comfort, superior energy efficiency, and the ability to use a condensing boiler or hydronic heat pump to its full potential. Radiant floors require the relatively low water temperatures that condensing boilers and hydronic heat pumps can provide. Radiant tubing can be incorporated into traditional concrete slabs, thin masonry slabs, or all-wood floors.

Despite the obvious advantages of radiant heat, it is easy to spend too much money on complicated heating options and not enough on insulation. This often leads to unnecessarily large expenditures on new heating equipment without significant reductions in heating energy cost and carbon emissions.

Chimney Modifications

Replacing an old furnace with a new one can require additional changes that are often overlooked by both contractors and homeowners. Chimneys lead the list of neglected items. Many existing furnaces are oversized, especially once the home's shell is improved. When a new smaller heating system is installed, the existing chimney is often too large for a new 80+ furnace. An 80+ furnace often produces a smaller volume of combustion gases than the old furnace, and these gases are cooler. This may require the re-lining of the existing chimney, which adds significantly to the cost of the new furnace. But neglecting this upgrade could result in acidic condensation that deteriorates the chimney.

The 90+ furnace doesn't use a standard vertical chimney but instead employs plastic pipe for venting. Combustion air is drawn from outdoors through another dedicated plastic pipe. This venting system provides superior health-and-safety benefits, compared to furnaces that vent into vertical chimneys and draw their combustion air from indoors.

One common problem you may encounter when installing a new plastic-piped vent for a 90+ furnace is that it often leaves a gas water heater venting into an existing chimney that was originally sized to accommodate both a furnace and water heater. The old chimney may be far too large for the water heater by itself, requiring a smaller chimney liner or a new chimney that is sized for the water heater alone. If you install a new furnace, be sure your technician tests the chimney draft at your water heater to ensure that it is adequate to exhaust combustion products.

SPACE HEATERS AND ZONE HEATING

Space heaters are inherently more efficient than central heaters because they don't have ducts or pipes to distribute the heat. The distribution of heat through pipes and ducts typically wastes 10 to 35 percent of the heat.

In the energy crises of the 1970s and early 1980s, many homeowners curtailed their use of central heating in favor of more efficient space heating to save money. As energy prices rise, more homeowners will begin using space heaters once again.

One disadvantage to using a space heater is the temperature variations that occur during cold weather between areas near the space heater and areas further away. This effect can be minimized by adding more insulation and making the home more airtight. The best-insulated homes are easily and comfortably heated by one or several space heaters.

Electric Zone Heating

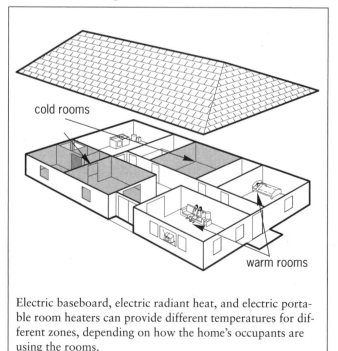

Electric baseboard, electric radiant heat, and electric portable room heaters can provide different temperatures for different zones, depending on how the home's occupants are using the rooms.

Zone Heating

We propose three home-zoning strategies for using electric space heaters. These strategies—by themselves or in combination—can reduce heating costs by 50 percent or more.

- Use a space heater that uses either gas or electricity to heat the core of the home. Allow the remainder of the home to be cooler. A portable electric space heater can easily heat a single room, and that may be sufficient when only a few people are home.
- Control the central heat with a programmable thermostat. Provide a comfortable temperature throughout the house during the main activity periods. Then program the thermostat to set back to a temperature of 50°F to 60°F at night and during low-activity periods. Consider installing electric radiant floor, a radiant panel, or heat lamp in the bathroom to provide comfort there.
- Install low-temperature electric radiant heating panels controlled by thermostats and ultrasonic occupancy sensors. The occupancy sensor won't allow heating unless the room is occupied. Radiant electric panels heat people directly, and gain efficiency because they produce heat quickly when turned on. Electric radiant heat saves at least 30 percent of the electricity used by electric convection heaters. This is probably the least expensive way to heat a superinsulated home.

Gas Space Heaters

Space heaters have no ductwork. Gas space heaters are very common in more temperate regions, but they also have an increasing role in super-efficient homes where small capacity is sufficient.

Space heaters can present safety problems, usually as a result of improper chimney function. The safest new space heaters draw outdoor air for combustion and have a sealed combustion chamber. This feature is called sealed-combustion or direct-vent. Space heaters that draw indoor air for combustion but use a fan to expel the combustion products are also safer than older models of gas space heaters. Unvented space heaters are dangerous, especially if you air-seal your home, and should be removed.

Old Gas Space Heaters   Most gas room heaters have efficiencies of between 60 percent and 75 percent. There are four common types of gas room heaters:

- Freestanding room heaters
- Floor furnaces
- Recessed wall furnaces
- Direct-vent wall furnaces

The first three models are older designs that may have obsolete safety controls. The oldest units may have no flame-safety device to shut the system off if the pilot light fails. These obsolete units should be replaced or retrofitted with modern combination gas valves equipped with flame-safety controls.

Room heaters with draft or combustion problems are particularly dangerous because they are located within the living space. Floor furnaces in particular often have backdrafting problems. This is due to their typical location in the middle of the room. They require a long horizontal vent connector, prone to poor draft, to reach the chimney that is always located at the edge of the room. All existing gas room heaters should be tested for CO and draft to ensure that they don't pose an immediate danger.

New Efficient Gas Space Heaters   The newest energy-efficient gas room heaters look very similar to the older models. However, they incorporate a variety of improvements to achieve efficiencies of 78 to 82 percent:

- Lighter metal heat exchangers
- Blowers to circulate room air
- Fan-controlled venting of combustion gases
- Intermittent pilot lights

The safest and most efficient models also have a power-draft blower and sealed combustion chamber.

Decorative Gas Stoves and Fireplaces   Gas-burning decorative stoves and fireplace inserts are very popular. They are valued for their visual appeal, but their annual fuel-utilization efficiencies are only 30 to 70 percent so they have no role in efficient homes.

Gas decorative stoves are more efficient than gas fireplaces. However, they are only a little more efficient than gas space heaters built eighty years ago.

Fireplace inserts, consisting of a ceramic log and gas burner inserted into a standard fireplace, are often both dangerous and inefficient. The fireplace's chimney draft is unpredictable, because it is a custom-built assembly. A vacuum in the home—caused by exhaust fans or other gas appliances—can easily backdraft the fireplace, polluting the home. None of the products mentioned in this section is appropriate for installation in an energy-efficient home.

Unvented Space Heaters

Unvented space heaters burn natural gas, propane, or kerosene to heat an individual room or a small home.

Unvented space heaters don't have a chimney, so they release all their combustion by-products into the home. These gases include carbon dioxide, carbon monoxide, water vapor, and other pollutants.

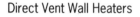

Direct Vent Wall Heaters

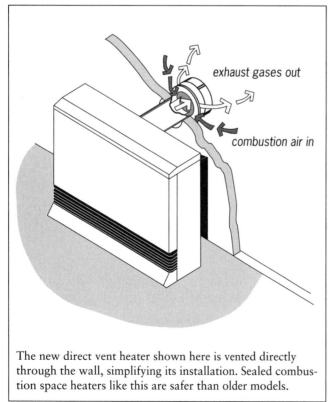

exhaust gases out

combustion air in

The new direct vent heater shown here is vented directly through the wall, simplifying its installation. Sealed combustion space heaters like this are safer than older models.

Carbon monoxide is of special concern, because high levels of this poisonous gas can cause injury or death. Unvented space heaters don't always produce carbon monoxide and other pollutants, but it is difficult to know how safely they are operating without testing them with a carbon monoxide detector. If your home has an un-vented space heater, you should, at a minimum, provide some protection to your family by installing a carbon monoxide alarm near the space heater.

The water vapor released by unvented space heaters can also contribute to moisture problems in the home, encouraging mold, mildew, and rot. This can cause respiratory ailments such as allergies and asthma, and it can deteriorate your home.

If you have an unvented space heater, consider replacing it with one of the new sealed-combustion space heaters. These power-vented wall units draw fresh air from the outdoors, and exhaust their combustion gases outside.

Pellet Stoves

Pellet stoves are making a strong comeback in response to higher fossil fuel costs. These stoves burn pelletized cellulose waste, which is more uniform and drier than average wood, giving these stoves an efficiency advantage. Pellet stoves are available as freestanding stoves or as fireplace inserts. All pellet stoves are fed automatically from internal storage containers holding from 40 to 100 pounds of pellets.

Pellet stoves have draft inducers that control draft and combustion air more precisely than wood stoves' atmospheric draft, making the pellet stove safer than a wood stove. Select a pellet stove that uses outdoor air for combustion. These stoves may also be described as sealed-combustion or direct-vent.

Wood Stoves and Fireplace Inserts

Wood stoves burn wood much more efficiently than fireplaces, by moving the fire into the center of the room and surrounding the firebox with room air. Air traveling through the combustion chamber is roughly controlled by a manual damper. Fireplace inserts are now designed to push more of the fire's heat out into the room.

The U.S. Environmental Protection Agency (EPA) and Canadian Standards Association (CSA) establish air pollution limits that have also boosted the efficiency of manufactured wood stoves and fireplace inserts. Look for a stove or insert rated as low-emission by the EPA and CSA. The new efficient wood stoves and inserts reduce emissions from 40 to 80 grams per hour to 2 to 5 grams. There is a similar reduction in heat waste up the chimney and creosote deposited in the chimney.

The habits of wood-burning users can greatly affect the emissions and efficiency of wood burning. Hot fires pollute less and are more efficient than smoldering fires. It's important to get the right size wood stove. If your stove is too large for your home and climate, you'll need to adjust the air intake to create a smoldering fire to keep from overheating your home. Unfortunately, smoldering fires use wood inefficiently and release more air pollutants.

If you plan to insulate your home to a high thermal resistance and to increase airtightness, wood heat is a poor choice because its typically large heat output, which is difficult to control, may easily overheat a home or lead the homeowner to smolder the fire. Wood stoves may also have problems obtaining enough combustion air and drafting properly in relatively airtight homes.

HEATING SYSTEMS OF THE FUTURE

The most interesting developments in heating systems are in integrated space and water heating systems and smaller, simpler heating systems for energy-efficient homes. Energy-efficient homes need whole-house ventilation systems, as discussed in *Ventilation Systems* on page 156. It makes sense to combine your home's heating and cooling systems with the ventilation system.

European manufacturers already produce these combined appliances. Canadian researchers are developing similar equipment. These systems include some or all of these functions:

Safe Wood Stove Installation

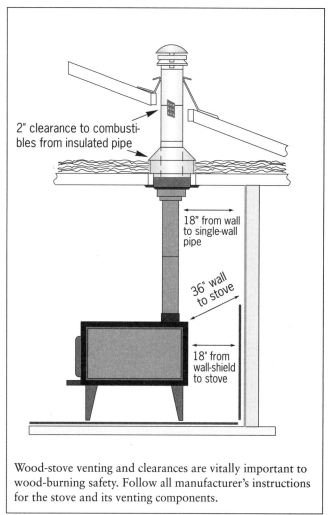

2" clearance to combustibles from insulated pipe

18" from wall to single-wall pipe

36" wall to stove

18" from wall-shield to stove

Wood-stove venting and clearances are vitally important to wood-burning safety. Follow all manufacturer's instructions for the stove and its venting components.

- An exhaust fan collects pollutants and discharges the air outdoors.
- A heat recovery ventilator (HRV) recovers some heat from the exhaust air, and transfers it to incoming fresh air.
- A heat pump extracts additional heat out of the exhaust air and imparts the heat through a heat exchanger to water in a storage tank.
- Incoming fresh air is heated as needed by a heat exchanger loop in the storage tank.
- Active solar heat is added to the storage tank through a heat exchanger.
- Electric auxiliary heat is added to the storage tank during high-demand periods.
- Domestic hot water is drawn directly out of the storage tank.

The Future of Combustion Appliances

The standard sizes for residential furnaces and boilers range from about 45,000 to 150,000 BTU per hour. What we need now is a new generation of heating systems with capacities in the range of 7,000 to 25,000 BTU per hour. These smaller systems will allow designers to fine-tune the heating systems for the next generation of efficient homes.

THE BOTTOM LINE

With fuel costs rising, heating improvements are always an excellent investment. But be sure to also consider ways to improve the efficiency of your home's building shell—such as upgrading insulation and doing air-sealing work—so your home won't need as much heat in the first place.

Professional Heating System Service

- Clean the furnace's combustion chamber and blower compartment if necessary.
- Confirm that the chimney removes combustion gases from the home under all conditions. Perform a carbon monoxide test and remedy the causes of carbon monoxide if present.

- Test the combustion efficiency, and adjust as needed.
- Inspect the duct system and seal any holes or cracks in ducts located in attics, crawl spaces, and attached garages as needed with high-quality duct mastic or metallic tape. You may choose to do this task yourself.

Buying and Installing a New Furnace

- Ask your heating contractor to select a furnace with an ENERGY STAR label. This new furnace should have an efficiency rating (AFUE) of greater than 90 percent, and it should have a sealed combustion chamber.
- Be sure your furnace is sized correctly to the house heating load. This sizing should account for any improvements you've made to the building shell, which may mean your new furnace can have a smaller capacity than your old one.
- Confirm that your chimney is sized correctly for the new system. Upgrade the chimney if needed.
- Test the duct system and seal any air leaks. Insulate the duct system if it is located in an attic or crawl space.

11 Photovoltaic Systems

Photovoltaic systems produce electricity from sunlight. This electricity can be used to operate the lights, appliances, and electronics in your home that normally consume electricity from the power grid. Photovoltaic (PV) systems have been used in homes and business for years, but are enjoying a resurgence in popularity due to technical advances in equipment, financial incentives, and increasing utility costs.

Photovoltaic systems embody two important characteristics: distributed generation and renewable energy. Distributed generation systems are located closer to the end user, and so incur fewer transmission losses than centralized power plants. Distributed systems are also less subject to system-wide outages than central systems. Renewable energy sources such as photovoltaic power utilize unlimited sources of energy rather than finite fuels such as coal, oil, and gas. Renewable energy sources are less subject to price fluctuations than non-renewables, and they also have a smaller environmental impact.

In this chapter we show how to evaluate your site for solar power, an analysis that will apply to both PV and solar hot water systems. We also explain how photovoltaic systems work and analyze the economics of installing PV systems.

EVALUATE YOUR HOME'S PV POTENTIAL

Have you improved the insulation in your home to the maximum possible extent? Your best conservation investment is to improve the thermal efficiency of your home. Invest in insulation and other shell improvements that have a short payback before making a long-term investment in photovoltaics.

Do you have a heating system that is powered by combustion fuels such as gas or oil rather then electricity? Electrically heated homes require more electrical

energy than can be provided by economically sized photovoltaic systems. If you have an electrically heated home, a better investment would be in switching your heat source from electricity to natural gas or solar thermal heat.

Does your combustion heating system operate at 90 percent efficiency or higher? If your home is heated by an older low-efficiency furnace or boiler, you should invest in its upgrade before installing a photovoltaic system.

Have you trimmed your annual electrical consumption to 2500 kilowatt-hours per person or less? Your investment in baseload conservation measures that reduce your electrical consumption will pay off by allowing you to install a smaller photovoltaic system.

Does your homesite receive sunlight for most of the day? Not every homesite is appropriate for the installation of a photovoltaic system. To get the best production from photovoltaics, you should have mostly un-obstructed access to the sun from 9 a.m. to 3 p.m.

Does your utility company or local government offer incentives for installing photovoltaic systems? Financial incentives that total up to half the cost of typical photovoltaic systems are available in many areas. These make the economics of photovoltaic power very attractive.

A PERSPECTIVE ON PV SYSTEMS

Since photovoltaic systems are relatively expensive and have a long payback of ten to thirty years, you should always spend your first home improvement dollars on simple conservation measures. These might include installing compact fluorescent lamps, upgrading the insulation in your attic, sealing air leaks, or replacing older inefficient appliances. These measures will reduce your electric load at a lower cost than installing a PV system, and some of them will also improve the comfort of your home. Once you've reduced your electrical load as much as possible with these basic improvements, it makes sense to consider a long-term investment in a PV system.

For families or business owners who want to reduce their environmental impact, PV power can be an important component of a personal energy plan. The average family in the U.S. today consumes about 11,000 kilowatt-hours (kWh) of electricity per year, though many get by comfortably on less than 5000 kWh. A modestly sized PV system can produce 2000 to 3000 kilowatt-hours of electricity per year, eliminating carbon dioxide emissions equal to driving about 10,000 miles in a typical automobile. Every PV system we install brings us closer to a sustainable energy future by reducing our dependence on both domestic and foreign nonrenewable sources of energy.

Some homeowners install photovoltaic (PV) systems because their buildings are located in remote areas beyond the reach of power lines. In these off-grid applications, the PV system may include batteries or a generator to provide electricity when the sun isn't shining. One advantage of these off-grid PV systems is that they allow property owners to avoid the cost of extending electric lines to their site.

But many consumers who are located within the service territory of an electric utility still invest in PV power. In these cases, the PV system is often connected to the electric grid. These grid-tied systems feed excess PV power into the grid when the system's production is greater than occupants' consumption, as during sunny weather. They draw power from the grid when the system's production is less than the consumption, such as at night and during cloudy weather.

Grid-tied systems are usually net-metered, with electric meters that record electricity going both into and out of the home. Many utility companies offer net metering agreements that compensate owners of qualified PV systems for power that is fed back into the electric grid.

PHOTOVOLTAIC ECONOMICS

Photovoltaic systems require a substantial economic investment, with the typical systems costing $15,000 to $30,000 before any incentives are applied. Over the life of the system, you'll pay about 25 cents per kilowatt-hour of electricity produced, compared to about 10 to 20 cents per kilowatt-hour for electricity currently purchased from North American utility companies. But as the cost of retail electricity increases, the financial return on photovoltaic systems will improve.

Fortunately, there are some incentives available for the installation of PV systems. Several utility companies offer grants to cover up to 50 percent of the cost of residential and/or commercial renewable energy systems. The Internal Revenue Service provides income tax credits for some PV installations, and many state governments and utility companies offer similar inducements. These incentives help bring the cost of PV systems within the reach of many building owners. And the financial viability of your PV system will improve in the future as electric costs inevitably increase.

Photovoltaic System Components

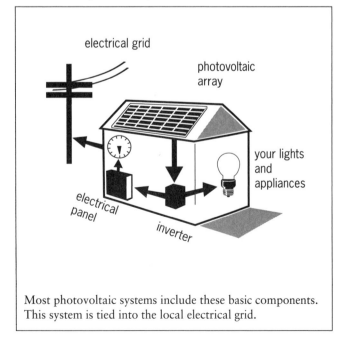

Most photovoltaic systems include these basic components. This system is tied into the local electrical grid.

PHOTOVOLTAIC POWER COMPONENTS

Solar cells are the smallest building blocks of photovoltaic systems. These silicon-based semiconductors utilize the reaction of sunlight within the cell to create an electrical current. Each cell produces a few watts of direct current (DC) electricity.

Photovoltaic modules include groups of solar cells that are electrically interconnected and mounted in lightweight frames. Modules are usually covered with glass and backed with a polymer or glass sheet that protects the cells from the elements. These modules are the basic PV components sold by most manufacturers. Typical modules produced for residential and light commercial installations produce 50 to 200 watts of power.

Solar arrays are the groups of these modules you see installed on the roofs of buildings or on ground-mounted racks. The electrical output of an array, usually measured in watts, is determined by how many modules it contains and the wattage of the individual modules.

Types of Solar Cells

The most common type of solar cells used in today's PV systems are crystalline solar cells. They are sliced into thin wafers several thousandths of an inch thick and a few inches long. You'll see these individual cells if you look closely at most solar panels. Among the various types of solar cells, crystalline cells convert sunlight to electricity the most efficiently, reducing the area needed for a given output. But their manufacturing cost is also the highest, requiring designers to balance the advantages of smaller area with cost.

Solar cells are also manufactured as thin-film materials, made by depositing a thin layer of PV material onto glass, plastic, or metal foil. The film is usually less than one ten-thousandth of an inch thick. Thin film materials can be integrated into building materials such as roof shingles. Thin film cells are less expensive per square foot than crystalline cells, though they require more area to achieve the same output.

Crystalline Solar Cells

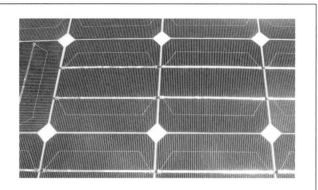

This most common type of solar cell is sliced into wafers that are interconnected and assembled into modules.

Integrated Inverter and Controller

This inverter/controller converts direct current to alternating current, controls the charging of a bank of batteries, and manages a net metering connection with the electrical grid.

Inverters

Solar cells produce direct current, which can be used immediately for some applications. Solar-powered calculators and battery chargers, for example, consume direct current (DC) power, and several manufacturers make DC refrigerators and other equipment for off-grid DC systems. But almost all the lights, appliances, and equipment in modern homes use the alternating current (AC) that is supplied by the electrical grid.

Inverters are electronic devices that convert DC power into AC power. If you intend to use your PV electricity to power your home's existing equipment, your system will require an inverter. An inverter is also necessary if you plan to connect your PV system to the utility grid. The majority of PV systems installed today utilize an inverter.

Inverters are specified by their capacity in kilowatts (this should meet or exceed the peak output of the array), and according to their output voltage (usually 120–240 volts AC). Inverters can convert input voltages of up to 600 volts from the PV array down to the 120–240 volts output needed by most equipment.

Most inverters also include relays and circuit breakers that manage the task of safely connecting your solar array to your home's existing electrical system and to the utility grid. They usually include a DC ground-fault circuit interrupter (GFCI) that disconnects the PV array if wiring defects are detected.

Backup Systems

Photovoltaic systems generate power only when the sun strikes the array. Backup systems provide an uninterrupted supply of solar electricity at night, during overcast weather, or during power failures.

If you install a stand-alone or off-grid system, you'll probably want to install a backup system that includes batteries, a gas-powered generator, or both. You'll also need an inverter that can manage the charging of your batteries and can start your generator when it's needed.

If you install a grid-tied system, you may not need a backup system, since you can usually rely on the grid to provide power when your PV system produces less power than you need.

Batteries

Open-cell lead-acid batteries are most commonly used for PV backup systems because they provide the best ratio of storage capacity per dollar of cost. These are similar to the open-cell batteries used in automotive applications. But PV batteries are designed for deep-cycle applications, rather than the brief load experienced when starting a vehicle, and so aren't damaged by the deep cycling—from fully charged to completely drained—common to backup systems. Open-cell batteries do require periodic maintenance to replace water lost to evaporation. Sealed batteries, though more expensive, are better where low-maintenance equipment is needed, such as in remote locations.

The installation and maintenance of a battery bank adds a considerable expense to a PV system. If you need to power only a stock-tank pump or office lights, for example, you may be able to utilize the daytime-only power produced by a system with no batteries. But most PV systems include either a battery bank, a backup generator, or a connection to the utility grid.

Battery Bank and Ventilated Enclosure

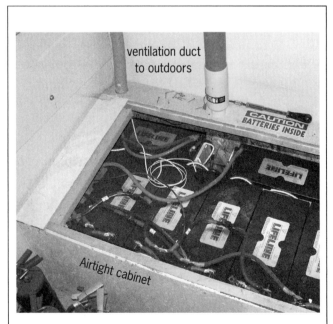

The open-cell batteries shown here are configured to match the 240 volts delivered by the grid. The cabinet is ventilated by a low-voltage fan that moves potentially explosive hydrogen gas to the outdoors.

Series and Parallel Wiring Configurations

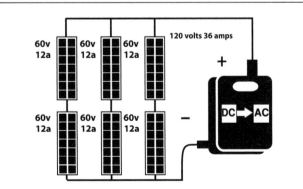

Modules are combined in *series* strings to produce higher voltage. In this drawing, each group of two 60-volt (60v) modules produces 120 volts. Modules are wired in *parallel* to produce higher amperage. In this drawing, the three series strings each produce 12 amps (12a), for a total of 36 amps.

SOLAR SITE ASSESSMENT

Some sites are better than others for producing photovoltaic power. The size and orientation of your home, the presence of shade, and possible zoning restrictions all affect the viability of PV systems for your site.

Photovoltaic systems are most commonly installed on the roofs of homes, garages, carports, and other structures. But they can also be installed vertically against a wall of your home, as part of an awning, or near the ground as a free-standing structure.

A preliminary site assessment will help you identify whether there are major obstacles to overcome. The information you'll gather in this process will be useful whether you plan to do the work yourself or hire a professional installer. And much of what you'll learn in this assessment, such as the effect of shading on your home, will tell you whether other solar thermal technologies, such as solar water heating and passive space heating, are viable options for you.

Access to the Sun

Your PV system will produce the most power when exposed to the longest solar window (shade-free sun) available at your site. A perfect solar window with no shadows all day allows 100 percent of the potential solar energy to strike your array. Any shading, as from trees or an adjoining building, will reduce your system's output from what it would be at this optimum exposure.

For the best performance your site should have an unobstructed solar window in the middle of the day. But a little shade is acceptable, especially if it crosses your array early or late in the day. An hour of shade at 8:00 a.m. will reduce your system's output a lot less than an hour of shade at 1:00 p.m.

Shade has a large effect on the PV output because of the series or parallel configuration in which solar cells are combined in the modules. A small strip of shade along the side of one module can reduce its output to zero since the shaded cells create resistance to the flow of current from the other cells in that module. In some configurations, an array that is shaded over 10 percent of its area could lose 80 percent of its output for as long as the shade persists.

Unobstructed Solar Window

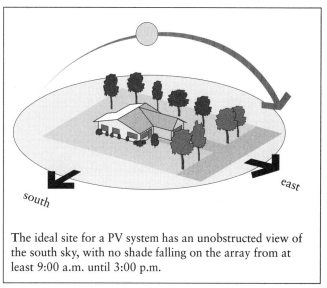

The ideal site for a PV system has an unobstructed view of the south sky, with no shade falling on the array from at least 9:00 a.m. until 3:00 p.m.

Shading issues are most apt to occur in the winter when the sun's altitude is lowest and shadows are the longest. You may be able to tolerate the shadow of an adjoining building, for example, if it only passes over one corner of your array for a few months in winter.

Solutions to Shade

If the site where you'll install your array receives some shade, you have three options to address its effects:

- Eliminate the shade by trimming the tree or moving the chimney.
- Move the array elsewhere, such as to a garage, patio cover, or barn.
- Increase the size of the array to make up for the impaired production.

Rooftop Versus Ground Installation

Your analysis of the sun's path across your site will give you a better idea of the best place to locate your array of PV modules.

For many building owners, the roof is the preferred site for a PV array because it's out of the way, close to the existing electrical system, and above many objects that cast shade. Most rooftop systems are mounted on racks that stand above the roof. These racks can hold modules at either the same slope as the roof surface, or at a steeper angle that optimizes the exposure to incoming solar energy. Rooftop systems can also utilize solar "shingles," thin-film modules that take the place of standard roofing shingles.

Ground-mounted systems have the advantage of easy and safe access, and, on some sites, more available room.

Rooftop Installation Considerations

Your site assessment should address these issues if you plan to mount a PV array on your roof:

- *What is the condition of your current roof?* If your roof will be ready for replacement within the next five or ten years, consider replacing the roofing before installing the array.
- *What type of roofing material is installed on your building?* Wood and tile roofs can be difficult to seal, for example, where the array's support rack penetrates the roof.
- *Are there chimneys and other utility penetrations that break up the space?* If you'll install the modules around obstructions, consider if those objects will cast shade on the array.
- *Which face of your roof has the best exposure?* You'll get the best performance when your array faces solar south, though you may be able to utilize east or west faces if you can accept diminished output.
- *How much room will PV installers and other workers need to work around the array?* Be sure workers have a safe walkway at the edges of the roof.
- *Do you plan to install new equipment in the future on your roof, such as a satellite dish or air conditioner?* You should avoid filling your entire roof with a PV system.
- *Do local zoning or building regulations limit the height or appearance of buildings?* You can limit these impacts by installing your array close to the pitch of your roof, or by choosing a roof face that is out of view.

Solar Module Space Requirements

Crystalline Silicone Cells require 100 to 150 square feet per kilowatt of output, so a typical two-kilowatt system will cover 200 to 300 square feet.

Thin Film Cells require 170 to 300 square feet per kilowatt of output, so a typical two-kilowatt system will cover 340 to 600 square feet.

Rooftop Solar Array

This solar array is installed to match the pitch of the roof. This simplifies the installation, compared to installing the modules on a sloped rack, and it minimizes wind load on the mounting system. The trade-off, on this low-slope 4-in-12-pitch roof, is a lower output in the winter when the sun is low in the sky.

Ground-Mount Considerations

If you mount a PV array on the ground, you should consider a different set of issues:

- *How far will the array be from the edge of your property? How high will it be?* Local ordinances or zoning regulations often control these dimensions.
- *Will the array be subject to vandalism?* This is a much greater issue for ground-mounted installations than for roof mounting.
- *Will you need to excavate for mounting racks or underground wiring?* Be sure to locate any underground utility lines before digging.

Describing Tilt Angles

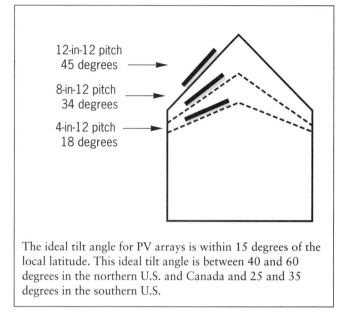

12-in-12 pitch
45 degrees

8-in-12 pitch
34 degrees

4-in-12 pitch
18 degrees

The ideal tilt angle for PV arrays is within 15 degrees of the local latitude. This ideal tilt angle is between 40 and 60 degrees in the northern U.S. and Canada and 25 and 35 degrees in the southern U.S.

Ground-Mounted Solar Array

This solar array takes advantage of a large south-facing yard. This installation solves the problem of a house roof that has no south-facing planes.

Options in Mounting Racks

Your choice in mounting racks will determine how closely your array is aligned with the sun throughout the day and across the seasons. Your array will produce the most power if it faces the sun directly at all times. This is difficult in practice since the sun crosses the sky from east to west each day, and the sun's path varies in distance above the horizon throughout the year.

Azimuth describes the sun's location on a horizontal plane that runs east and west. The sun's azimuth changes from morning to night as it rises in the east, crosses solar south, and sets in the west.

Altitude describes the sun's location in a vertical plane above the horizon. The sun's altitude above the horizon varies throughout the day as it rises from the horizon, passes high in the sky, and descends again to the horizon. Its altitude also varies throughout the year. In the northern hemisphere, you'll see it at its highest altitude on June 21, the summer solstice. Its lowest altitude will be on December 21, the winter solstice.

Your mounting rack will also affect the outward appearance of the array. A fixed rack will be the least obtrusive, especially if it's mounted parallel to the roof surface. Tracking arrays take up additional space, and are usually used in ground-mount installations.

Fixed Mounting Rack

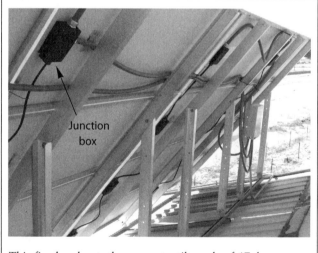

Junction box

This fixed rack sets the array at a tilt angle of 47 degrees, matching the site's latitude. Waterproof flexible conduit connects the modules to one another.

Fixed Racks Fixed racks are the cheapest, strongest, and most common choice, especially for rooftop installations where space is at a premium. They hold the modules in an unchangeable orientation, usually facing an azimuth of 180 degrees, or due south. Their tilt, or altitude, can be set parallel to the roof surface on which they're mounted for the easiest installation. But on low-pitch roofs they are often raised above the roof angle to optimize output.

Manually Adjustable Racks Racks that are manually adjustable can be changed throughout the year to follow the sun's changing altitude. Their azimuth is usually fixed at due south. If adjusted faithfully—perhaps four times per year—they can increase the annual system output by 10 to 12 percent when compared to fixed-rack systems. This benefit must be weighed against the adjustable rack's increased cost and space requirements.

Single-Axis Trackers Single-axis trackers rotate east to west following the sun's daily path. Their altitude remains fixed throughout the year. Their motion is driven by either a small motor that is guided by a sun-seeking photocell, or by a passive gas-charge system in which a canister of refrigerant is heated by the sun and expands or contracts to move the array. Single-axis tracking systems can increase annual output by up to 25 percent over fixed racks.

Dual-Axis Trackers Dual-axis trackers follow both the sun's altitude and azimuth throughout the day and year. These most complicated systems can produce up to 30 percent more energy than fixed-rack systems.

COSTS AND BENEFITS OF PHOTOVOLTAIC SYSTEMS

The size of your investment in photovoltaic power will depend primarily upon the output of your system. This peak output is usually measured in watts. Residential systems can range from one to five thousand watts (one to five kilowatts), while commercial systems range up to thirty kilowatts or more.

Your Initial Investment

The typical installed cost for PV systems, including labor and materials, varies from $8 to $10 per watt. For a typical 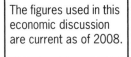 two-kilowatt (2 kw) system, the total cost is usually about $15,000 to $20,000. This base cost is for grid-tied systems with no battery storage or other backup system. Your cost will vary depending on the ease of access to your site, whether you choose to install a

The figures used in this economic discussion are current as of 2008.

backup system, your choice of mounting racks, whether you install PV shingles or other architectural array options, and other factors.

Expected Power Production

The electrical power generated by a typical two-kilowatt system is usually about 2500 to 3000 kilowatt-hours per year. The value of the energy produced by your system will vary depending on the cost of electricity in your area.

The average household in the United States uses about 11,000 kilowatt-hours of electricity per year. Thus this example two-kilowatt system can be expected to produce about 25 to 30 percent of a typical household's needs. Families who have already improved the efficiency of their homes will find that a PV system can meet a larger portion of their electrical needs.

Equipment Lifespan

Modern PV systems have proven to be very long-lasting. The solar modules which make up about half the cost of most systems and can be expected to have a lifespan of 25 years or more, though their output tends to deteriorate about 1 percent per year. Inverters, which make up less than a quarter of the cost of most systems, should last just as long, though like all electronic devices, they may sometimes fail prematurely. The remainder of the system—mounting racks, wiring, and disconnect equipment—should last as long as the building that they are mounted on.

Predicting PV Output

Given that probable lifespan, much of the burden of determining whether a PV system investment makes sense becomes an estimation of its annual output. One of the easiest ways to predict your system's annual output is with an online calculator called PVWatts. The PVWatts website, hosted by the National Renewable Energy Lab, includes a simple calculator that allows you to predict how much energy your planned system will produce, as measured in either kilowatt-hours of electricity or in dollars' worth of savings.

The PVWatts program can produce an approximate estimate of your system's output with just two factors: your location, and the peak output of your system's modules.

The rough calculation you'll make with this information can give you an idea of your site's PV potential. But as you learn more about your system, you can fine-tune your PVWatts calculation by including other factors:

- Whether your array tracks the sun's path.
- The direction your collectors will face in relation to solar south.
- The tilt of your collectors in relation to your latitude.
- The losses inherent in your system's inverter and wiring.
- The cost of the grid-provided electricity your system will replace.

See the *Resources* on page 173 for more information about the PVWatts calculator and other solar design tools.

GRID-TIED PV SYSTEMS

Many utility companies allow their customers to connect properly installed photovoltaic systems onto the existing electrical grid. These grid-tied systems can feed excess PV power back into the power grid any time the customer uses less power than the PV system produces. This is typically during the day when the sun is out and the occupants aren't home or have minimal demands. These systems then draw power back from the utility grid when the customer consumes more than the PV system produces, such as during cloudy weather, at night, or when the system is out of operation.

Grid-tied systems do not require batteries, making them the most economical and popular type of PV system, though batteries can be included to provide service if the electric grid fails.

Net Metering

The net meter plugs into the standard meter-base on your electrical panel. The net meter measures current flow both into and out of your home, and so registers your net electrical consumption.

Net Metering Agreements

If you have a grid-tied PV system, you may be eligible for a net-metering agreement with your utility company. Net metering allows you to benefit from the excess power your system feeds into the electric grid. With net metering, you can effectively "bank" your power for later use without the use of batteries. Your utility company will credit your account at retail rates for the excess power you produce.

WORKING WITH PV INSTALLERS

Almost all photovoltaic systems are installed by electrical contractors. Your understanding of PV basics will help you choose a competent contractor and effectively supervise their work. This is the best approach unless you have a lot of expertise with complicated electrical installations.

Finding a Contractor

Do some research before you hire a contractor to install your system. Ask for written proposals from contractors who bid for your job. Be sure that each is bidding on the same size and type of system. If the bids don't specify similar details, you may need to go back and ask for adjustments so you can make an accurate comparison.

Don't buy on price alone. Evaluate your contractor based on her entire proposal, and be sure to ask some specific questions:

- How long has the contractor been in business?
- Has the contractor installed PV systems before? Have you contacted previous customers?
- Does the contractor have a valid electrical contractor's license? Does he have any industry PV certifications?
- Has the contractor provided a rough estimate of the power the system will produce?
- Will the contractor apply for the proper permits?
- Will the contractor provide an installation warranty that goes beyond the equipment manufacturer's warranty?

THE BOTTOM LINE

Solar energy can be an appealing solution to your electrical needs. But if your home is built to typical current standards, you'll see a much more favorable payback for improved insulation, tighter air-sealing, and the purchase of efficient appliances. Once you make these improvements, and your home is at the pinnacle of efficiency, a photovoltaic system can be an important next step toward crafting a home that uses no net electrical energy from the grid.

- Focus your first conservation dollars on reducing your home's consumption for heating, cooling, and water heating.
- Trim your baseload electrical consumption to the bare minimum. If you use less than 2500 kilowatt-hours annually for each person in your family, you have done a good job of conserving electricity, and should consider installing a photovoltaic system.
- Evaluate your homesite's potential for solar power by considering climate, shade, and the presence of a good place to mount solar panels.
- Contact your utility company and state energy office to learn if financial incentives are available for photovoltaic systems.
- Work with an experienced PV contractor to design and install a high-quality system that will be long-lived and trouble-free.

12 Moisture Management and Ventilation

Your home should be a healthy and safe place to live. Over the course of a lifetime, most of us spend more time in our homes than anywhere else. Your well-being will depend in part on how you manage your home environment.

When excess moisture accumulates in your home, it can cause health problems, deteriorate building materials, and increase your energy consumption. The management techniques we describe in the first part of this chapter can help you keep moisture under control.

Most homes are ventilated by air leakage, with help from kitchen and bath exhaust fans. But air leakage isn't a reliable or efficient way to control moisture in your home since it provides excessive ventilation during severe weather and inadequate ventilation during mild weather. The best way to maintain good indoor air quality is with a whole-house ventilation system that provides fresh air when and where it's needed. We describe ventilation systems in the second part of this chapter.

EVALUATE YOUR HOME'S MOISTURE MANAGEMENT AND VENTILATION

Do you have problems with mold or mildew in your home? You can often control these problems by managing moisture in and around your home.

Do you have exhaust fans installed in your kitchen and bathrooms? Exhaust fans are an important first line of defense against moisture and odors in the home. They become even more important as you improve the efficiency and airtightness of your home.

Does your home have a dirt-floored crawl space or basement? The ground under your home is often the largest source of moisture in your home.

Does runoff from rain or snowmelt ever puddle against your home's foundation? This water can seep into your home and cause moisture problems.

Does your home have any plumbing or roof leaks? These sources of moisture are easy to control. Give roof and plumbing repair your highest priority.

Does your home have odors and high relative humidity? Your home may be fairly airtight and may need a whole-house ventilation system to provide good indoor air quality.

MOISTURE BASICS

Excess moisture is a problem in many modern homes. Airborne water vapor isn't a problem by itself. But when the water vapor condenses to liquid water, this condensation can cause a number of problems.

- Wet homes are not healthy. Excess moisture encourages the growth of mold, mildew, fungus, and other biological contaminants. These "biocontaminants" thrive in warm, dark, moist environments such as building cavities. Biocontaminants are responsible for a range of human health problems such as allergies and asthma. Many people have strong responses to these organisms, with effects ranging from annoying sniffles to dangerous asthmatic attacks.

- Wet homes are not durable. Wet building materials may support termites, carpenter ants, and other insects. Water rusts metal building components, leaches cement out of masonry walls, and damages building materials if it freezes in cold weather. Your home will last longer if it is dry.

- Excess moisture increases energy consumption. When moisture condenses in your home's insulation, heat can travel through the insulation more easily. And both heating systems and cooling systems use extra energy when they must dry out your home. During the heating season, the air that is warmed by your furnace causes excess moisture in your home to evaporate, cooling the air and requiring more heating. During the cooling season, the cold evaporator coil in your air conditioner causes water to condense out of the indoor air that circulates through it. This process of condensation releases heat, which causes your cooling system to run longer. Your heating and cooling systems use more energy when they must dry out your home.

Measuring Moisture

Airborne moisture is measured in percent relative humidity (RH). Air at 0 percent relative humidity contains no water vapor. Air at 100 percent relative humidity is totally saturated with water vapor. Saturated air causes condensation when it flows near cool surfaces.

The tiny water droplets that coat the walls and ceiling of a bathroom after you shower are the result of the room air reaching 100 percent relative humidity. The bathroom's cool walls and ceiling provide condensing surfaces where water vapor becomes liquid water.

Vapor Migration in Building Cavities

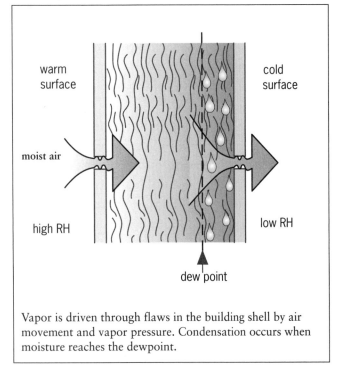

Vapor is driven through flaws in the building shell by air movement and vapor pressure. Condensation occurs when moisture reaches the dewpoint.

All homes contain condensing surfaces that are hidden within the walls, in the attic and crawl space, and around carpet, wallpaper, and furnishings. Water vapor travels to these hidden areas driven by differences in air pressure or humidity. Your home's relative humidity is an important determinant of how much moisture condenses.

Most authorities agree that an indoor relative humidity of 45 to 65 percent is best. Relative humidity lower than this range is normal in drier regions. Low relative humidity can cause uncomfortably dry skin in some people. High relative humidity encourages moisture condensation. If you're curious about the relative humidity in your home, we recommend that you purchase a simple hygrometer, or moisture meter, to monitor your home's relative humidity. If the relative humidity is too high, you can take steps to counteract it as outlined here.

How Moisture Travels in Your Home

Moisture moves through your home in four distinct ways:

- Liquid water flows downwards through openings in the building. Rain may fall on your roof, for example, and leak into your home around a poorly sealed chimney.
- Liquid water wicks through solid materials in all directions by the process known as capillary action. Water can travel up through the ground, then wick through your concrete foundation, and into the wooden structure of your home. Water seeps horizontally too—through the wood siding on your home, for example—when the siding becomes saturated after a rainstorm.
- Water vapor is carried by moving air. Humid air from indoors or outdoors can migrate into building cavities where the water vapor may encounter a cold surface and condense. In summer, the humid air moves from outdoors and the condensing surface is the back side of the drywall. In winter, the humid air comes from indoors and the condensing surface is the back side of the exterior sheathing. In either case, moisture will accumulate inside the wall.

• Water vapor moves through porous materials such as drywall, concrete, and wood by the process called vapor diffusion. It can then condense on hidden cold surfaces.

When water moves through your home by any of these mechanisms, it can accumulate and cause problems. A good moisture management plan keeps moisture in check.

HOW TO CONTROL OUTDOOR MOISTURE

Don't let water leak into your home. Rainwater or snowmelt that leaks through your roof, flows in around doors and windows, or seeps through your siding can damage your home. Fixing these leaks should be your first defense against moisture problems.

If you have standing water in your basement or crawl space, you should take immediate action to dry it out. If you have gutters and downspouts, be sure they direct water away from your home. You might also limit irrigation around your foundation. If all else fails, consider installing a sump pump to move water away from the foundation.

Moisture that enters the home through foundations and crawl spaces contributes to indoor humidity even when no wet areas are apparent. Moisture moves easily through the home, by air movement and by seeping through permeable wood and concrete. Radon and other soil gases may also migrate into dirt crawl spaces.

We recommend that you cover the ground in all dirt-floored crawl spaces and basements with a ground-moisture barrier. This plastic sheeting should be sealed at the seams and foundation walls. Standard polyethylene plastic, either clear or black, is acceptable, but reinforced high-density polyethylene is better. This tough moisture barrier won't tear if a tradesperson needs to crawl around on it.

A ground moisture barrier also helps to control radon, methane, and other soil gases. Seal the edges to the foundation with polyurethane or butyl sealant. Seal the seams with sealant or acrylic builder's tape (not duct tape).

Sources of Moisture in the Home

Moisture source	Typical amount, in pints
Ground moisture, basement or crawl space	0–105 per day
Respiration and perspiration, 4 people	10-12 per day
Dryer vented indoors	4–6 per load
Cooking, 4 people	2–4 per day
Showering, 4 people	2 per day
Dishwashing	1–2 per day

Exterior Moisture Control

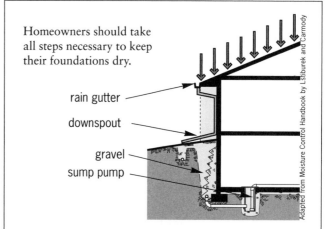

Homeowners should take all steps necessary to keep their foundations dry.

rain gutter
downspout
gravel
sump pump

Adapted from Moisture Control Handbook by Lstiburek and Carmody

Protect your foundation from water damage. Be sure that your gutters and downspouts direct water away from the foundation. Grade the soil around your home so water runs away from the foundation. Avoid watering plants that are against the foundation.

Well-Sealed Crawl Space

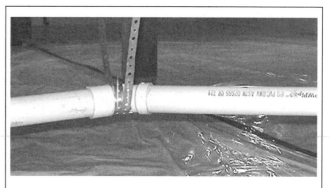

A ground moisture barrier slows the flow of moisture and other soil gases into your home. The seams should be sealed with builder's tape, and the edges fastened to the foundation wall with polyurethane caulk.

HOW TO CONTROL INDOOR MOISTURE

Your normal home activities release some moisture into the air. Cleaning the house, doing laundry, breathing, and bathing all release moisture. But you should take a few precautions to keep this indoor moisture production to a minimum.

- Don't allow plumbing leaks to go unchecked. Even minor leaks can release substantial amounts of moisture and cause structural damage. Repair these right away. If your home has a crawl space, take time periodically to go in there with a flashlight and look around for plumbing leaks and other problems.

- Be sure that your clothes dryer is vented to the outdoors. It may be tempting to leave your dryer vent un-hooked and allow this hot, humid air to heat and humidify your home. But the moisture released from a load of drying clothes—averaging half a gallon per load—is too much for most homes. Dryer exhaust is full of lint and chemicals, too. If you have a gas dryer (a good idea from a conservation point of view), it's even more critical that it's vented to the outdoors since the dryer exhaust also contains combustion by-products.

- Always run your bathroom fan after taking a bath or shower. Run your kitchen fan when doing a lot of water-based cooking, or anytime that you use a gas range. These fans should be ducted to the outdoors, and not just into the attic.

If you notice condensation on your windows during cold weather, or mildew growing on the walls in your bathrooms and bedrooms, it's a sure sign that you should reduce moisture sources.

VENTILATION SYSTEMS

Your efforts to control moisture and indoor pollutants should always focus on source control—keeping them out of your home in the first place. This is easier and more efficient than removing them with ventilation. So be sure that you've taken all the source-control steps we've described here.

Small amounts of moisture and pollutants are unavoidable and can be controlled to safe levels with ventilation. In most homes, this is the job of the common bathroom and kitchen fans. In the most efficient homes, it's advisable to upgrade to a whole-house ventilation system that ventilates every room. Unfortunately, most homes still rely instead upon air leakage to carry away moisture and pollutants. We don't recommend this approach.

The Trouble with Air Leakage

Wind, temperature differences, chimneys, and heating and cooling systems force air into and out of a building through unintentional air leaks in walls, floors, ceilings, windows, and doors.

Air leakage is a questionable source of fresh air because of the contaminated path it may take into the home. Air leaking from the crawl-space, for example, may contain moisture, biological pollutants, or radon. Air leaking through wall cavities and attics may contain environmental dust, insulation particles, and formaldehyde.

The timing of air leakage rarely fits the needs of a house's occupants. Air leakage over-ventilates the home during severe weather and under-ventilates it

Indoor Sources of Moisture

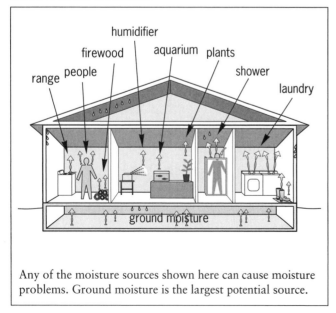

Any of the moisture sources shown here can cause moisture problems. Ground moisture is the largest potential source.

during mild weather. Air leakage often successfully dilutes pollutants, but it's an unreliable and expensive method of air-quality management.

Though uncontrolled ventilation may have been sufficient to remove moisture and other pollutants in the past, indoor air quality problems are now increasingly common in modern homes. Excessive air leakage also incurs higher energy costs than in the past. Yet air sealing can sometimes encourage pollutants to accumulate.

The solution to these problems is to seal the home's air barrier and provide controlled, planned ventilation. It is considerably cheaper to provide a little ventilation to control pollutants than it is to heat and cool a home that is exchanging air with the outdoors at an uncontrollable rate. A whole-house ventilation system consumes electrical energy, but it allows you to seal your home with the assurance that your indoor air remains healthy. Your savings from reduced heating and cooling costs can be up to twenty times greater than the cost of running your ventilation equipment.

Uncontrolled Air Leakage

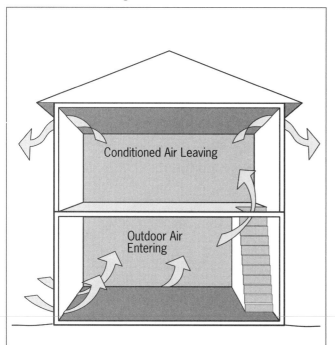

Air is driven through holes and cracks in the building shell. This increases utility costs, carries moisture into building cavities, and compromises indoor air quality.

The Role of Ventilation Systems

The best designers and builders now recognize that whole-house ventilation is an integral part of modern home design.

Properly designed whole-house ventilation systems perform several tasks:

- They discourage the growth of dust mites and mold.
- They protect human health by diluting airborne pollutants and by supplying fresh air.
- They preserve structures by controlling indoor relative humidity.
- They improve comfort by eliminating odors and reducing drafts.

Mechanical ventilation systems are different than the passive vents installed in attics and crawl spaces to control moisture and heat. The mechanical ventilation systems we discuss here move air through the home using fans and ducts. Electric controls regulate these systems to provide ventilation where and when it's needed.

Your home's ventilation system can be as simple as having an exhaust fan in the kitchen and one in each bathroom. We recommend this installation as a bare minimum for every home. In the most efficient homes, advanced whole-house ventilation systems are becoming the norm.

Ventilation systems are grouped generally into three categories that are defined by which way air flows through them: exhaust, supply, and balanced heat recovery ventilation.

Exhaust Ventilation

Kitchen and bathroom exhaust fans are the most common type of ventilation equipment, and are installed in the majority of homes in North America. They are simple, inexpensive, and can control moisture and odors reasonably well in homes that are only moderately airtight.

Exhaust systems create negative pressure within the home, drawing replacement air into the home through holes and cracks in the building shell. This flow of outdoor air into the home does incur some energy cost, since the outdoor air must be heated or cooled during parts of the year. This doesn't matter much for the occasional use that is common in most homes. But if you craft a superinsulated home that is designed to have constant controlled ventilation, the cost of this replacement air can add up. Heat-recovery ventilators, which reclaim some of this energy from the exiting air stream, should be considered in these most efficient homes to help offset this loss.

We recommend that every home should have a high-quality exhaust fan installed in the kitchen and in each bathroom. These fans should be ducted to outdoors so that moisture is not just moved elsewhere in your home. Even if your home has a central heat recovery ventilator, you should install exhaust fans to provide spot ventilation where it is needed the most.

Avoid the use of recirculating or ductless range hoods. These may have filters that collect odors and grease, but the filter often clogs or becomes ineffective in short order. Recirculating fans don't remove moisture, either.

The cost of installing a kitchen or bath exhaust fan will range from $200 to $500 including installation.

Central exhaust-only systems use a single multi-port ventilating unit to exhaust air from several rooms. They can be assembled from individual components (fan, duct, and controls) or installed as a packaged system. Central exhaust systems are installed in the attic, crawl space, or basement, with ducting that leads to bathrooms, kitchens, or utility rooms. The fan may be a packaged multi-port unit or a stand-alone fan with site-installed branch ducting.

Central exhaust systems are not usually designed to accommodate the grease collected by range hoods. Install separate exhaust fans, ducted to the outdoors, over the cooking area.

Supply Ventilation

Supply ventilation systems move air into the home. Unlike exhaust ventilation, they provide whole-house fresh-air distribution rather than collecting pollutants at the source.

The most common supply ventilation systems utilize the existing blower and ductwork that are associated with the heating or cooling system. A small supply

duct is run from outdoors to the return plenum of the air handler. This supply duct often includes a motorized damper that opens when the fan operates in either heating or cooling mode. This duct brings outdoor air into the furnace where it is mixed with return air and supplied to the house. This setup has the disadvantage that no ventilation air is provided during the off seasons when heating and cooling aren't needed.

Central Exhaust Ventilator

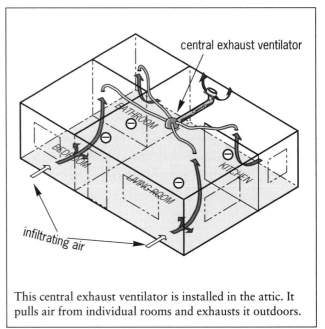

This central exhaust ventilator is installed in the attic. It pulls air from individual rooms and exhausts it outdoors.

Ducted Exhaust Fan

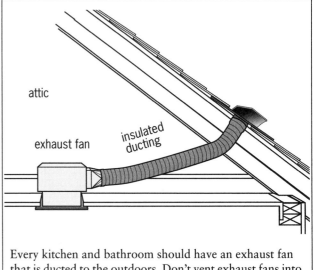

Every kitchen and bathroom should have an exhaust fan that is ducted to the outdoors. Don't vent exhaust fans into attics or crawl spaces. This can cause structural damage if moisture condenses on the wooden structure.

Advanced modern "fan cycler" controls are available that allow the system to operate in a low-flow ventilation mode when neither heating nor cooling are required. Under this control method, the blower is activated by an electronic control, timing its cycles to deliver a controlled ventilation rate throughout the year.

Using the heating or cooling system for ventilation is not always ideal. Some fans are noisy and inefficient because forced-air blowers are designed to move approximately ten times more air than is needed for ventilation. An electronically controlled blower reduces this inefficiency by operating at a lower power and speed when ventilating without heating or cooling.

The best supply ventilation systems may be those that utilize a small standalone fan that is installed in a closet or the attic. They usually have small dedicated ducting that leads to rooms within the home. Homes that are moderately airtight should have either supply or exhaust ventilation systems. These systems usually cost between $300 and $1000 including installation.

Balanced Heat Recovery Ventilators

Balanced ventilation systems exhaust stale air and provide fresh air through a ducted distribution system. Of all the ventilation schemes, they do the best job of controlling pollutants in the home, and they are the best choice for today's most efficient and airtight homes.

Balanced systems move equal amounts of air into and out of the home. Most balanced systems incorporate heat recovery ventilators (HRVs) that reclaim some of the heat from the exhaust air stream. The HRV has a flat-plate aluminum or polyethylene air-to-air heat exchanger at its core in which the supply and exhaust airstreams pass one another with minimal mixing. Heat travels through the core, by conduction, from the warmer to the cooler airstream. In heating climates this means that heat contained in the exhaust air warms the incoming supply air. In cooling climates, the heat of the incoming supply air is passed to the outgoing exhaust. This reduces the energy penalty associated with ventilation systems.

Energy recovery ventilators (ERVs) are a further refinement of HRV technology. While HRVs transfer only heat between the airstreams, ERVs transfer both heat and moisture. In hot and humid regions, this reduces the cost of air conditioning by maintaining the dry indoor conditions needed for efficient operation of air conditioners. A ducted HRV or ERV system will cost between $1500 and $4000, including installation.

Supply Ventilation

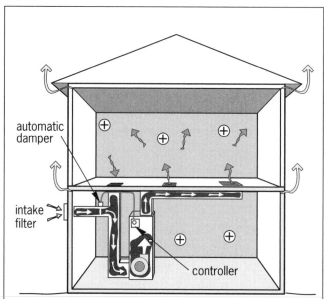

The air handler draws filtered outdoor air into the home, pressurizing it. Stale indoor air exits through air leaks in the building shell. The automatic damper opens when the air handler comes on. The controller opens and closes the damper and cycles the air handler as needed to ventilate the home.

Ducting Design for a Heat Recovery Ventilator

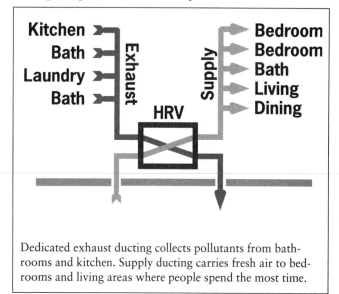

Dedicated exhaust ducting collects pollutants from bathrooms and kitchen. Supply ducting carries fresh air to bedrooms and living areas where people spend the most time.

Heat Recovery Ventilator

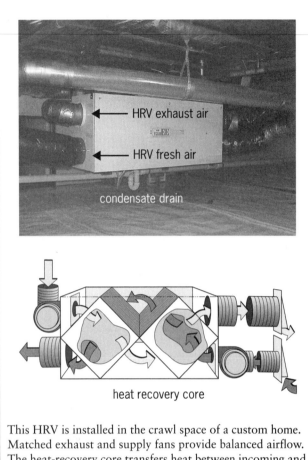

This HRV is installed in the crawl space of a custom home. Matched exhaust and supply fans provide balanced airflow. The heat-recovery core transfers heat between incoming and outgoing air to minimize the energy penalty of ventilation.

CONTROLS FOR VENTILATION EQUIPMENT

Accessible controls for your ventilation system let you choose when it runs and how much air it moves based on the conditions in your house at the moment. Don't shortchange this important component.

Manual Controls

Simple on/off manual controls allow you to ventilate as needed. These are often used for exhaust fans in bathrooms and kitchens.

Manual controls sometimes include countdown or time-delay timers occupants can activate to run the system for a specific period of time.

Humidity Controls

Humidity controls will operate your fan when indoor humidity levels reach a set level. They are used with either simple exhaust fans or central ventilation equipment. They can be set for a range of humidity levels, and have the advantage of automatic operation that doesn't require much management. They should be set to keep indoor humidity low enough to prevent indoor condensation in the winter. This level will vary from 30 percent to 50 percent relative humidity.

Combination Controls

Central ventilation systems are often operated by a combination of manual and automatic controls. The most common strategy utilizes a multispeed fan that runs on low or medium speed to provide continuous ventilation. Override switches in the kitchen and bathrooms activate high-speed operation during moisture-producing activities such as cooking, bathing, or cleaning.

INSTALLING VENTILATION EQUIPMENT

Properly installed ventilation systems should be unobtrusive and long-lived. To achieve this standard, we recommend that you choose the best-quality fans you can afford, and that you pay careful attention to the installation details. Installing a simple exhaust fan is a reasonable project if you have basic carpentry and electrical skills.

Buy only equipment that has a laboratory-measured sound rating. This should be included in the manufacturer's literature or stamped on the unit. These sound ratings are specified in sones. A quiet refrigerator, for example, produces about 1 sone. The best bathroom fans produce $\frac{1}{2}$ to $1\frac{1}{2}$ sones, though many mass-marketed fans produce 3 to 4 sones. Many codes and standards specify a maximum noise rating of 1 to 2 sones for ventilation fans. Quieter is always better: the noise made by cheap bearings and imbalanced fan blades will translate into shorter service life. Besides, a noisy fan will rarely be used.

Be sure to install the unit on flexible mountings to reduce vibration and noise. Mount it so it doesn't touch framing members if possible. Use vibration isolating pads, gaskets, or straps where contact is unavoidable.

Run ductwork from the fan to the outside of the house. In the most common installation, the fan is installed in the ceiling below an attic, and the ductwork can be run to a roof vent so it discharges outdoors. Don't use the white vinyl ducting that is designed for dryers, since it tends to impede airflow and often collapses over time. The most permanent choice is hard steel or aluminum ductwork, though flexible aluminum is acceptable. If you live in a cold region, insulate the ductwork so that condensation doesn't accumulate inside.

THE BOTTOM LINE

The management of your home provides a unique opportunity to control the health of your immediate environment.

Homes built with the right combination of good air barriers, high levels of insulation, and mechanical ventilation are safe, comfortable, and affordable. Wouldn't you like to describe your home this way?

- **Interior Moisture Management.** Repair any plumbing leaks in your home. Be sure that your dryer is ducted to the outdoors. Run your exhaust fans whenever you create excess moisture in your home.

- **Exterior Moisture Management.** Repair your roof if it leaks. Be sure the ground outside your home slopes away from the foundation. If you have gutters and downspouts, be sure the downspouts lead water away from your home's foundation. If you have a dirt-floored basement or crawl space, install a ground moisture barrier over the soil.

- **Exhaust Ventilation.** Install exhaust fans in your kitchen and bathrooms if you don't already have them. Be sure they are ducted to the outdoors.

- **Whole House Ventilation.** If you have performed advanced air sealing on your home, or if a blower door test shows that your home has little natural air infiltration, consider installing a central ventilation system with a heat recovery ventilator.

Building a New Home

If you build a new home, you'll have the opportunity to create a house that is exceedingly comfortable, efficient, and durable. It will take foresight and commitment to do so, because the homebuilding process is littered with pitfalls that can derail your attempts to build an energy-efficient home. Your knowledge can help assure that you get the best house possible.

Much of the information in this chapter has been addressed to some degree elsewhere in the book. But here we show how the best construction practices can be implemented when not constrained by the impediments of remodel work. We also describe some materials and methods that are used only in new construction. Finally, we identify specific energy-efficiency details that are specified in building codes.

Building an Efficient and Sustainable Home

The most efficient homes are crafted by homebuilders who understand how to facilitate communication between the owner, the designers, and the trade specialists.

NEW HOME BASICS

The efficiency of conventional frame dwellings built in North America hasn't changed much in the last fifty years. We have added many incremental improvements such as insulated glass, high-efficiency heating systems, and improved refrigerator technology. But one thing that has changed little is the design of the thermal boundary: the critical assembly of insulation and air barrier that is your primary defense against temperature extremes.

The best homebuilders now have ready-to-go designs for homes that will use 50 to 80 percent less energy than the average. These are comfortable homes that look no different than others in the same neighborhood. They vary in size and style, but they all include a common set of traits:

- A simple building shell
- Very high insulation levels
- Airtight construction
- Energy-efficient windows and doors
- A whole-house ventilation system
- A small heating system
- Little or no air-conditioning
- Efficient lighting and appliances
- Energy-efficient landscaping

The most efficient homes are small—the best predictor of energy consumption is size. We cannot emphasize this principle enough. *No matter how well you engineer a huge house, it will consume large amounts of energy.*

The largest barriers to building low-energy homes are consumer tastes and contractor habit. For years, many of us have purchased large homes with complex construction details and luxury options that maximize energy use. Most homebuyers have not been interested in high insulation levels and other low-visibility efficiency measures. We have asked for fashion, not efficiency.

The solution is simple. If you plan to build a new home, we recommend that you educate yourself on the process of efficient construction. You may have talented designers and builders working on your behalf, but your knowledge will assure that you get the energy efficiency you expect and are paying for. You should also work hard to find a builder who already builds energy-efficient homes. You will be spending your hard-earned money on this project, and you should not have to pay for the education of your homebuilder.

INSULATION FOR NEW HOMES

Insulation is the key to energy efficiency in most American climates. In cold and hot climates, insulation is essential to providing comfort. In mild climates such as the American Southwest, superior insulation can eliminate the need for heating and cooling altogether.

Attic Insulation

Plan to insulate your attic to between R-40 and R-60. Standard roof trusses limit the amount of insulation that can be placed directly over the perimeter of the exterior walls. A raised-heel or "energy" truss allows 8 to 16 inches of insulation or more to be placed over the outer wall.

Efficient Roof Edge Details

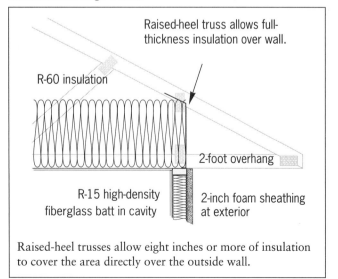

Raised-heel truss allows full-thickness insulation over wall.

R-60 insulation

2-foot overhang

R-15 high-density fiberglass batt in cavity

2-inch foam sheathing at exterior

Raised-heel trusses allow eight inches or more of insulation to cover the area directly over the outside wall.

Another way to improve the thermal integrity of this hard-to-insulate area is to blow foam insulation against the bottom of the roof sheathing above the exterior walls. Since foam insulation has almost double the R-value of fiberglass or cellulose, it makes it possible to maintain a high R-value in this area without installing a raised-heel truss.

Make sure the air leakage sites into the attic are sealed before installing attic insulation.

Cathedral Ceilings

No building component has generated so much trouble and controversy in recent years as cathedral ceilings. They are too shallow to insulate well. Conventional builders and building inspectors insist that they must be ventilated. Building scientists argue that the narrow ventilation space can't dry the cavity effectively, and that the only hope of keeping moisture out of the cavity is to seal it up. Electricians are forced to wreck the effectiveness of the insulation by installing recessed light fixtures. Retrofitters complain that cathedral ceilings represent a severe weakness in the home's thermal boundary, costing thousands of dollars to fix.

We recommend that you build a home with flat ceilings so you can take advantage of the myriad benefits of an open attic. But if you do choose to build a cathedral ceiling, you can avoid expensive repairs by choosing one of the following options.

Scissor Truss Cathedral Ceilings

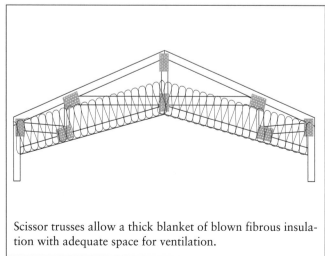

Scissor trusses allow a thick blanket of blown fibrous insulation with adequate space for ventilation.

- Install scissor trusses. Insulate the section of the roof over the exterior wall with spray foam or buy trusses that have room for a full-depth blanket of insulation over the exterior wall.
- Install structural insulated panels. This sandwich of wood sheeting and polystyrene foam forms both structure and seamless insulation.
- Build a ventilated roof cavity. Make it absolutely airtight and install foam board between the drywall and rafters for a thermal break, and to create a high R-value over the entire roof assembly.

Above-Ground Walls

Most energy codes require a minimum wall insulation of R-13 to R-21. The best homes utilize a much higher insulation level.

Most North American homes have wood-framed walls. The insulation should fill the wall cavity from top to bottom, side to side, and front to back. Here are a few common ways to increase the thermal resistance (R-value) of exterior walls.

- Always use wood frame two-by-six walls, filled with high density R-21 fiberglass batts.

Structural Insulated Panels for Cathedral Ceilings

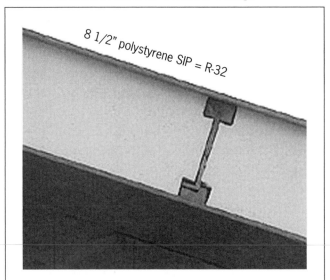

Structural insulated panels (SIPs) are used here to form an engineered cathedral ceiling. The inner core of expanded polystyrene is protected by an outer skin of oriented stand board (OSB), a composite wood product similar to plywood.

- Install at least 2 inches of insulated foam sheathing underneath the siding to reduce heat flow through the walls and prevent condensation in the wall cavities. When installed over a two-by-six wall, this assembly will deliver R-30.
- Frame wood walls with 24-inch spacing, rather than 16-inch spacing.
- Frame exterior-wall corners, and intersections with interior walls, with as much insulation and as little wood as possible.
- Build insulated headers above doors and windows.

New Methods of Wall Construction

In the past twenty years, structural insulated panels (SIPs) and insulated concrete forms (ICFs) have become common in some parts of the United States. Both construction methods provide exceptional thermal performance.

Structural Insulated Panel Walls

Homes made with structural insulated panels (SIPs) are among the most airtight and well-insulated buildings in North America. SIPs provide both structure and insulation, eliminating the standard wood frame wall.

SIPs are less expensive and a little easier to build for the conventional building work force compared to ICFs. However, they are less foolproof and could be damaged by moisture unless they are very carefully protected.

ICFs are probably the best way to build a home in a warm, sunny climate. The combination of high thermal resistance and high thermal mass will provide superior comfort and low energy bills. Use an ICF system that features at least 2 inches of foam on each side of the wall.

Sprayed Foam Wall Insulation

Here the walls and roof have been filled with sprayed urethane foam insulation for an extremely airtight assembly. Additional foamboard has been installed over the walls to create a thermal break at the studs.

Insulated Concrete Forms

Insulated concrete forms (ICFs) are ideal in climates with large daily temperature variations because of their combination of thermal mass with continuous insulation.

Foundations and Floors

Our most severe moisture problems are related to crawl spaces and basements. Builders should avoid these foundation types in regions with high water tables, poor soil drainage, and the possibility of flooding. Crawl spaces in particular can trap water and water vapor under the home, leading to building deterioration and indoor air quality problems.

When homes are built over crawl spaces, they should be insulated at either the floor (above the crawl space), or at the foundation walls (around the crawl space). In any case, take steps to control moisture in the crawl space by installing a ground moisture barrier, such as polyethylene sheeting, over the bare soil. If flooding is common in your region, don't build on a crawl space. When it eventually floods, the resulting pond under your home will likely damage your home, encourage the growth of mold and mildew, and cause respiratory distress for your family. Instead, build your home on stilts using any of the excellent designs for flood-resistant foundations available from your local HUD office.

Floor Insulation

If you choose to insulate your conventional frame floor, the unfaced fiberglass batt should fill the floor cavity and be in continuous contact with the floor sheathing. Choose a batt size that matches the depth of your floor joists—for example, a 9½ inch batt for a 2-by-10 floor cavity. Provide permanent support such as wood strips, twine, or stainless-steel wire for this type of floor-insulation installation.

Trussed floor joists are insulated most effectively with blown fiberglass insulation, rather than fiberglass batts. The floor cavity is first sheeted on the bottom with vapor-permeable house wrap or lightweight perforated foam sheathing to contain the insulation. See *Insulation* on page 81, for more information.

Foundation-Wall and Slab Insulation

The best homes have 2 to 4 inches of foam on the crawl space walls to achieve a minimum of R-10. The foam must be protected from ultraviolet light and moisture if installed on the exterior. On the interior, foam must usually be covered by an ignition barrier like drywall to protect against and slow the spread of fire.

In cold climates, concrete slabs should be insulated with extruded polystyrene at the perimeter and with extruded or expanded polystyrene underneath. Many builders and homeowners don't recognize the value of slab insulation and end up with homes that are uncomfortable and expensive to heat.

In cold climates, insulate both the crawl-space walls and the floor. For information on basement insulation, see on page 97.

AIR-SEALING AND VENTILATION FOR NEW HOMES

Over the past thirty years, a consensus has developed about the role of air-sealing and insulation in high-performance homes. The best homes now include high levels of insulation to keep interior surfaces warm and reduce condensation. An air barrier is installed immediately adjacent to the exterior insulation to slow the loss of conditioned air and to prevent moisture from moving into the insulation. The air barrier can include plastic sheeting, airtight drywall, building paper, or air-tight exterior sheathing, but it must be thoroughly sealed at the edges, seams, doors and windows, and utility penetrations.

All openings in the outside walls should be sealed as the home is constructed. This includes window and door frames, utility penetrations for pipes and wires, and the junctions of walls, ceilings, and floors. Sealing air leaks significantly reduces energy loss and keeps airborne moisture from entering building cavities, where it can encourage mold and mildew growth. Airtight homes are also cleaner and quieter.

Some homebuilders still believe you can build "tight but not too tight." Such an approach is a recipe for disaster. New homes tend to accumulate moisture, and they are filled with building materials, cabinets, and furniture that emit volatile organic compounds. Without a mechanical ventilation system, most new homes are already too airtight for acceptable health and building durability.

Exterior Insulation on Crawl-Space Walls

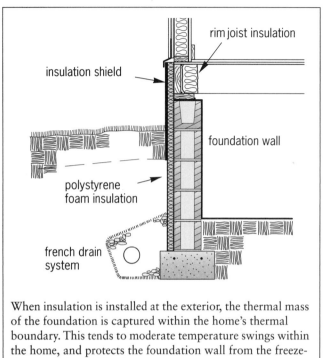

When insulation is installed at the exterior, the thermal mass of the foundation is captured within the home's thermal boundary. This tends to moderate temperature swings within the home, and protects the foundation wall from the freeze-thaw cycle in the North.

Sealing Framing Junctions with Spray Foam

Leaky perimeter of truss-joist floor

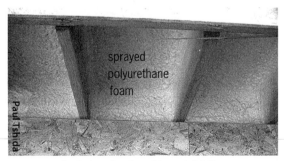

Sealed perimeter of truss-joist floor

Two-part sprayed foam is an excellent material for insulating and air-sealing difficult areas like rim joists and cantilevered floors.

Continuous Thermal Boundary

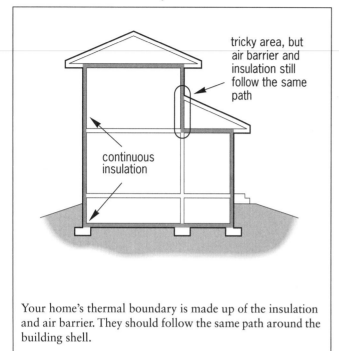

tricky area, but air barrier and insulation still follow the same path

continuous insulation

Your home's thermal boundary is made up of the insulation and air barrier. They should follow the same path around the building shell.

Major Air Leakage Follows the Utilities

floor framing connected to outdoors

ductwork installed here will be prone to excessive heat loss

Architectural protrusions such as bay windows, built-in porches, and cantilevered floors, make air-sealing difficult. Follow the plumbers and heating contractors—and their reciprocating saws—to find many of your home's biggest air leaks.

If you build a new home, we recommend that you install a whole-house heat recovery ventilator system (HRV). These move a balanced amount of air into and out of the home, and include ducting throughout the home for both exhaust and supply air. The system will cost $1500 to $4000, and will be well worth the expense because you will then be able to build a truly efficient and well-sealed home that does not depend on infiltration to control indoor air quality. This approach will be far cheaper in the end because of the reduced utility expense.

WINDOWS FOR NEW HOMES

The number and size of windows have a great effect on a home's efficiency. In general, the window area of new homes should not exceed 12 percent of the floor area. If they are well-placed, this many windows will provide ample view, sun, and ventilation.

When choosing windows, look closely at: U-factor (a measure of heat loss through the window), and solar heat-gain coefficient (SHGC, a measure of solar heat gain through the window).

A low U-factor means that heat will travel through the window slowly. The primary benefit of low U-factor is reduced cost of home heating in the winter. Buy windows with a U-factor of 0.32 or less for greater winter comfort and lower heating bills.

A low SHGC means that less solar heat will enter your home than through a window with a higher SHGC. This keeps your home cool in the summer when the sun strikes your windows. The Energy Code specifies an average SHGC of 0.40 or less for residential windows. Choose windows with a SHGC of 0.40 or even 0.30 to keep your home cool in summer and to reduce air-conditioning costs. Roof overhangs or built-in awnings should be included on south, east, and west windows to prevent summer overheating.

The visible transmittance (VT) is the fraction of visible light admitted to the home by the window glass. Normally for north and south windows, you want a high VT of 0.65 or more. However, for east and west windows in hot, sunny climates, low-angle sun may create oppressive glare. In this case, you may want a lower VT for the windows facing in these directions to cut glare while still preserving your view.

MOISTURE PROTECTION FOR NEW HOMES

There is no reason to have moisture problems in a brand new home. Yet the owners of tens of thousands of recently built homes in the U.S. are struggling to control mold and mildew that threatens both their structures and their health. This is one of the most severe health hazards you can create for your family. And most insurance companies will disclaim coverage for this hazard.

Many moisture problems originate at the foundation. Concrete basements, crawl spaces, and slabs are the most common types of foundations. However, these common foundation types aren't suitable for wet soils and flood-prone areas. There are numerous good flood-resistant foundations that put the home's structure above the ground, with no contact with the wet ground. Having an open car port under a home-on-stilts is a fine idea if the soil in your region ever gets saturated or if flooding is a possibility.

Concrete foundations should be carefully water-proofed, and this includes the edge of slabs. The contractor should also use as much gravel as necessary to assure good drainage, especially when building in silt and clay soils. Gravel is inexpensive compared to moisture problems.

Design your home with deep overhangs to protect your walls and foundation from rainwater. Two feet is minimum, and three feet is better. Large overhangs also reduce air conditioning costs significantly by minimizing the amount of sun that reaches house walls.

Don't plant your landscaping against your home's foundation, and never allow spray from a sprinkler to touch your home. This encourages wood-eating termites, ants, and fungus. These pests cause billions of dollars of damage each year, yet they can't thrive if deprived of water. Don't aid and abet them.

WATER HEATING FOR NEW HOMES

Water heating is always one of the top three residential energy users. It will be worth your time and effort to make some accommodations in your house plans for installing the water heater in a central location. Many homeowners want to put mechanical systems as far out of sight and mind as possible. However, research into both conventional and solar water heating shows clearly that central storage location is a very big factor in achieving a good water-heating efficiency. For efficient water heating, house plans should concentrate the plumbing rather than spreading it from one end of a home to another.

Be sure to insist on good insulation for pipes traveling through concrete slabs. Uninsulated pipes running through slabs can make you wait a couple minutes for hot water. Polyethylene plastic pipes, more reliable than older plastic plumbing, are less thermally conductive and more energy-efficient than copper pipes. Smaller diameter pipes are sometimes installed, usually $\frac{3}{8}$ inch rather than $\frac{1}{2}$ inch, to speed hot-water delivery while saving energy and water. All hot-water pipes should be carefully insulated, including those hidden inside building cavities.

Solar Domestic Hot Water

Solar heating for domestic hot water systems is a viable option in many regions. This is a tried-and-true technology that has been used for more than a century, and recent advances in equipment have made it all the more reliable. The economics of solar hot water are best in new construction since installers don't have to deal with the difficulties of fitting the system onto an existing home.

You'll be able to optimize the installation of a solar water system in your new home. Consider designing the roof at a pitch to optimize the collection of solar energy in winter. This will allow you to mount solar collectors flat against the roof rather than on a tilted rack. The result will be a fairly steep roof, a design change that also allows for more attic insulation and will extend the life of your roofing material. Frame in a chaseway that leads from the roof to the mechanical room where the water heating tank will be located. This will ease the installation of pipes and wires. All of these accommodations will benefit the installation of a photovoltaic system, too. And if you don't plan to install any type of solar system, you can still make these simple changes on the chance that you'll install the equipment in the future.

Evacuated-Tube Solar Water Collector

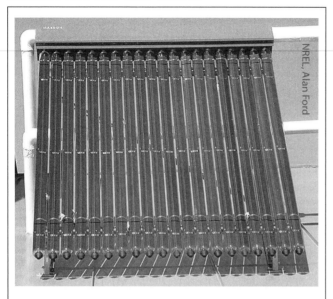

Solar heating is becoming more competitive with gas and electricity for producing domestic hot water. The evacuated-tube collector shown here utilizes a vacuum to provide a high level of insulation around the circulating fluid and increase hot water production in cold weather.

New Compact Heat and Ventilation Units

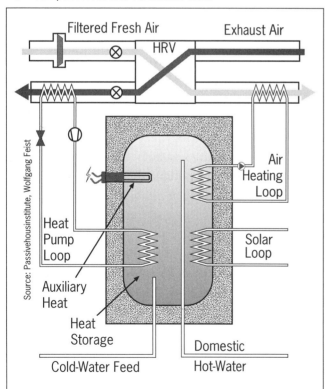

These combined systems are designed for smaller and more energy-efficient homes. They will be the equipment of choice for the most efficient homes of the future.

HEATING AND COOLING FOR NEW HOMES

The ideal size and design of the heating and cooling system for a new home depends on the home's energy efficiency and size. A majority of new homes use forced-air heating and cooling systems. These are usually oversized by a large margin, a practice that was acceptable when fuel was cheap. But oversizing reduces the efficiency of any heating or cooling system because of the resultant frequent cycling. There is a simple solution to this problem: the installer of every new heating or cooling system should perform a heat loss calculation that estimates the proper size of equipment and ducting.

You should include a requirement to produce a written sizing calculation when negotiating with your heating and cooling contractor. It's the law in many jurisdictions. If you have designed an efficient shell for your home, the sizing calculation will show just how small a heating and cooling system you can install. This small system will be a key determinant of future energy costs.

Locate your heating, cooling, water heating, and ventilation equipment inside your home. This includes all your ductwork. If you locate these systems outside your home's insulated space in an uninsulated attic, crawl space, or attached garage, you will not be building an energy-efficient home.

Testing Duct Systems

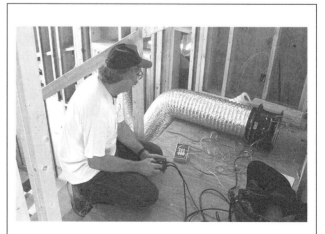

This technician is testing the airtightness of ducts using a duct tester. This test is required in many jurisdictions.

Do You Need Air-Conditioning?

The need for cooling depends more on homesite, home design, and habit than does heating. Even in the deep South where the weather is hot for months on end, families get by with little or no air-conditioning because they have shaded lots, homes with deep overhangs, reflective roofs, and fans in every room. It is quite possible to design homes for every climate that don't need air-conditioning. Many of the details are included in this book. These homes are comfortable year-round, they are inexpensive to operate, and they have great resale value.

Central Versus Space Heat

Although many lending institutions, and even some energy codes, require central heating, many highly efficient homes have heating loads that are much smaller than the smallest available furnaces. With homes this efficient, many designers also question whether a home needs a central furnace and all its potentially leaking ductwork.

Many builders and home owners are choosing to heat the most energy-efficient homes with space heaters. The energy-efficient homes we've describe here are too airtight for old-fashioned open-combustion heating equipment. The space heaters for energy-efficient homes must have sealed combustion chambers, with combustion air coming from outdoors. It's not uncommon, for example, for the most efficient new homes in Montana to be heated by one or two space heaters with capacities 10,000 to 20,000 BTUs per hour (roughly the output of two stove-top burners). In comparison, the smallest furnace you can buy from most manufacturers is rated at about 40,000 BTUs per hour.

One intermediate approach is to select a small furnace, and design an abbreviated super-efficient duct system. Well insulated homes don't need to have heated or cooled air delivered at the exterior walls. The supply registers can instead be located along interior walls, allowing the ducts to be shorter and straighter, and resulting in less air leakage and thermal losses in the ducts. The heating and cooling equipment itself should also be located within the thermal boundary of the home, and not in a garage, attic, or crawl space.

Another viable option for the most efficient homes is to install electric heat. Even though the cost per unit of delivered heat is higher than for gas heating systems, this difference will account for relatively few dollars in a home with a minimal need for heat. Electric heat has the advantage that it is cheaper to buy, cheaper to install, offers trouble-free service, and has no issues of combustion safety. But this economy of electric heat only holds true if you build a truly efficient super-insulated home.

THE BOTTOM LINE

If you build a new home, you'll be faced with both tremendous opportunities and sobering responsibilities. Over recent years, our knowledge of construction science has progressed quickly. Our choice of building materials has never been so extensive. And we have never had so much financial wealth available for the construction of homes.

Yet many who hope to build a home struggle with the simplest questions. *How much insulation is enough? Is a high-efficiency heating system worth the extra expense? Does it make sense to install a black roof in a sunny region?* And then comes the most general question, one which reveals much about our sense of family, our places in the community, and our commitment to the globe. *Is it possible to be perfectly happy in a modest home of less than 2000 square feet?* For there is no greater way to squander energy at home than by constructing a too-big house.

We sense that a profound shift is taking place in how many of us view our homes. That shift is driven by the cost of energy, by the recognition that we all share a finite set of natural resources, and by the hope that our homes could house us but not burden us. We hope the advice we offer here helps you create a shelter that is safe, secure, and sustainable, and that you can move one step closer to claiming control of your own housing. We wish you luck in the endeavor.

Resources

SATURN ONLINE

Saturn Online offers follow-up resources for readers of this book. Free tip sheets provide additional information about the procedures described here, and online seminars guide homeowners through the process of crafting an efficient home. The courses stress specific solutions for making deep reductions in energy consumption and carbon emission. An online forum allows participants to discuss home energy solutions with industry experts. Saturn Online also offers courses that cater to professionals and advanced do-it-yourselfers.

For more information, visit *www.saturnonline.biz*

ORGANIZATION CONTACTS

American Council for an Energy-Efficient Economy (ACEEE) - 1001 Connecticut Ave. NW, Suite 801, Washington, DC 20036. 202-429-8873. *www.aceee.org* ACEEE collaborates with other groups on research into the benefits of energy efficiency, and publishes many reports. Publishes the excellent book *Consumer Guide to Home Energy Savings*.

American Solar Energy Society, Inc. (ASES) - 2400 Central Ave. G-1, Boulder, CO 80301. 303-443-3130. *www.ases.org* ASES is a nonprofit educational organization that encourages the use of solar energy technologies. ASES publishes the magazine *Solar Today*.

Building Performance Institute - 107 Hermes Road Suite 110, Malta, NY 12020. 518-899-2727. *www.bpi.org* Certifies energy auditors and related professionals working in the weatherization and home performance fields. Provides accreditation for home performance contractors. Manages both written and field testing of technicians. Maintains a list of accredited home performance contractors.

California Energy Commission (CEC) - 1516 Ninth Street, P.O. Box 944295, Sacramento, CA 94244-2950. 916-654-4287. *www.energy.ca.gov* The CEC publishes extensive written and web-based resources on building technology and energy efficiency.

Centers for Disease Control and Prevention (CDC) - 1600 Clifton Rd, Atlanta, GA 30333. 800-311-3435. *www.cdc.gov* Provides written and web-based information on home health hazards such as asbestos, radon, carbon monoxide, and household chemicals.

Department of Housing and Urban Development (HUD) - 451 7th Street S.W., Washington, DC 20410 (202) 708-1112. *www.hud.gov* HUD manages a vast information network on homeownership in general, with topics that include buying and selling homes, identifying the most favorable mortgages, and improving home efficiency.

ENERGY STAR® - The ENERGY STAR website is one of the best online resources for information on building efficiency. *www.energystar.gov*

The Energy & Environmental Building Association (EEBA) - 6520 Edenvale Boulevard, Suite 112, Eden Prairie, MN 55346 952-881-1098. *www.eeba.org* EEBA's goal is to provide education and resources to transform the residential design and construction industry to profitably deliver energy efficient and environmentally responsible buildings and communities.

Florida Solar Energy Center (FSEC) - 1679 Clearlake Rd., Cocoa, FL 32922. 321-638-1015. *www.fsec.ucf.edu* FSEC is an important resource for anyone who owns a home in a hot, humid climate. They offer publications on topics such as passive cooling, radiant barriers, moisture control in hot climates, shading techniques, air leakage, air-conditioner performance, and more.

Home Energy - PMB 95, 2124 Kittredge St., Berkeley, CA 94704. 510-524-5405. *www.homeenergy.org* Publishers of *Home Energy Magazine*, the premier U.S. publication on home energy efficiency.

Journal of Light Construction - 186 Allen Brook Lane, Williston, VT. 802-879-3335. *www.jlconline.com* JLC publishes an excellent professional journal for the construction trades.

National Renewable Energy Laboratory (NREL) - 1617 Cole Blvd., Golden, CO 80401-3393. 303-275-3000. *www.nrel.gov* The DOE's solar and renewable energy laboratory. Performs many kinds of building energy research. Produces publications for both professionals and consumers.

North American Technical Excellence (NATE) - 4100 North Fairfax Drive #210, Arlington, VA 2220 3(703) 276-7247. *www.natex.org* NATE provides a national certification for the most skilled heating and cooling technicians. They maintain an online database of certified technicians.

Passive House Institute U.S. - 110 S. Race St. Ste 202, Urbana, IL 61801. *www.passivehouse.us* The Passive House Institute works to establish European super-efficient construction standards in the U.S. They provide technical assistance, offer training, and certify homes that are built to Passive House standards.

PVwatts, National Renewable Energy Lab - *www.rredc.nrel.gov/solar/calculators/PVWATTS* The online PVWatts calculator allows you to estimate the output of solar electric systems. The website also includes other solar design tools and research materials.

Residential Energy Services Network (RESNET) - P.O. Box 4561, Oceanside, CA92052. 760-806-3448. *www.resnet.us* National organization of home energy raters (HERS Raters) and rating organizations. Their mission is to develop a national market for home energy rating systems and energy efficient mortgages. Maintains a list of certified HERS Raters.

Solar Energy International (SEI) - P.O. Box 715, Carbondale, CO 81623 970-963-8855. *www.solarenergy.org* SEI offers the industry's best hands-on workshops and online courses on renewable energy and sustainable construction.

Southface Energy Institute - 241 Pine St. NE, Atlanta, GA 30308. 404-872-3549. *www.southface.org* Nonprofit educational institute focuses on energy-efficient building for the southern states. Website has a good question-and-answer section.

U.S. Green Building Council (USGBC) - 1800 Massachusetts Ave. NW Suite 300, Washington, DC 20036. 202-828-7422. *www.usgbc.org* USGBC administers the LEED program (Leadership in Energy and Environmental Design), an educational and rating system for green buildings.

INTERNET KEYWORD SEARCHES

The Internet offers an unlimited amount of information on the topics covered in this book. We've included some keywords here to help you find what you're looking for a quickly as possible.

For tips on conducting effective Internet searches, visit *www.google.com/help/basics.html*

Chapter 1: - Developing a Plan for Your Home
Home Performance with Energy Star
home performance contractor
online energy audit
home energy rater
energy auditor

Chapter 2: - Lighting and Appliances
efficient lighting
energy star lighting
energy star appliance
energy star refrigerator

Chapter 3: - Water Heating
energy star water heating
energy factor
on-demand water heater
solar water heating
solar energy international

Chapter 4: - Heating and Cooling: First Steps
cool roof coatings
whole-house fan
programmable thermostat
high efficiency furnace
high efficiency air conditioner

Chapter 5: - Landscaping
arborist
energy star landscaping
landscaping water conservation
shade trees
xeriscaping

Chapter 6: - Finding and Sealing Air Leaks
energy star air sealing
blower door test
air sealing
one-part foam insulation
spray foam kit

Chapter 7: - Insulation
where to insulate
attic insulation
energy star insulation
heat loss calculation
wall insulation

Chapter 8: - Windows and Doors
energy star windows
energy star doors
sliding glass door hardware
installation masters

Chapter 9: - Cooling Systems
energy star cooling
evaporative cooler
evaporative cooler parts
air conditioning efficiency

Chapter 10: - Heating Systems
energy star heating
high-efficiency heating equipment
hydronic heating
NATE service technician

Chapter 11: - Photovoltaic Systems
solar energy international
pvwatts calculator
solar panels
grid tied pv systems
net metering

Chapter 12: - Moisture Management and Ventilation
energy star ventilation
ground moisture barrier
polyethylene vapor barrier
exhaust ventilation
heat recovery ventilator

Chapter 13: - Building a New Home
energy star new homes
home energy rating
energy efficient building
green building materials
sustainable building

Index

Saturn Bookstore

Residential Energy: Cost Savings and Comfort for Existing Buildings

Discusses the principles of residential energy conservation in greater detail than *The Homeowner's Handbook to Energy Efficiency*. This is the standard textbook used to train energy auditors and building performance contractors. Includes checklists, tables, a glossary, dozens of useful appendices, and illustrations on almost every page. 320 pages.

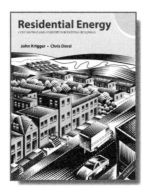

Your Home Cooling Energy Guide

Explores all the options for reducing the cost of air conditioning. Illustrates solutions that include shading, ventilation, evaporative cooling, awnings, sun screens, window films, radiant barriers, insulation, reflective coatings, and shade trees. 80 pages.

Your Mobile Home: Energy and Repair Guide for Manufactured Housing

Summarizes the collective experience of many experts who work with manufactured housing. Describes the construction process, outlines common repair tasks, and identifies the best weatherization measures to reduce utility costs. Includes many illustrated step-by-step procedures. A must-have book for all mobile home owners. 256 pages.

Residential Ventilation Systems

Outlines step-by-step procedures for properly choosing, designing and installing ventilation systems. Provides critical information for homeowners who want to control mold, mildew, and moisture problems in their homes. 26 pages.

Hydronic Heating Systems

Includes solid technical advice on installing, maintaining, and troubleshooting hydronic home heating systems. Covers both modern hot-water heating systems and legacy steam systems. Includes an analysis of installation options for new homes. 40 pages.

Visit our website to learn more about these publications or to place an order.

We offer free same-day shipping for orders placed online.

www.homeownershandbook.biz

Download free conservation tip sheets, listen to free podcasts, or sign up for online classes that show you how to reduce your utility bills now.